The
BLESSED
CHRISTIAN
LIFE

J.-23
1-

CHRISTIAN ART
PUBLISHERS

Published by Christian Art Publishers
PO Box 1599, Vereeniging, 1930, RSA

© 2014
First LuxLeather edition 2014

Cover designed by Christian Art Publishers

Cover images used under license from Shutterstock.com

Scripture quotations are taken from the New King James Version.
Copyright © 1979, 1980, 1982 by Thomas Nelson, Inc.
Used by permission. All rights reserved.

Scripture quotations marked NIV are taken from
the *Holy Bible*, New International Version® NIV®.
Copyright © 1973, 1978, 1984 by International Bible Society.
Used by permission of Zondervan Publishing House.
All rights reserved.

Scripture quotations set in italics indicate the author's emphasis.

Set in 11 on 14 pt Calibri
by Christian Art Publishers

Printed in China

ISBN 978-1-4321-1247-9

© All rights reserved. No part of this book may be reproduced in
any form without permission in writing from the publisher,
except in the case of brief quotations in critical articles or reviews.

14 15 16 17 18 19 20 21 22 23 – 10 9 8 7 6 5 4 3 2 1

Contents

Book 1

HOW TO SUCCEED IN THE CHRISTIAN LIFE

by

R. A. TORREY

Contents

Dedicated to
the many thousands in many
lands who have professed
Christ in our meetings.

Introduction

I have for years felt the need of a book to put in the hands of those beginning the Christian life that would tell them just how to make a complete success of this new life upon which they were entering. I could find no such book, so I have been driven to write one. This book aims to tell the young convert exactly what he needs to know. I hope that pastors, evangelists and other Christian workers may find it a useful resource to hand to young converts. I hope that it may also prove a helpful book to many who have long been Christians but have not made that headway in the Christian life that they long for.

1

Beginning Right

*T*HERE is nothing more important in the Christian life than beginning right. If we begin right we can go on right. If we begin wrong the whole life that follows is likely to be wrong. If anyone who reads these pages has begun wrong, it is a very simple matter to begin over again and begin right. John 1:12 tells us what the right beginning in the Christian life is, "But as many as received Him, to them He gave the right to become children of God, to those who believe in His name." The right way to begin the Christian life is by receiving Jesus Christ. To anyone who receives Him, He at once gives power to become a child of God. If the reader of this book should be the wickedest person on earth and should at this moment receive Jesus Christ, that very instant this person would become a child of God. God says so in the most unqualified way in the verse quoted above. No one can become a child of God in any other way. No person, no matter how carefully they have been reared, no matter how well they have been sheltered from the vices and evils of this world, is a child of God until they receive Jesus Christ. We are "sons of God through faith in Christ Jesus" (Galatians 3:26), and in no other way.

What does it mean to receive Jesus Christ? It means to take Christ to be to yourself all that God offers Him to be to everybody. Jesus Christ is God's gift. "For God so loved the world that He gave His only begotten Son, that whoever believes in Him should not perish but have everlasting life" (John 3:16). Some accept this wondrous gift of God. Everyone who does accept this gift becomes a child of God. Many others refuse this wondrous gift of God, and everyone who refuses this gift perishes. He is condemned already. "He who believes in Him is not condemned; but he who does not believe is condemned already, because he has not believed in the name of the only begotten Son of God" (John 3:18).

What does God offer His Son to be to us?

1. First of all, *God offers Jesus to us to be our sin-bearer*. We have all sinned. There is not a man or woman or a boy or girl who has not sinned (see Romans 3:22-23). If any of us say that we have not sinned we are deceiving ourselves and giving the lie to God (see 1 John 1:8, 10). Now we must each of us bear our own sin or some one else must bear it in our place. If we were to bear our own sins, it would mean we must be banished forever from the presence of God, for God is holy. "God

is light and in Him is no darkness at all" (1 John 1:5). But God Himself has provided another to bear our sins in our place so that we should not need to bear them ourselves. This sin-bearer is God's own Son, Jesus Christ, "He made Him who knew no sin to be sin for us, that we might become the righteousness of God in Him" (2 Corinthians 5:21).

When Jesus Christ died upon the cross of Calvary He redeemed us from the curse of the law by being made a curse in our stead (see Galatians 3:13). To receive Christ then is to believe this testimony of God about His Son, to believe that Jesus Christ did bear our sins in His own body on the cross (see 1 Peter 2:24), and to trust God to forgive all our sins because Jesus Christ has borne them in our place. "All we like sheep have gone astray; we have turned, every one, to his own way; and the LORD has laid on Him the iniquity of us all" (Isaiah 53:6).

Our own good works, past, present or future have nothing to do with the forgiveness of our sins. Our sins are forgiven, not because of any good works that we do; they are forgiven because of the atoning work of Christ upon the cross of Calvary in our place. If we rest in this atoning work we shall do good works, but our good works will be the outcome of our being saved and the outcome of our believing on Christ as our sin-bearer. Our good works will not be the ground of our salvation, but the result of our salvation, and the proof of it. We must be very careful not to mix in our good works at all as the ground of salvation. We are not forgiven because of Christ's death *and our good works*, we are forgiven solely and entirely because of Christ's death. To see this clearly is the right beginning of the true Christian life.

2. *God offers Jesus to us as our deliverer from the power of sin.* Jesus not only died, He rose again. Today He is a living Savior, He has all power in heaven and on earth (see Matthew 28:18). He has power to keep the weakest sinner from falling (see Jude 24). He is able to save not only from the uttermost but "to the uttermost" all that come unto the Father through Him. "Therefore He is also able to save to the uttermost those who come to God through Him, since He always lives to make intercession for them" (Hebrews 7:25). "If the Son makes you free, you shall be free indeed" (John 8:36).

To receive Jesus is to believe what God tells us about Him in His Word, to believe that He did rise from the dead, to believe that He does now live, to believe that He has power to keep us from falling, to believe that He has power to keep us from the power of sin day by day, and trust Him to do it.

This is the secret of daily victory over sin. If we try to fight sin in our own strength, we are bound to fail. If we just look up to the risen Christ to keep us every day and every hour, He will keep us. Through the crucified Christ we get deliverance from the guilt of sin, our sins are all blotted out, we are free from all condemnation; but it is through the risen Christ that we get daily victory over the power of sin. Some receive Christ as a sin-bearer and thus find pardon, but do not get beyond that, and so their lives are characterized by daily failure. Others receive Him as their risen Savior and thus enter into an experience of victory over sin. To begin right we must take Him not only as our sin-bearer, and thus find pardon. We must also take Him as our risen Savior, our Deliverer from the power of sin, our Keeper, and thus find daily victory over sin.

3. But *God offers Jesus to us, not only as our sin-bearer and our Deliverer from the power of sin, but He also offers Him to us as our Lord and King.* We read in Acts 2:36, "Let all the house of Israel know assuredly that God has made this Jesus, whom you crucified, both Lord and Christ." Lord means Divine Master, and Christ means anointed King. To receive Jesus is to take Him as our Divine Master, as the One to whom we yield the absolute confidence of our intellects, the One whose word we believe absolutely, the One whom we will believe though many of the wisest of men may question or deny the truth of His teachings; and as our King to whom we gladly yield the absolute control of our lives, so that the question from this time on is never going to be, what would I like to do or what do others tell me to do, or what do others do, but the whole question is WHAT WOULD MY KING JESUS HAVE ME DO? A right beginning involves an unconditional surrender to the lordship and kingship of Jesus.

The failure to realize that Jesus is Lord and King, as well as Savior, has led to many a false start in the Christian life. We begin with Him as our Savior, as our sin-bearer and our Deliverer from the power of sin, but we must not end with Him merely as Savior, we must know Him as Lord and King. There is nothing more important in a right beginning of the Christian life than an unconditional surrender, both of the thoughts and the conduct, to Jesus. Say from your heart and say it again and again, "*All* for Jesus." Many fail because they shrink back from this entire surrender. They wish to serve Jesus with half their heart, and part of themselves and part of their possessions. To hold back anything from Jesus means a wretched life of stumbling and failure.

The life of entire surrender is a joyous life all along the way. If you have never done it before, go alone with God today, get down on your knees and say, "All for Jesus," and mean it. Say it very earnestly; say it from the bottom of your heart. Stay there until you realize what it means and what you are doing. It is a wondrous step forward when one really takes it. If you have taken it already, take it again, take it often. It always has fresh meaning and brings fresh blessedness. In this absolute surrender is found the key to the truth. Doubts rapidly disappear for one who surrenders all (see John 7:17). In this absolute surrender is found the secret of power in prayer (see 1 John 3:22). In this absolute surrender is found the supreme condition of receiving the Holy Ghost (see Acts 5:32).

Taking Christ as your Lord and King involves obedience to His will as far as you know it in each smallest detail of life. There are those who tell us that they have taken Christ as their Lord and King who at the same time are disobeying Him daily in business, in domestic life, in social life and in personal conduct. Such persons are deceiving themselves. You have not taken Jesus as your Lord and King if you are not striving to obey Him in everything each day. He Himself says, "Why do you call Me 'Lord, Lord,' and not do the things which I say?" (Luke 6:46).

To sum it all up, the right way to begin the Christian life is to accept Jesus Christ as your sin-bearer and to trust God to forgive your sins because Jesus Christ died in your place; to accept Him as your risen Savior who ever lives to make intercession for you, and who has all power to keep you, and to trust Him to keep you from day to day; and to accept Him as your Lord and King to whom you surrender the absolute control of your thoughts and of your life. This is the right beginning, the only right beginning of the Christian life. If you have made this beginning, all that follows will be comparatively easy. If you have not made this beginning, make it now.

2

The Open Confession
of Christ

*H*AVING begun the Christian life right by taking the proper attitude towards Christ in a private transaction between Himself and yourself, the next step is an open confession of the relationship that now exists between yourself and Jesus Christ. Jesus says in Matthew 10:32, "Whoever confesses Me before men, him I will also confess before My Father who is in heaven." He demands a public confession. He demands it for your own sake. This is the path of blessing. Many attempt to be disciples of Jesus and not let the world know it. No one has ever succeeded in that attempt. To be a secret disciple means to be no disciple at all. If one really has received Christ he cannot keep it to himself. "For out of the abundance of the heart the mouth speaks" (Matthew 12:34). So important is the public confession of Christ that Paul puts it first in his statement of the conditions of salvation. He says, "If you *confess with your mouth* the Lord Jesus and believe in your heart that God has raised Him from the dead, you will be saved. For with the heart one believes unto righteousness, and with the mouth confession is made unto salvation" (Romans 10:9-10). The life of confession is the life of full salvation. Indeed, the life of confession is the life of the only real salvation. When we confess Christ before men here on earth, He confesses us before the Father in heaven and the Father gives us the Holy Spirit as the seal of our salvation.

It is not enough that we confess Christ just once, as, for example, when we are confirmed, or when we unite with the church, or when we come forward in a revival meeting. We should confess Christ constantly. We should not be ashamed of our Lord and King. We should let people know that we are on His side. In the home, in the church, at our work, and at our play, we should let others know where we stand. Of course, we should not parade our Christianity or our piety, but we should leave no one in doubt whether we belong to Christ. We should let it be seen that we glory in Him as our Lord and King.

The failure to confess Christ is one of the most frequent causes of backsliding. Christians get into new relationships where they are not known as Christians and where they are tempted to conceal the fact; they yield to the temptation and they soon find themselves drifting. The more you make of Jesus Christ, the more He will make of you. It will save you from many a temptation if the fact is clearly known that you are one who acknowledges Christ as Lord in all things.

3

Assurance of Salvation

*I*F one is to have the fullest measure of joy and power in Christian service, he must know that his sins are forgiven, that he is a child of God, and that he has eternal life. It is the believer's privilege to *know* that he has eternal life. John says in 1 John 5:13, "These things I have written to you ... *that you may know* that you have eternal life, and that you may continue to believe in the name of the Son of God." John wrote this first epistle for the express purpose that anyone who believes in the name of the Son of God *might know* that he has eternal life.

There are those who tell us that no one can know that he has eternal life until he is dead and has been before the judgment seat of God, but God Himself tells us that we may know. To deny the possibility of the believer's knowing that he has eternal life is to say that the First Epistle of John was written in vain, and it is to insult the Holy Spirit who is its real author. Again Paul tells us in Acts 13:39, "By Him [Christ] everyone who believes *is justified* from all things." So everyone who believes in Jesus may know that he is justified from all things. He may know it because the Word of God says so. Again John tells us in John 1:12, "But *as many as received Him* [Jesus Christ], to them He gave the right to become children of God, to those who believe in His name." Here is a definite and unmistakable declaration that everyone who receives Jesus becomes a child of God. Therefore every believer in Jesus may know that he is a child of God. He may know it on the surest of all grounds, because the Word of God asserts that he is a child of God.

But how may any individual know that he has eternal life? He may know it on the very best ground of knowledge; that is, through the testimony of God Himself as given in the Bible. The testimony of Scripture is the testimony of God. What the Scriptures say is absolutely sure. What the Scriptures say God says. In John 3:36 the Scriptures say, "He who believes in the Son *has* everlasting life." Any one of us may know whether we believe in the Son or not, whether we have that real faith in Christ that leads us to receive Him. If we have this faith in Christ we have God's own written testimony that we have eternal life, that our sins are forgiven, that we are the children of God. We may feel forgiven, or we may not feel forgiven, but that does not matter. It is not a question of what we feel but of what

God says. God's Word is always to be believed. Our own feelings are oftentimes to be doubted. There are many who are led to doubt their sins are forgiven, to doubt that they have everlasting life, to doubt that they are saved, because they do not feel forgiven, or do not feel that they have everlasting life, or do not feel that they are saved. Because you do not feel it is no reason why you should doubt it.

Suppose that you were sentenced to imprisonment and that your friends secured a pardon for you. The legal document announcing your pardon is brought to you. You read it and know you are pardoned because the legal document says so, but the news is so good and so sudden that you are dazed by it. You do not realize that you are pardoned. Someone comes to you and says, "Are you pardoned?" What would you reply? You would say, "Yes, I am pardoned." Then he asks, "Do you feel pardoned?" You reply, "No, I do not feel pardoned. It is so sudden, it is so wonderful, I cannot realize it." Then he says to you, "But how can you know that you are pardoned if you do not feel it?" You would hold out the document and you would say, "This says so." The time would come, after you had read the document over and over again and believed it, when you would not only know you were pardoned because the document said so, but you would feel it. The Bible is God's authoritative document declaring that everyone who believes in Jesus is justified; declaring that everyone who believes in the Son has everlasting life; declaring that everyone who receives Jesus is a child of God. If anyone asks you if your sins are all forgiven, reply, "Yes, I know they are because God says so." If they ask you if you know that you are a child of God, reply, "Yes, I know I am a child of God because God says so." If they ask you if you have everlasting life, reply, "Yes, I know I have everlasting life because God says so. God says, 'He who believes in the Son has everlasting life.' I know I believe in the Son, and therefore I know I have eternal life – because God says so." You may not feel it yet, but if you will keep meditating upon God's statement and believing what God says, the time will come when you will feel it.

For one who believes in the Son of God to doubt that he has eternal life is for him to make God a liar. "He who believes in the Son of God has the witness in himself; he who does not believe God has made Him a liar, because he has not believed the testimony that God has given of His Son. And this is the testimony: that God has given us eternal life, and this life is in His Son. He who has the Son has life; he who does not have the Son of God does not have life" (1 John 5:10-12). Anyone who does not believe God's testimony that He has given unto us eternal life and that this life is in His Son and that he who has the Son has life, makes God a liar.

It is sometimes said, "It is presumption for anyone to say that he knows he is saved, or to say that he knows that he has eternal life." But is it presumption to believe God? Is it not rather presumption not to believe God, to make God a liar? When you who believe in the Son of God and yet doubt that you have eternal life, you make God a liar. When Jesus said to the woman who was a sinner, "Your sins are forgiven" (Luke 7:48), was it presumption for her to go out and say, "I know my sins are all forgiven"? Would it not have been presumption for her to have doubted for a moment that her sins were all forgiven? Jesus had said that they were forgiven. For her to doubt it would have been for her to give the lie to Jesus. Is it then any more presumption for the believer today to say, "My sins are all forgiven, I have eternal life," when God says in His written testimony to everyone who believes, "You are justified from all things" (Acts 13:39), "You have eternal life" (John 3:36; 1 John 5:13)?

Be very sure first of all that you really do believe on the name of the Son of God; that you really have received Jesus. If you are sure of this then never doubt for a moment that your sins are all forgiven, never doubt for a moment that you are a child of God, never doubt for a moment that you have everlasting life. If Satan comes and whispers, "Your sins are not forgiven," point Satan to the Word of God and say, "God says my sins are forgiven and I know they are." If Satan whispers, "Well, perhaps you don't believe in Him," then say, "Well, if I never did before, I will now." And then go out rejoicing, knowing that your sins are forgiven, knowing that you are a child of God, knowing that you have everlasting life.

There are doubtless many who say they know they have eternal life who really do not believe in the name of the Son of God, who have not really received Jesus. This is not true assurance. It has no sure foundation in the Word of God, which cannot lie. If we wish to get assurance of salvation we must first get saved. The reason why many don't have the assurance that they are saved is because they are not saved. They ought not to have assurance. What they need first is salvation. But if you have received Jesus in the way described in the first chapter, you are SAVED, you are a child of God, your sins are forgiven. Believe it, know it. Rejoice in it.

Having settled it, let it remain settled. Never doubt it. You may make mistakes, you may stumble, you may fall, but even if you do, if you have really received Jesus, know that your sins are forgiven and rise from your fall and go forward in the glad assurance that there is nothing between you and God.

4

Receiving the Holy Spirit

*W*HEN the apostle Paul came to Ephesus, he found a little group of twelve disciples of Christ. There was something about these twelve disciples that struck Paul unfavorably. We are not told what it was. It may be that he did not find in them that overflowing joyfulness that one learns to expect in all Christians who have really entered into the fullness of blessing that there is for them in Christ. It may be that Paul was troubled at the fact that there were only twelve of them, thinking that if these twelve were what they ought to be, there would certainly have been more than twelve of them by this time. Whatever it may have been that impressed Paul unfavorably, he went right to the root of the difficulty at once by putting to them the question, "Did you receive the Holy Spirit when you believed?" (Acts 19:2). It came out at once that they had not received the Holy Ghost, that in fact they did not know that the Holy Ghost had been given. Then Paul told them that the Holy Ghost had been given, and also showed them just what they must do to receive the Holy Ghost then and there, and before that gathering was over the Holy Ghost came upon them. From that day on there was a different state of affairs in Ephesus. A great revival sprang up at once so that the whole city was shaken, "So the word of the Lord grew mightily and prevailed" (Acts 19:20). Paul's question to these young disciples in Ephesus should be put to young disciples everywhere: "Have you received the Holy Spirit?" In *receiving the Holy Spirit* is the great secret of joyfulness in our own hearts, of victory over sin, of power in prayer, and of effective service.

Everyone who has truly received Jesus must have the Holy Spirit dwelling in him in some sense; but in many believers, though the Holy Spirit dwells in them, He dwells way back in some hidden sanctuary of their being, deep in their subconsciousness. It is something quite different, something far better than this, to receive the Holy Spirit in the sense that Paul meant in his question. To receive the Holy Spirit in such a sense that one knows experimentally that he has received the Holy Spirit, to receive the Holy Spirit in such a sense that we are conscious of the joy with which He fills our hearts different from any joy that we have ever known in the world; to receive the Holy Spirit in such a sense that He rules our life and produces within us in ever increasing measure the fruit of the Spirit, love, joy, peace, long-suffering, gentleness, goodness, faith, meekness, temperance; to receive the Holy Spirit in such a sense that we are conscious of His drawing our hearts out in prayer in a way that is not of ourselves; to receive the Holy Spirit in such a sense that we are conscious of His help when we witness for Christ, when we speak to others individually and try to lead them to accept Christ, or when we teach a Sunday school class, or speak in public, or do any other work for the Master. Have you received the Holy Spirit? If you have not, let me tell you how you may.

1. First of all, in order to receive the Holy Spirit, one must be resting in the death of Christ on the cross for us as the sole and all-sufficient ground upon which God pardons all our sins and forgives us.
2. In order to receive the Holy Spirit we must put away every known sin. We should go to our heavenly Father and ask Him to search us through and through and to bring to light anything in our life, our outward life or our inward life, that is wrong in His sight, and if He does bring anything to light that is displeasing to Him, we should put it away, no matter how dear it is to us. There must be a complete renunciation of all sin in order to receive the Holy Spirit.
3. In the third place, in order to receive the Holy Spirit there must be an open confession of Christ before the world. The Holy Spirit is not given to those who are trying to be disciples in secret, but to those who obey Christ and publicly confess Him before the world.

4. In the fourth place, in order to receive the Holy Spirit, there must be an absolute surrender of our lives to God. You must go to Him and say, "Heavenly Father, here I am. You have bought me with a price. I am Your property. I renounce all claim to do my own will, all claim to govern my own life, all claim to have my own way. I give myself up unreservedly to You – all I am and all I have. Send me where You wish, use me as You wish, do with me what You wish – I am Yours." If we hold anything back from God, no matter how small it may seem, that spoils it all. But if we surrender all to God, then God will give all that He has to us. There are some who shrink from this absolute surrender to God, but absolute surrender to God is simply absolute surrender to infinite love. Surrender to the Father, to the Father whose love is not only wiser than any earthly father's, but more tender than any earthly mother's.

5. In order to receive the Holy Spirit there should be definite asking for the Holy Spirit. Our Lord Jesus says in Luke 11:13, "If you then, being evil, know how to give good gifts to your children, how much more will your heavenly Father give the Holy Spirit to those who ask Him!" Just ask God to give you the Holy Spirit and expect Him to do it, because He says He will.

6. Last of all, in order to receive the Holy Spirit, there must be faith, simply taking God at His word. No matter how positive any promise of God's word may be, we enjoy it personally only when we believe. Our

Lord Jesus says, "Whatever things you ask when you pray, believe that you receive them, and you will have them" (Mark 11:24). When you pray for the Holy Spirit you have prayed for something according to God's will and therefore you may know that your prayer is heard and that you have what you asked of Him (see 1 John 5:14-15). You may feel no different, but do not look at your feelings but at God's promise. Believe the prayer is heard, believe that God has given you the Holy Spirit and you will afterwards have in actual experience what you have received in simple faith on the bare promise of God's Word.

It is well to go often alone and kneel down and look up to the Holy Spirit and put into His hands anew the entire control of your life. Ask Him to take control of your thoughts, control of your imagination, control of your affections, control of your desires, control of your ambitions, control of your choices, control of your purposes, control of your words, control of your actions, control of everything, and just expect Him to do it. The whole secret of victory in the Christian life is letting the Holy Spirit who dwells within you have undisputed right of way in the entire conduct of your life.

5

Looking unto Jesus

*J*F we are to run with patience the race that is set before us, we must always keep looking unto Jesus (see Hebrews 12:1-3). One of the simplest and yet one of the mightiest secrets of abiding joy and victory is to *never lose sight of Jesus*.

1. First of all *we must keep looking at Jesus as the ground of our acceptance before God*. Over and over again Satan will make an attempt to discourage us by bringing up our sins and failures and thus try to convince us that we are not children of God, or not saved.

If he succeeds in getting us to keep looking at and brooding over our sins, he will soon get us discouraged, and discouragement means failure. But if we will keep looking at what God looks at, the death of Jesus Christ in our place that completely atones for every sin that we ever committed, we will never be discouraged because of the greatness of our sins. We shall see that while our sins are great, very great, they have all been atoned for. Every time Satan brings up one of our sins, we shall see that Jesus Christ has redeemed us from its curse by being made a curse in our place (see Galatians 3:13). We shall see that while in ourselves we are full of unrighteousness, nevertheless in Christ we are made the righteousness of God, because Christ was made to be sin in our place (see 2 Corinthians 5:21). We will see that every sin that Satan taunts us about has been borne and settled forever (see 1 Peter 2:24; Isaiah 53:6). We shall always be able to sing,

> "Jesus paid my debt,
> All the debt I owe;
> Sin had left a crimson stain.
> He washed it white as snow."

If you are this moment troubled about any sin that you have ever committed, either in the past or in the present, just look at Jesus on the cross; believe what God tells you about Him, that this sin which troubles you was laid upon Him (see Isaiah 53:6). Thank God that the sin is all settled; be full of gratitude to Jesus who bore it in your place and trouble about it no more. It is an act of base ingratitude to God to brood over sins that He in His infinite love has canceled. Keep looking at Christ on the cross and walk always in the sunlight of God's favor. This favor of God has been purchased for you at great cost. Gratitude demands that you should always believe in it and walk in its light.

2. In the second place, *we must keep looking at Jesus as our risen Savior, who has all power in heaven and on earth and is able to keep us every day and every hour.* Are you tempted to do some wrong at this moment? If you are, remember that Jesus rose from the dead, remember that at this moment He is living at the right hand of God in the glory; remember that He has all power in heaven and on earth, and that, therefore, He can give you victory right now. Believe what God tells you in His Word that Jesus has power to save you this moment "to the uttermost" (Hebrews 7:25). Believe that He has power to give you victory over this sin that now besets you. Ask Him to give you victory, expect Him to do it. In this way by looking unto the risen Christ for victory you may have victory over sin every day, every hour, every moment. "Remember that Jesus Christ was raised from the dead" (2 Timothy 2:8).

God has called every one of us to a victorious life, and the secret of this victorious life is always looking to the risen Christ for victory. Through looking to Christ crucified we obtain pardon and enjoy peace. Through looking to the risen Christ we obtain present victory over the power of sin. If you have lost sight of the risen Christ and have yielded to temptation, confess your sin and know that it is forgiven because God says so (see 1 John 1:9) and look to Jesus, the risen One, again, to give you victory now and keep looking to Him.

3. In the third place, *we must keep looking to Jesus as the One whom we should follow in our daily conduct.*

Our Lord Jesus says to us, His disciples today, as He said to His early disciples, "Follow Me." The whole secret of true Christian conduct can be summed up in these two words: "Follow Me." "He who says he abides in Him ought himself *also to walk just as He walked*" (1 John 2:6).

One of the commonest causes of failure in Christian life is found in the attempt to follow some good man whom we greatly admire. No man and no woman, no matter how good, can be safely followed. If we follow any man or woman, we are bound to go astray. There never has been but one absolutely perfect Man upon this earth – the Man Christ Jesus. If we try to follow any other man we are more sure to imitate his faults than his excellencies. Look at Jesus and Jesus only as your Guide.

If at any time you are in any perplexity as to what to do, simply ask the question, what would Jesus do? Ask God by His Holy Spirit to show you what Jesus would do. Study your Bible to find out what Jesus did do and follow Jesus. Even though no one else seems to be following Jesus, be sure that you follow Him. Do not spend your time or thought in criticizing others because they do not follow Jesus. See that you follow Him yourself. When you are wasting your time criticizing others for not following Jesus, Jesus is always saying to you, "What is that to you? You follow Me" (John 21:22). The question for you is not what following Jesus may involve for other people. The question is what does following Jesus mean for you?

This is the really simple life, the life of simply following Jesus. Many perplexing questions will come to you, but the most perplexing question will soon become as clear as day if you determine with all your heart to follow Jesus in everything. Satan will always be ready to whisper to you, "Such and such a good man does it," but all you need to do is to answer, "It matters not to me what this or that man may do or not do. The only question to me is, what would Jesus do?"

There is wonderful freedom in this life of simply following Jesus. This path is straight and plain. But the path of the one who tries to shape his conduct by observing the conduct of others is full of twists and turns and pitfalls. Keep looking at Jesus. Follow on trustingly where He leads. This is the path of the just which shines ever brighter unto the perfect day (see Proverbs 4:18). He is the Light of the World; anyone who follows Him shall not walk in darkness, but shall have the light of life all along the way (see John 8:12).

6

Church Membership

$\mathcal{N}$O young Christian and no old Christian can have real success in the Christian life without the fellowship of other believers. The church is a divine institution, built by Jesus Christ Himself. It is the one institution that abides. Other institutions come and go; they do their work for their day and disappear, but the church will continue to the end. "The gates of Hades shall not prevail against it" (Matthew 16:18). The church is made up of men and women, imperfect men and women, and consequently is an imperfect institution, but none the less it is of divine origin and God loves it, and every believer should realize that he belongs to it and should openly take his place in it and bear his responsibilities regarding it.

The true church consists of all true believers, all who are united to Jesus Christ by a living faith in Himself. In its outward organization at the present time, it is divided into numberless sects and local congregations, but in spite of these divisions the true church is one. It has one Lord, Jesus Christ. It has one faith, faith in Him as Savior, Divine Lord and only King; one baptism, the baptism in the one Spirit into the one body (see Ephesians 4:4-5; 1 Corinthians 12:13). But each individual Christian needs the fellowship of individual fellow believers. The outward expression of this fellowship is in membership in some organized body of believers. If we hold aloof from all organized churches, hoping thus to have a broader fellowship with all believers belonging to all the churches, we deceive ourselves. We will miss the helpfulness that comes from intimate union with some local congregation. I have known many well-meaning persons who have held aloof from membership in any specific organization, and I have never known a person who has done this whose own spiritual life has not suffered by it.

On the Day of Pentecost the three thousand who were converted were at once baptized and were added to the church (see Acts 2:41, 47), and "They continued steadfastly in the apostles' doctrine and fellowship, in the breaking of bread, and in prayers" (Acts 2:42). Their example is the one to follow. If you have really received Jesus Christ, hunt up as soon as possible some company of others who have received Jesus Christ and unite yourself with them.

In many communities there may be no choice of churches, for there is only one. In other communities one will be faced with the question, "With what body of believers shall I unite?" Do not waste your time looking for a perfect church. There is no perfect church. If you wait until you find a perfect church before you unite with any, you will unite with none, and thus you will belong to a church in which you are the only member and that is the most imperfect church of all. I would rather belong to the most imperfect Christian church I ever knew than not to belong to any church at all.

The local churches in Paul's day were very imperfect institutions. Let one read the epistles to the Corinthians and see how imperfect was the church in Corinth, see how much there was that was evil in it, and yet Paul never thought of advising any believer in Corinth to get out of this imperfect church. He did tell them to come out of heathenism, to come out from fellowship with infidels (see 2 Corinthians 6:14-18), but not a word on coming out of the imperfect church in Corinth. He did tell the church in Corinth to separate from their membership certain persons whose lives were wrong (see 1 Corinthians 5:11-12), but he did not tell the individual members of the church in Corinth to get out of the church because these persons had not yet been separated from their fellowship.

As you cannot find a perfect church, find the best church you can. Unite with a church where they believe in the Bible and where they preach the Bible. Avoid the churches where words are spoken open or veiled that have a tendency to undermine your faith in the Bible as a reliable revelation from God Himself, the all-sufficient rule of faith and practice. Unite with a church where there is a spirit of prayer, where the prayer-meetings are well kept up. Unite with a church that has a real active interest in the salvation of the lost, where young Christians are looked after and helped, where minister and people have a love for the poor and outcast, a church that regards its mission in this world to be the same as the mission of Christ, "to seek and to save the lost."

As to denominational differences, other things being equal, unite with that denomination whose ideas of doctrine and of government and of the ordinances are most closely akin to your own. But it is better to unite with a live church of some other denomination than to unite with a dead church of your own. We live in a day when denominational differences are becoming ever less and less, and oftentimes they are of no practical consequence whatever; and one will often feel more at home in a church of some other denomination than in any accessible church of his own denomination. The things that divide the denominations are insignificant compared with the great fundamental truths and purposes and faith that unite them.

If you cannot find the church that agrees with the pattern set forth above, find the church that comes nearest to it. Go into that church and by prayer and by work try to bring that church as nearly as you can to the pattern of what you think a church of Christ ought to be. But do not waste your strength in criticism against either church or minister. Seek for what is good in the church and in the minister and do your best to strengthen it. Hold aloof firmly, though unobtrusively, from what is wrong and seek to correct it. Do not be discouraged if you cannot correct it in a day or a week or a month or a year. Patient love and prayer and effort will tell in time. Drawing off by yourself and snarling and grumbling will do no good. They will simply make you and the truths for which you stand repulsive.

7

Bible Study

*T*HERE is nothing more important for the development of the spiritual life of the Christian than regular, systematic Bible study. It is as true in the spiritual life as it is in the physical life that health depends upon what we eat and how much we eat. The soul's proper food is found in one book, the Bible. Of course, a true minister of the gospel will feed us on the Word of God, but that is not enough. He feeds us but one or two days in the week and we need to be fed every day. Furthermore, it will not do to depend upon being fed by others. We must learn to feed ourselves. If we study the Bible for ourselves as we ought to study it, we shall be in a large measure independent of human teachers. Even if we are so unfortunate as to have for our minister a man who is himself ignorant of the truth of God we shall still be safe from harm.

We live in a day in which false doctrine abounds on every hand and the only Christian who is safe from being led into error is the one who studies his Bible for himself daily. The Apostle Paul warned the elders of the church in Ephesus that the time was soon coming when grievous wolves should enter in among them, not sparing the flock. When of their own selves men should arise, speaking perverse things to draw away the disciples after them, he told them how to be safe even in such perilous times as these. He said, "I commend you to God and to the word of His grace, which is able to build you up and give you an inheritance among all those who are sanctified" (Acts 20:32). Through meditation on the Word of God's grace they would be safe even in the midst of abounding error on the part of the leaders in the church (see Acts 20:29-32).

Writing later to the Bishop of the church in Ephesus, Paul said, "But evil men and impostors will grow worse and worse, deceiving and being deceived" (2 Timothy 3:13), but he goes on to tell Bishop Timothy how he and his fellow believers could be safe even in such times of increasing peril as were coming. That way was through the study of the Holy Scriptures, which are able to make wise unto salvation (see 2 Timothy 3:14-15). "All Scripture," he adds, "is given by inspiration of God, and is profitable for doctrine, for reproof, for correction, for instruction in righteousness, that the man of God may be complete, thoroughly equipped for every good work" (2 Timothy 3:16-17). That is to say, through the study of the Bible one will be sound in doctrine, will be led to see his sins and put them away, will find discipline in the righteous life and attain unto complete equipment for all good works. Our spiritual health, our growth, our strength, our victory over sin, our soundness in doctrine, our joy and peace in Christ, our cleansing from inward and outward sin, our fitness for service, all depend upon the study of the Word of God. The one who neglects his Bible is bound to make a failure of the Christian life. The one who studies his Bible in the right spirit and by a true method is bound to make a success of the Christian life.

This brings us face to face with the question, "What is the right way to study the Bible?"

1. First of all, we should *study it daily* (see Acts 17:11). This is of prime importance. No matter how good the methods of Bible study that one follows may be, no matter how much time one may put into Bible study now and then, the best results can only be secured when one makes it a matter of principle never to let a single day go by without earnest Bible study. This is the only safe course. Any day that is allowed to pass without faithful Bible study is a day thrown open to the advent into our hearts and lives of error or of sin.

The writer has been a Christian for more than a quarter of a century and yet today he would not dare to allow even a single day to pass over his head without listening to the voice of God as it speaks to him through the pages of His Book. It is at this point that many fall away. They grow careless and let a day pass, or even several days pass, without going alone with God and letting Him speak to them through His Word.

Mr Moody once wisely said, "In prayer we talk to God. In Bible study, God talks to us, and we had better let God do most of the talking."

A regular time should be set apart each day for the study of the Bible. I do not think it is well as a rule to say that we shall study so many chapters in a day, for that leads to undue haste and skimming and thoughtlessness, but it is well to set apart a certain length of time each day for Bible study. Some can give more time to Bible study than others, but no one ought to give less than fifteen minutes a day. I set the time so low in order that no one may be discouraged at the outset. If a young Christian should set out to give an hour or two hours a day to Bible study, there is a strong probability that he would not keep to the resolution and he might become discouraged. Yet I know of many very busy people who have given the first hour of every day for years to Bible study and some who have given even two hours a day.

The late Earl Cairns, Lord Chancellor of England, was one of the busiest men of his day, but Lady Cairns once told me that no matter how late he reached home at night he always arose at the same early hour for prayer and Bible study. She said, "We would sometimes get home from Parliament at two o'clock in the morning, but Lord Cairns would always arise at the same early hour to pray and study the Bible." Lord Cairns is reported as saying, "If I have had any success in life, I attribute it to the habit of giving the first two hours of each day to Bible study and prayer."

It is important that one choose the right time for

this study. Wherever it is possible, the best time for this study is immediately after arising in the morning. The worst time of all is the last thing at night. Of course, it is well to give a little while just before we retire to Bible reading, in order that God's voice may be the last to which we listen, but the bulk of our Bible study should be done at an hour when our minds are clearest and strongest. Whatever time is set apart for Bible study should be kept sacredly for that purpose.

2. We should *study the Bible systematically*. Much time is frittered away in random study of the Bible. The same amount of time put into systematic study would yield far larger results. Have a definite place where you are studying and have a definite plan of study. A good way for a young Christian to begin the study of the Bible is to read the Gospel of John. When you have read it through once, begin and read it again until you have gone over the Gospel five times. Then read the Gospel of Luke five times in the same way; then read Acts five times, then 1 Thessalonians five times, then 1 John five times, then Romans five times, then Ephesians five times.

By this time you will be ready to take up a more thorough method of Bible study. A good method is to begin at Genesis and read the Bible through chapter by chapter. Read each chapter through several times and then answer the following questions on the chapter:

(a) What is the principal subject of the chapter? (State the principal contents of the chapter in a single phrase or sentence.)

(b) What is the truth most clearly taught and most em-
phasized in the chapter?

(c) What is the best lesson?

(d) What is the best verse?

(e) Who are the principal people mentioned?

(f) What does the chapter teach about Jesus Christ?

Go through the entire Bible in this way.

Another and more thorough method of Bible chapter
study, which cannot be applied to every chapter in the
Bible, but which will yield excellent results when applied
to some of the more important chapters of the Bible, is
as follows:

(a) Read the chapter for today's study five times, reading it aloud at least once. Each new reading will
bring out some new point.

(b) Divide the chapter into its natural divisions and find
headings for each division that describes in the most
striking way the contents of that division. For example, suppose the chapter studied is 1 John 5. You
might divide it in this way: First division, verses 1-3,
The Believer's Noble Parentage. Second division,
verses 4-5, The Believer's Glorious Victory. Third division, verses 6-10, The Believer's Sure Ground of
Faith. Fourth division, verses 11-12, The Believer's
Priceless Possession. Fifth division, verse 13, The
Believer's Blessed Assurance. Sixth division, verses
14-15, The Believer's Unquestioning Confidence.
Seventh division, verses 16-17, The Believer's Great

Power and Responsibility. Eighth division, verses 18-19, The Believer's Perfect Security. Ninth division, verse 20, The Believer's Precious Knowledge. Tenth division, verse 21, The Believer's Constant Duty.

(c) Write down the leading facts of the chapter in their proper order.

(d) Make a note of the persons mentioned in the chapter and of any light thrown upon their character.

(e) Note the principal lessons of the chapter. It would be well to classify these. For instance, lessons about God, lessons about Christ, lessons about the Holy Spirit, etc.

(f) Find the central truth of the chapter.

(g) The key verse of the chapter, if there is one.

(h) The best verse in the chapter. Mark it and memorize it.

(i) Write down what new truth you have learned from the chapter.

(j) Write down what truth already known has come to you with new power.

(k) What definite thing have you resolved to do as a result of studying this chapter? It would be well to study in this way all the chapters in Matthew, Mark, Luke, John and Acts; the first eight chapters of Romans; 1 Corinthians 12, 13 and 15; the first six chapters of 2 Corinthians; all the chapters in Galatians, Ephesians, Philippians, First Thessalonians and the First Epistle of John.

It would be well at times to vary this by taking up other methods of study for a time.

Another profitable method of Bible study is the topical method. This was Mr Moody's favorite method of study. Take up the great topics of which the Bible teaches, such as the Holy Spirit, Prayer, the Blood of Christ, Sin, Judgment, Grace, Justification, the New Birth, Sanctification, Faith, Repentance, the Character of Christ, the Resurrection of Christ, the Ascension of Christ, the Second Coming of Christ, Assurance, Love of God, Love (to God, to Christ, to Christians, to all men), Heaven, Hell. Get a Bible text book and go through the Bible on each one of these topics.

3. We should *study the Bible comprehensively* – the whole Bible. Many who read their Bibles make the great mistake of confining all their reading to certain portions of the Bible that they enjoy, and in this way they get no knowledge of the Bible as a whole. They miss altogether many of the most important phases of Bible truth. Begin and go through the Bible again and again – a certain portion each day from the Old Testament and a portion from the New Testament. Read carefully at least one Psalm every day.

It is well oftentimes to read a whole book of the Bible through at a single sitting. Of course, with a few books of the Bible this would take one or two hours, but with most of the books of the Bible it can be done in a few minutes. With the shorter books of the Bible they should be read through again and again at a single sitting.

4. *Study the Bible attentively.* Do not hurry. One of

the worst faults in Bible study is haste and heedlessness. The Bible only does good by the truth that it contains. It has no magic power. It is better to read one verse attentively than to read a dozen chapters thoughtlessly. Sometimes you will read a verse that takes hold of you. Don't hurry on. Linger and ponder that verse. As you read, mark in your Bible what impresses you most. One does not need an elaborate system of Bible marking, simply mark what impresses you. Meditate upon what you mark. God pronounces that man blessed who "meditates" in God's law day and night (see Psalm 1:2).

It is wonderful how a verse of Scripture will open if one reads it over and over again and again, paying attention to each word as he reads it, trying to get its exact meaning and its full meaning. Memorize the passages that impress you most (see Psalm 119:11). When you memorize a passage of Scripture, memorize its location as well as its words. Fix in your mind chapter and verse where the words are found. A busy but spiritually-minded man who was hurrying to catch a train once said to me, "Tell me in a word how to study my Bible." I replied, "Thoughtfully."

5. *Study your Bible comparatively.* Compare Scripture with Scripture. The best commentary on the Bible is the Bible itself. Wherever you find a difficult passage in the Bible, there is always some passage elsewhere that explains its meaning. It is well to take up some book of the Bible and go through that book verse by verse. This is a very fruitful method of Bible study. It is also well in studying the Bible by chapters to look up the

references on the more important verses in the chapter.

6. *Study your Bible believingly.* The apostle Paul in writing to the Christians in Thessalonica says, "For this reason we also thank God without ceasing, because when you received the Word of God which you heard from us, you welcomed it not as the word of men, but as it is in truth, the Word of God, which also effectively works in you who believe" (1 Thessalonians 2:13). Happy is the one who receives the Word of God as these believers in Thessalonica received it, who receives it for what it really is, the Word of God. In such a one it "effectively works." The Bible is the Word of God and we get the most out of any book by studying it for what it really is. It is often said that we should study the Bible just as we study any other book. That principle contains a truth, but it also contains a great error. The Bible, it is true, is a book as other books are books, the same laws of grammatical and literary construction hold here as in other books, but the Bible is a unique book. It is what no other book is, the Word of God. This can be easily proven to any candid man. The Bible ought then to be studied as no other book is. It should be studied as the Word of God. This involves five things:

(a) A greater eagerness and more careful and candid study to find out just what it teaches than is bestowed upon all other books. It is important to know the mind of man. It is absolutely essential to know the mind of God. The place to discover the mind of God is the Bible. This is the book in which

God reveals His mind.

(b) A prompt and unquestioning acceptance of, and submission to, its teachings when definitely ascertained. These teachings may appear to us unreasonable or impossible, nevertheless we should accept them. If this book is the Word of God, how foolish it is to submit its teachings to the criticism of our finite reasoning. A little boy who discredits his wise father's statements simply because to his infant mind they appear unreasonable, is not a philosopher, but a fool. But the greatest of human thinkers is only an infant compared with the infinite God. And to discredit God's statements found in His Word because they appear unreasonable to our infantile minds is not to act the part of the philosopher, but the part of a fool. When we are once satisfied that the Bible is the Word of God, its clear teachings must be for us the end of all controversy and discussion.

(c) Absolute reliance upon all its promises in all their length and breadth and depth and height. The one who studies the Bible as the Word of God will say of any promise, no matter how vast and beyond belief it appears, "God who cannot lie has promised this, so I will claim it for myself." Mark the promise you thus claim. Look each day for some new promise from your infinite Father. He has put "His riches in glory" at your disposal (see Philippians 4:19). I know of no better way to grow rich spiritually than to search daily for promises, and when you find them appropriate them to yourself.

(d) Obedience. Be a doer of the Word and not a hearer only deceiving your own soul (see James 1:22). Nothing goes further to help one understand the Bible than the purpose to obey it. Jesus said, "If anyone wills to do His will, he shall know concerning the doctrine" (John 7:17). The surrendered will means the clear eye. If our eye is good (that is, our will is absolutely surrendered to God) our whole body shall be full of light. But if our eye be bad (that is, if we are trying to serve two masters and are not absolutely surrendered to one Master, God) our whole body shall be full of darkness (see Matthew 6:22-24). Many a passage that looks obscure to you now would become as clear as day if you were willing to obey in all things what the Bible teaches. Each commandment discovered in the Bible that is really intended as a commandment to us should be obeyed instantly. It is remarkable how soon one loses his relish for the Bible and how soon the mind becomes obscured to its teachings when we disobey the Bible at any point.

Many a time I have known persons who have loved their Bibles and have been useful in God's service and clear in their views of the truth who have come to something in the Bible that they were unwilling to obey, some sacrifice was demanded that they were unwilling to make, and their love for the Bible has rapidly waned, their faith in the Bible began to weaken, and soon they were drifting farther and farther away from clear views of the truth. Nothing clears the mind like obedience; nothing darkens the mind like disobedience. To obey a truth you see prepares you to see other truths. To disobey a truth you see darkens your mind to all truths.

Cultivate prompt, exact, unquestioning, joyous obedience to every command that it is evident from its context applies to you. Be on the lookout for new orders from your King. Blessing lies in the direction of obedience to them. God's commands are but signboards that mark the road to present success and blessedness and to eternal glory.

(e) Studying the Bible as the Word of God involves studying it as His own voice speaking directly to you. When you open the Bible to study, realize that you have come into the very presence of God and that now He is going to speak to you. Realize that it is God who is talking to you as much as if you saw Him standing there. Say to yourself, "God is now going to speak to me." Nothing goes farther to give a freshness and gladness to Bible study than the realization that as you read, God is actually talking to you.

In this way Bible study becomes personal companionship with God Himself. That was a wonderful privilege that Mary had one day, of sitting at the feet of Jesus and listening to His voice, but if we will study the Bible as the Word of God and as if we were in God's very presence, then we shall enjoy the privilege of sitting at the feet of God and having Him talk to us every day.

How often what would otherwise be a mere mechanical performance of a duty would become a wonderfully joyous privilege if one would say as he opens the Bible, "Now God, my Father, is going to speak to me." Oftentimes it helps us to a realization of the presence of God to read the Bible on our knees. The Bible became in some measure a new book to me when I took to reading it on my knees.

7. *Study the Bible prayerfully.* God, who is the author of the Bible, is willing to act as interpreter of it. He does so when you ask Him to. The one who prays with earnestness and faith the Psalmist's prayer, "Open my eyes, that I may see wondrous things from Your law" (Psalm 119:18) will get his eyes opened to see new beauties and wonders in the Word of God that he never dreamed of before.

Be very definite about this. Each time you open the Bible to study it, even though it is but for a few minutes, ask God to give you an open and discerning eye, and expect Him to do it. Every time you come to a difficulty in the Bible, lay it before God and ask an explanation and expect it. How often we think as we puzzle over hard passages, "Oh, if I only had some great Bible teacher here to explain this to me!" God is always present. He understands the Bible better than any human teacher. Take your difficulty to Him and ask Him to explain it. Jesus said, "When He, the Spirit of truth, has come, He will guide you into all truth" (John 16:13).

It is the privilege of the humblest believer in Christ to have the Holy Spirit for his guide in his study of the Word. I have known many very humble people, people with almost no education, who got more out of their

Bible study than most of the great theological teachers that I have known; simply because they had learned that it was their privilege to have the Holy Spirit for their teacher as they studied the Bible. Commentaries on the Bible are oftentimes of great value, but one will learn more of real value from the Bible by having the Holy Spirit for his teacher when he studies his Bible than he will from all the commentaries that were ever published.

8. *Improve spare moments for Bible study.* In almost every man's life many minutes each day are lost, while waiting for meals, riding on trains, going from place to place in cars and so forth. Carry a pocket Bible with you and save these golden moments by putting them to the very best use, listening to the voice of God.

9. *Store away the Scripture in your mind and heart.* It will keep you from sin (see Psalm 119:11); from false doctrine (see Acts 20:29, 30, 32; 2 Timothy 3:13-15). It will fill your heart with joy (see Jeremiah 15:16) and peace (see Psalm 85:8). It will give you victory over the evil one (see 1 John 2:14); it will give you power in prayer (see John 15:7); it will make you wiser than the aged and your enemies (see Psalm 119:98, 100, 130); it will make you "complete, thoroughly equipped for every good work" (2 Timothy 3:17). Try it. Do not memorize at random but memorize Scripture in a connected way; memorize texts bearing on various subjects in proper order; memorize by chapter and verse that you may know where to put your finger on the text if anyone disputes it. You should have a good Bible for your study.

8

Difficulties in the Bible

*S*OONER or later every young Christian comes across passages in the Bible which are hard to understand and difficult to believe. To many a young Christian, these difficulties become a serious hindrance in the development of their Christian life. For days and weeks and months oftentimes faith suffers partial or total eclipse. At just this point wise counsel is needed. We have no desire to conceal the fact that these difficulties exist. We rather desire to frankly face and consider them. What shall we do concerning these difficulties that every thoughtful student of the Bible will sooner or later encounter?

1. *The first thing we have to say about these difficulties is that from the very nature of the case difficulties are to be expected.* Some people are surprised and staggered because there are difficulties in the Bible. I would

be more surprised and more staggered if there were not. What is the Bible? It is a revelation of the mind and will and character and being of the infinitely great, perfectly wise, and absolutely holy God. But to whom is this revelation made? To men and women like you and me, to finite beings. To men who are imperfect in intellectual development and consequently in knowledge, and in character and consequently in spiritual discernment.

There must, from the very necessities of the case, be difficulties in such a revelation made to such persons. When the finite tries to understand the infinite there is bound to be difficulty. When the ignorant contemplate the utterances of one perfect in knowledge there must be many things hard to be understood and some things which to their immature and inaccurate minds appear absurd.

When sinful beings listen to the demands of an absolutely holy being they are bound to be staggered at some of His demands, and when they consider His dealings they are bound to be staggered at some of His dealings. These dealings will necessarily appear too severe, stern, harsh, terrific. It is plain that there must be difficulties for us in such a revelation as the Bible is proven to be. If someone should hand me a book that was as simple as the multiplication table and say, "This is the Word of God, in which He has revealed His whole will and wisdom," I would shake my head and say, "I cannot believe it. That is too easy to be a perfect revelation of infinite wisdom." There must be in any complete revelation of God's mind and will and character and being, things hard for a beginner to understand, and the wisest and best of us are but beginners.

2. *The second thing to be said about these difficulties is that a difficulty in a doctrine, or a grave objection to a doctrine, does not in any wise prove the doctrine to be untrue.* Many thoughtless people fancy that it does. If they come across some difficulty in the way of believing in the divine origin and absolute inerrancy and infallibility of the Bible, they at once conclude that the doctrine is exploded. That is very illogical. Stop a moment and think and learn to be reasonable and fair.

There is scarcely a doctrine in science commonly believed today that has not had some great difficulty in the way of its acceptance. When the Copernican theory, now so universally accepted, was first proclaimed, it encountered a very grave difficulty. If this theory were true the planet Venus should have phases as the moon has. But no phases could be discovered by the best glass then in existence. But the positive argument for the theory was so strong that it was accepted in spite of this apparently unanswerable objection. When a more powerful glass was made, it was discovered that Venus had phases after all.

The whole difficulty arose, as all those in the Bible arise, from man's ignorance of some of the facts in the case. According to the common sense logic recognized in every department of science, if the positive proof of a theory is conclusive, it is believed by rational men, in spite of any number of difficulties in minor details. Now the positive proof that the Bible is the Word of

God, that it is an absolutely trustworthy revelation from God Himself of Himself, His purposes and His will, of man's duty and destiny, of spiritual and eternal realities, is absolutely conclusive. Therefore every rational man and woman must believe it in spite of any number of difficulties in minor details. He is a shallow thinker who gives up a well-attested truth because of some facts which he cannot reconcile with that truth. And he is a very shallow Bible scholar who gives up the divine origin and inerrancy of the Bible because there are some supposed facts that he cannot reconcile with that doctrine.

3. *The third thing to be said about the difficulties in the Bible is that there are many more and much greater difficulties in the way of a doctrine that holds the Bible to be of human origin, and hence fallible, than are in the way of the doctrine that holds the Bible to be of divine origin and hence altogether trustworthy.* A man may bring you some difficulty and say, "How do you explain that if the Bible is the Word of God?" and perhaps you may not be able to answer him satisfactorily. Then he thinks he has you, but not at all.

Turn on him and ask him how do you account for the fulfilled prophecies of the Bible if it is of human origin? How do you account for the marvelous unity of the Book? How do you account for its inexhaustible depth? How do you account for its unique power in lifting men up to God? How do you account for the history of the Book, its victory over all men's attacks, etc., etc., etc. For every insignificant objection he can bring to your view, you can bring many deeply significant objections to his view, and no candid man will have any difficulty in deciding between the two views. The difficulties that confront one who denies that the Bible is of divine origin and authority are far more numerous and weighty than those that confront the ones who believes it is of divine origin and authority.

4. *The fourth thing to be said about the difficulties in the Bible is this: the fact that you cannot solve a difficulty does not prove that it cannot be solved, and the fact that you cannot answer an objection does not prove at all that it cannot be answered.* It is passing strange how often we overlook this very evident fact. There are many who, when they meet a difficulty in the Bible and give it a little thought and can see no possible solution, at once jump at the conclusion that a solution is impossible by anyone, and so throw up their faith in the reliability of the Bible and in its divine origin.

A little more of that modesty that is becoming in beings so limited in knowledge as we all are would have led them to say, "Though I see no possible solution to this difficulty, someone a little wiser than I might easily find one." Oh! if we would only bear in mind that we do not know everything, and that there are a great many things that we cannot solve now that we could easily solve if we only knew a little more.

Above all, we ought never to forget that there may be a very easy solution to infinite wisdom of that which to our finite wisdom – or ignorance – appears absolutely insoluble. What would we think of a beginner in algebra who, having tried in vain for half an hour to solve a difficult problem, declared that there was no possible solution to the problem because he could find none? A man of much experience and ability once left his work and came a long distance to see me in great perturbation of spirit because he had discovered what seemed to him a flat contradiction in the Bible. It had defied all his attempts at reconciliation, but in a few moments he was shown a very simple and satisfactory solution to the difficulty.

5. *The fifth thing to be said about the difficulties in the Bible is that the seeming defects in the Book are exceedingly insignificant when put in comparison with its many and marvelous excellencies.* It certainly reveals great perversity of both mind and heart that men spend so much time expatiating on the insignificant points that they consider defects in the Bible, and pass by absolutely unnoticed the incomparable beauties and wonders that adorn and glorify almost every page.

What would we think of any man, who, in studying some great masterpiece of art, concentrated his entire attention upon what looked to him like a fly-speck in the corner? A large proportion of what is vaunted as "critical study of the Bible" is a laborious and scholarly investigation of supposed fly-specks and an entire neglect of the countless glories of the Book.

6. *The sixth thing to be said about the difficulties in the Bible is that the difficulties in the Bible have far more weight with superficial readers of it than with profound students.* Take a man who is totally ignorant of the real

contents and meaning of the Bible and devotes his whole strength to discovering apparent inconsistencies in it. To such superficial students of the Bible these difficulties seem of immense importance; but to the one who has learned to meditate on the Word of God day and night, they have scarce any weight at all. That mighty man of God, George Müller, who had carefully studied the Bible from beginning to end more than a hundred times, was not disturbed by any difficulties he encountered. But to the one who is reading it through carefully for the first or second time there are many things that perplex and stagger.

7. *The seventh thing to be said about the difficulties in the Bible is that they rapidly disappear upon careful and prayerful study.* How many things there are in the Bible that once puzzled us and staggered us that have been perfectly cleared up, and no longer present any difficulty at all! Is it not reasonable to suppose that the difficulties that still remain will also disappear upon fur- ther study?

How shall we deal with the difficulties which we do find in the Bible?

(a) First of all, *honestly*. Whenever you find a difficulty in the Bible, frankly acknowledge it. If you cannot give a good honest explanation, do not attempt as yet to give any at all.

(b) *Humbly*. Recognize the limitations of your own mind and knowledge, and do not imagine there is no solution just because you have found none. There is in all probability a very simple solution. You will find it some day, though at present you can find no solution at all.

(c) *Determinedly*. Make up your mind that you will find the solution if you can by any amount of study and hard thinking. The difficulties in the Bible are your heavenly Father's challenge to you to set your brains to work.

(d) *Fearlessly*. Do not be frightened when you find a difficulty, no matter how unanswerable it appears upon first glance. Thousands have found such before you. They were seen hundreds of years ago and still the old Book stands. You are not likely to discover any difficulty that was not discovered and probably settled long before you were born, though you do not know just where to lay your hand upon the solution.

The Bible, which has stood eighteen centuries of rigid examination and incessant and awful assault, is not going under before any discoveries that you make or any attacks of modern infidels. All modern infidel attacks upon the Bible are simply a revamping of old objections that have been disposed of a hundred times in the past. These old objections will prove no more effective in their new clothes than they did in the cast-off garments of the past.

(e) *Patiently*. Do not be discouraged because you do not solve every problem in a day. If some difficulty defies your best effort, lay it aside for awhile. Very likely when you come back to it, it will have disappeared and you will wonder how you were ever perplexed by it.

The writer often has to smile today when he thinks how sorely he was perplexed in the past over questions which are now as clear as day.

(f) *Scripturally.* If you find a difficulty in one part of the Bible, look for other Scripture to throw light upon it and dissolve it. Nothing explains Scripture like Scripture. Never let apparently obscure passages of Scripture darken the light that comes from clear passages; rather let the light that comes from the clear passage illuminate the darkness that seems to surround the obscure passage.

(g) *Prayerfully.* It is wonderful how difficulties dissolve when one looks at them on his knees. One great reason why some modern scholars have learned to be destructive critics is because they have forgotten how to pray.

9

Prayer

*T*HE one who would succeed in the Christian life must lead a life of prayer. Very much of the failure in Christian living today, and in Christian work, results from neglect of prayer. Very few Christians spend as much time in prayer as they ought. The apostle James told believers in his day that the secret of the poverty and powerlessness of their lives and service was neglect of prayer. "You have not," says God through the apostle James, "because you ask not." So it is today. Why is it, many a Christian is asking, that I make such poor headway in my Christian life? Why do I have so little victory over sin? Why do I accomplish so little by my effort? And God answers, "You have not because you ask not."

It is easy enough to lead a life of prayer if one only sets about it. Set apart some time each day for prayer.

The rule of David and of Daniel is a good one: three times a day. "Evening and morning and at noon," says David, "I will pray, and cry aloud, and He shall hear my voice" (Psalm 55:17). Of Daniel we read, "Now when Daniel knew that the writing was signed, he went home. And in his upper room, with his windows open toward Jerusalem, he knelt down on his knees three times that day, and prayed and gave thanks before his God, as was his custom since early days" (Daniel 6:10).

Of course, one can pray while walking the street, or riding in the car, or sitting at his desk, and one should learn to lift his heart to God right in the busiest moments of his life, but we need set times of prayer, times when we go alone with God, shut to the door and talk to our Father in the secret place (see Matthew 6:6). God is in the secret place and will meet with us there and listen to our petitions.

Prayer is a wonderful privilege. It is an audience with the King. It is talking to our Father. How strange it is that people should ask the question, "How much time ought I to spend in prayer?" When a subject is summoned to an audience with his king, he never asks, "How much time must I spend with the king?" His question is rather, "How much time will the king give me?" And with any true child of God who realizes what prayer really is, that it is an audience with the King of kings, the question will never be, "How much time must I spend in prayer?" but "How much time may I spend in prayer with a due regard to other duties and privileges?"

Begin the day with thanksgiving and prayer. Thanksgiving for the definite mercies of the past, prayer for the definite needs of the present day. Think of the temptations that you are likely to meet during the day; ask God to show you the temptations that you are likely to meet and get from God strength for victory over these temptations before the temptations come. The reason why many fail in the battle is because they wait until the hour of battle. The reason why others succeed is because they have gained their victory on their knees long before the battle came. Jesus conquered in the awful battles of Pilate's judgment hall and of the cross because He had the night before in prayer anticipated the battle and gained the victory before the struggle really came.

He had told His disciples to do the same. He had bidden them to "pray that you may not enter into temptation" (Luke 22:40), but they had slept when they ought to have prayed, and when the hour of temptation came they fell. Anticipate your battles, fight them on your knees before temptation comes and you will always have victory. At the very outset of the day, get counsel and strength from God Himself for the duties of the day.

Never let the rush of business crowd out prayer. The more work that any day has to do, the more time must be spent in prayer in preparation for that work. You will not lose time by it, you will save time by it. Prayer is the greatest time saver known to man. The more the work crowds you, the more time take for prayer.

Stop in the midst of the bustle and hurry and temptation of the day for thanksgiving and prayer. A few minutes spent alone with God at midday will go far to keep you calm in the midst of the worries and anxieties of modern life.

Close the day with thanksgiving and prayer. Review all the blessings of the day and thank God in detail for them. Nothing goes farther to increase faith in God and in His Word than a calm review at the close of each day of what God has done for you that day. Nothing goes farther towards bringing new and larger blessings from God than intelligent thanksgiving for blessings already granted.

The last thing you do each day is to ask God to show you if there has been anything in the day that has been displeasing in His sight. Then wait quietly before God and give God an opportunity to speak to you. Listen. Do not be in a hurry. If God shows you anything in the day that has been displeasing in His sight, confess it fully and frankly as to a holy and loving Father. Believe that God forgives it all, for He says He does (see 1 John 1:9).

Thus at the close of each day all your accounts with God will be straightened out. You can lie down and sleep in the glad consciousness that there is not a cloud between you and God. You can arise the next day to begin life anew with a clean balance sheet.

Do this and you can never backslide for more than twenty-four hours. Indeed, you will not backslide at all. It is very hard to straighten out accounts in business that have been allowed to get crooked through a prolonged period. No bank ever closes its business day until its balance is found to be absolutely correct. And no Christian should close a single day until his accounts with God for that day have been perfectly adjusted alone with Him.

There should be special prayer in special temptation – that is when we see the temptation approaching. If you possibly can, get at once alone somewhere with God and fight your battle out. Keep looking to God. "Pray without ceasing" (1 Thessalonians 5:17). It is not needful to be on your knees all the time, but the heart should be on its knees all the time. We should be often on our knees or on our faces literally. This is a joyous life, free from worry and care. "Be anxious for nothing, but in everything by prayer and supplication, with thanksgiving, let your requests be made known to God; and the peace of God, which surpasses all understanding, will guard your hearts and minds through Christ Jesus" (Philippians 4:6-7).

There are three things for which one who would succeed in the Christian life must especially pray.

- For wisdom. "If any of you lacks wisdom [and we all do], let him ask of God" (James 1:5).
- For strength. "Those who wait on the LORD shall renew their strength" (Isaiah 40:31).
- For the Holy Spirit. "How much more will your heavenly Father give the Holy Spirit to those who ask Him!" (Luke 11:13).

Even if you have received the Holy Spirit, you should constantly pray for a new filling with the Holy Spirit and definitely expect to receive it. We need a new filling with the Spirit for every new emergency of Christian life and Christian service. The apostle Peter was baptized and filled with the Holy Spirit on the Day of Pentecost (see Acts 2:1-4), but he was filled anew in Acts 4:8 and Acts 4:31.

There are many Christians in the world who once had a very definite baptism with the Holy Spirit and had great joy and were wonderfully used, but who have tried to go ever since in the power of that baptism received years ago, and today their lives are comparatively joyless and powerless. We need constantly to get new supplies of oil for our lamps. We get these new supplies of oil by asking for them.

It is not enough that we have our times of secret prayer to God alone with Him, we also need fellowship with others in prayer. If they have a prayer-meeting in your church, attend it regularly. Attend it for your own sake; attend it for the sake of the church. If it is a prayer-meeting only in name and not in fact, use your influence quietly and constantly (not obtrusively) to make it a real prayer-meeting. Keep the prayer-meeting night sacredly for that purpose. Refuse all social engagements for that night.

A major-general in the United States army once took command of the forces in a new district. A reception was arranged for him for a certain night in the week. When he was informed of this public reception he replied that it was prayer-meeting night and everything else had to give way for prayer-meeting, that he could not attend the reception on that night. That general had proved himself a man that could be depended upon. The Church of Christ in America owes more to him than to almost any other officer in the American army.

Ministers learn to depend upon their prayer-meeting members. The prayer-meeting is the most important meeting in the church. If your church has no prayer-meeting, use your influence to have one. It does not take many members to make a good prayer-meeting. You can start with two but work for many.

It is well to have a little company of Christian friends with whom you are in real sympathy and with whom you meet regularly every week simply for prayer. There has been nothing of more importance in the development of my own spiritual life than a little prayer-meeting of less than a dozen friends who have met every Saturday night for years. We met and together we waited upon God. If my life has been of any use to the Master, I attribute it largely to that prayer-meeting. Happy is the young Christian who has a little band of friends like that who meet together regularly for prayer.

10

Working for Christ

*O*NE of the important conditions of growth and strength in the Christian life is work. No man can keep up his physical strength without exercise and no man can keep up his spiritual strength without spiritual exercise. The working Christian is the happy Christian. The working Christian is the strong Christian.

Some Christians never backslide because they are too busy about their Master's business to backslide. Many professed Christians do backslide because they are too idle to do anything but backslide. Jesus said to the first disciples, "Follow Me, and I will make you fishers of men" (Matthew 4:19). Anyone who is not a fisher of men is not following Christ. Bearing fruit in bringing others to the Savior is the purpose for which Jesus has chosen us and is one of the most important conditions of power in prayer. Jesus says in John 15:16,

"You did not choose Me, but I chose you and appointed you *that you should go and bear fruit*, and that your fruit should remain, *that whatever you ask the Father in My name He may give you*." These words of Jesus are very plain. They tell us that the one who is bearing fruit is the one who can pray in the name of Christ and get what he asks in that name.

In the same chapter Jesus tells us that bearing fruit in His strength is the condition of fullness of joy. He says, "These things I have spoken to you [that is, the things about abiding in Him and bearing fruit in His strength], that My joy may remain in you, and that your joy may be full" (John 15:11). Experience abundantly proves the truth of these words of our Master. Those who are full of activity in winning others to Christ are those who are full of joy in Christ Himself.

If you wish to be a happy Christian, if you wish to be a strong Christian, if you wish to be a Christian who is mighty in prayer, begin at once to work for the Master and never let a day pass without doing some definite work for Him.

But how can a young Christian work for Him? How can a young Christian bear fruit? The answer is very simple and very easy to follow. You can bear fruit for your Master by going to others and telling them what your Savior has done for you, and by urging them to accept this same Savior and showing them how to do it.

There is no other work in the world that is so easy to do, so joyous, and so abundant in its fruitfulness, as personal hand-to-hand work. The youngest Christian can do personal work. Of course, he cannot do it so well as he will do it later, after he has had more practice. But the way to learn how to do it is by doing it. I have known thousands of Christians all around the world who have begun to work for Christ, and to bring others to Christ, the very day that they were converted. How often young men and young women, yes, and old men and old women too, have come to me and said, "I accepted Jesus Christ last night as my Savior, my Lord and my King, and tonight I have led a friend to Christ." Then the next day they would come and tell me of someone else they had led to Christ.

When we were in Sheffield, a young man working in a warehouse accepted Christ. Before the month's mission in Sheffield was over he had led thirty others to Christ, many of them in the same warehouse where he himself worked. This is but one instance among many. There are many books that tell how to do personal work.

But one does not need to wait until they have read some book on the subject before they begin. One of the commonest and greatest mistakes that is made is that of frittering one's life away in getting ready to get ready to get ready. Some never do get ready. The way to get ready is to begin at once. Make up your mind that you will speak about accepting Christ to at least one person every day.

Early in his Christian life Mr Moody made this resolution that he would never let a day pass over his head without speaking to at least one person about Christ. One night he was returning late from his work. As he got near home it occurred to him that he had not spoken to anyone that day. He said to himself, "It is too late now. I will not get an opportunity. Here will be one day gone without my speaking to anyone about Christ." But a little ways ahead of him he saw a man standing under a lamp post. He said, "Here is my last opportunity." The man was a stranger to him, though he knew who Mr Moody was.

Mr Moody hurried up to him and asked him, "Are you a Christian?" The man replied, "That is none of your business. If you were not a sort of a preacher I would knock you into the gutter." But Mr Moody spoke a few faithful words to him and passed on.

The next day this man called on one of Mr Moody's business friends in Chicago in great indignation. He said, "That man Moody of yours over on the Northside is doing more harm than he is good. He has zeal without knowledge. He came up to me last night, a perfect stranger, and asked me if I was a Christian. He insulted me. I told him if he had not been a sort of preacher I would have knocked him into the gutter."

Mr Moody's friend called him in and said to him, "Moody, you are doing more harm than good. You have zeal without knowledge. You insulted a friend of mine on the street last night." Mr Moody went out somewhat crestfallen, feeling that perhaps he was doing more harm than good, that perhaps he did have zeal without knowledge.

But some weeks after, late at night, there was a great pounding on his door. Mr Moody got out of bed and rushed to the door supposing that the house was on fire. That same man stood at the door. He said, "Mr Moody, I have not had a night's rest since you spoke to me that night under the lamp post and I have come around for you to tell me what to do to be saved." Mr Moody had the joy that night of leading that man to Christ.

It is better to have zeal without knowledge than to have knowledge without zeal, but it is better yet to have zeal with knowledge, and anyone may have this. The way to get knowledge is by experience, and the way to get experience is by doing the work. The man who is so afraid of making blunders that he never does anything, never learns anything. The man who goes ahead and does his best and is willing to risk the blunders, is the man who learns to avoid the blunders in the future. Some of the most gifted men I have ever known have never really accomplished anything, they were so fearful of making blunders. Some of the most useful men I have ever known were men who at the outset were the least promising, but who had a real love for souls and went on, at first in a blundering way, but they blundered on until they learned by experience to do things well.

Do not be discouraged by your blunders. Pitch in and keep pegging away. Every honest mistake is but a stepping-stone to future success. Try every day to lead someone else to Christ. Of course, you will not succeed every day, but the work will do you good any way, and years after you will often find that where you thought you have made the greatest blunders, you have ac- complished the best results. The man who gets angriest at you, will often turn out in the end the man who is most grateful to you. Be patient and hope on. Never be discouraged.

Make a prayer list. Go alone with God. Write down at the top of a sheet of paper, "God helping me, I promise to pray daily and to work persistently for the conversion of the following persons." Then kneel down and ask God to show you who to put on that list. Do not make the list so long that your prayer and work become mechanical and superficial. After you have made the list, keep your covenant, really pray for them every day.

Watch for opportunities to speak to them – improve these opportunities. You may have to watch long for your opportunities with some of them, and you may have to speak often, but never give up. I prayed about fifteen years for one man, one of the most discouraging men I ever met, but I saw that man converted at last, and I saw him a preacher of the gospel, and many others were converted through his preaching, and now he is in the Glory.

Learn to use tracts. Get a few good tracts that are fitted to meet the needs of different kinds of people. Then hand these tracts out to the people whose needs they are adapted to meet. Follow your tracts up with prayer and with personal effort.

Go to your pastor and ask him if there is some work he would like to have you do for him in the church. Be a person that your pastor can depend upon. We live in a day in which there are many kinds of work going on outside the church, and many of these kinds of work are good and you should take part in them as you are able, but never forget that your first duty is to the church of which you are a member.

Be a person that your pastor can count on. It may be that your pastor may not want to use you, but at least give him the chance of refusing you. If he does refuse you, don't be discouraged, but find work somewhere else. There is plenty to do and few to do it. It is as true today as it was in the days of our Savior: "The harvest truly is plentiful, but the laborers are few" (Matthew 9:37). "Pray the Lord of the harvest to send out laborers into His harvest" (Matthew 9:38). Pray that He will send you.

The right kind of men are needed in the ministry. The right kind of men and women are needed for foreign mission work, but you may not be the right kind of a man or woman for foreign missionary work, but none the less there is work for you to do just as important in its place as the work of the minister or the missionary is. See that you fill your place, and fill it well.

11

Foreign Missions

*I*N order to have the largest success in the Christian life one must be interested in foreign missions. The last command of our Lord before leaving this earth was, "Go therefore and make disciples of all the nations, baptizing them in the name of the Father and of the Son and of the Holy Spirit, teaching them to observe all things that I have commanded you; and lo, I am with you always, even to the end of the age" (Matthew 28:19-20).

Here is a command and a promise. It is one of the sweetest promises in the Bible. But the enjoyment of the promise is conditioned upon obedience to the command. Our Lord commands every one of His disciples to go and "make disciples" of all the nations. This command was not given to the apostles alone, but to every member of Christ's church in all ages. If we go, then Christ will be with us even unto the end of the age; but, if we do not go, we have no right to count upon His companionship. Are you going? How can we go? There are three ways in which we can go, and in at least two of these ways we must go if we are to enjoy the wonderful privilege of the personal companionship of Jesus Christ every day unto the end of the age.

1. First, *many of us can go in our own persons*. Many of us ought to go. God does not call every one of us to go as foreign missionaries, but He does call many of us to go who are not responding to the call. Every Christian should offer himself for the foreign field and leave the responsibility of choosing him or refusing him to the all-wise One, God Himself. No Christian has a right to stay at home until he has gone and offered himself definitely to God for the foreign field.

If you have not done it before, do it today. Go alone with God and say, "Heavenly Father, here I am. Your property, purchased by the precious blood of Christ. I belong to You. If You wish me in the foreign field, make it clear to me and I will go." Then keep watching for the leading of God. God's leading is clear leading. He is light and in Him is no darkness at all (see 1 John 1:5).

If you are really willing to be led, He will make it clear as day. Until He does make it clear as day, you need have no morbid anxiety that perhaps you are staying at home when you ought to go to the foreign field. If He wants you, He will make it clear as day in His own way and time. If He does make it clear, then prepare to go step by step as He leads you. And when His hour comes, go, no matter what it costs. If He does not make it clear that you ought to go in your own person, stay at home and do your duty at home and go in the other ways that will now be told.

2. *We all can go, and all ought to go to the foreign field by our gifts.* There are many who would like to go to the foreign field in their own person, but whom God providentially prevents, but who are still going in the missionaries they support or help to support. It is possible for you to preach the gospel in the remotest corners of the earth by supporting or helping to support a foreign missionary or a native worker in that place.

Many who read this book are able financially to support a foreign missionary out of their own pocket. If you are able to do it, do it. If you are not able to support a foreign missionary, you may be able to support a native helper – do it. You may be able to support one missionary in Japan and another in China, and another in India and another in Africa and another somewhere else – do it. Oh! the joy of preaching the gospel in lands that we shall never see with our own eyes.

How few in the church of Christ today realize their privilege of preaching the gospel and saving men and women and children in distant lands by sending substitute missionaries to them, that is, by sending some one that goes for you where you cannot go yourself. They could not go but for your gifts by which they are supported and you could not go but for them, by their going in your place. You may be able to give but very little to foreign missions, but every little counts. Many insignificant streams together make a mighty river. If you cannot be a river, at least be a stream.

Learn to give largely. The large giver is the happy Christian. "The generous soul will be made rich" (Proverbs 11:25), "He who sows sparingly will also reap sparingly, and he who sows bountifully will also reap bountifully," "God is able to make all grace abound toward you, that you, always having all sufficiency in all things, may have an abundance for every good work" (2 Corinthians 9:6, 8).

Success and growth in the Christian life depend upon few things more than upon liberal giving. The stingy Christian cannot be a growing Christian. It is wonderful how a Christian man begins to grow when he begins to give.

Power in prayer depends on liberality in giving. One of the most wonderful statements about prayer and its answers is 1 John 3:22. John says there that, whatsoever he asked of God he received; and he tells us why, because he on his part kept God's commandments and did those things which were pleasing in His sight. The immediate context shows that the special commandments he was keeping were the commandments about giving.

He tells us in the twenty-first verse that when our heart condemns us not in the matter of giving, then have we confidence in our prayers to God. God's answers to our prayers come in through the same door that our gifts go out to others, and some of us open the door such a little ways by our small giving that God is not able to pass on to us any large answers to our prayers.

One of the most remarkable promises in the Bible is found in Philippians 4:19: "My God shall supply all your need according to His riches in glory by Christ Jesus," but this promise was made to believers who had distinguished themselves above their fellows by the largeness and the frequency of their giving (see vv. 14-18). Of course, we should not confine our giving to foreign missions. We should give to the work of the home church. We should give to rescue work in our large cities. We should do good to all men as we have opportunity, especially to those who are of the household of faith (see Galatians 6:10). But foreign missions should have a large part in our gifts.

Give systematically. Set aside for Christ a fixed proportion of all the money or goods you get. Be exact and honest about it. Don't use that part of your income for yourself under any circumstances. The Christian is not under law, and there is no law binding on the Christian that he should give a tenth of his income, but as a matter of free choice and glad gratitude a tenth is a good proportion to begin with. Don't let it be less than a tenth. God required that of the Jews, and the Christian ought not to be more selfish than a Jew. After you have given your tenth, you will soon learn the joy of giving free will offerings in addition to the tenth.

3. There is another way in which we can go to the foreign field, and that is by our prayers. We can all go in this way. Any hour of the day or night you can reach any corner of the earth by your prayers. I go to Japan, to China and to Australia and to Tasmania and to New

Zealand and to India and to Africa and to other parts of the earth every day, by my prayers. And prayer really brings things to pass where you go. Do not make prayer an excuse for not going in your own person if God wishes you, and do not make prayer an excuse for small giving. There is no power in that kind of prayer. If you are ready to go yourself if God wishes you, and if you are actually going by your gifts as God gives you ability, then you can go effectually by your prayers also. The greatest need of the work of Jesus Christ today is prayer. The greatest need of foreign missions today is prayer. Foreign missions are a success, but they are no such success as they ought to be and might be. They are no such success as they would be if Christians at home, as well as abroad, were living up to the full measure of their opportunity in prayer.

Be definite in your prayers for foreign missions. Pray first of all that God will send forth laborers into His harvest, the right sort of laborers. There are many men and women in the foreign field that ought never to have gone there. There was not enough prayer about it. More foreign missionaries are greatly needed, but only more of the right kind of missionaries. Pray to God daily and believingly to send forth laborers into the harvest.

Pray for the laborers who are already on the field. No class of men and women need our prayers more than foreign missionaries. No class of men and women are objects of more bitter hatred from Satan than they. Satan delights to attack the reputation and the character of the brave men and women who have gone to the front in the battle for Christ and the Truth. No persons are subjected to so numerous and to such subtle and awful temptations as foreign missionaries. We owe it to them to support them by our prayers. Do not merely pray for foreign missionaries in general. Have a few special missionaries of whose work you make a study that you may pray intelligently for them.

Pray for the native converts. We Christians at home think we have difficulties and trials and temptations and persecutions, but the burdens that we have to bear are nothing to what the converts in heathen lands have to bear. The obstacles oftentimes are enormous and discouragements crushing. Christ alone can make them stand, but He works in answer to the prayers of His people. Pray often, pray earnestly, pray intensely and pray believingly for native converts. How wonderfully God has answered prayer for native converts we are beginning to learn from missionary literature.

It is well to be definite here again and to have some definite field about whose needs you keep yourself informed and pray for the converts of that field. Do not have so many that you become confused and mechanical. Pray for conversions in the foreign field. Pray for revivals in definite fields. The last few years have been years of special prayer for special revival in foreign fields and from every corner of the earth tidings have come of how amazingly God is answering these prayers. But the great things that God is beginning to do are small indeed in comparison with what He will do if there is more prayer.

12

Companions

*O*UR companions have a great deal to do with determining our character. The companionships that we form create an intellectual, moral and spiritual atmosphere that we are constantly breathing, and our spiritual health is helped or hindered by it.

Every young Christian should have a few wisely chosen friends, intimate friends with whom he can talk freely. Search out for yourself a few persons of about your own age with whom you can associate intimately. Be sure that they are spiritual persons in the best sense, persons who love to study the Bible, persons who love to converse on spiritual themes, persons who know how to pray and do pray, persons who are really working to bring others to Christ.

Do not be at all uneasy about the fact that some Christian people are more agreeable to you than others.

God has made us in that way. Some are attracted to some persons and some to others, and it proves nothing against the others and nothing against yourself that you are not attracted to them as you are to some people. Cultivate the friendship of those whose friendship you find helpful to your own spiritual life.

On the other hand, avoid the companionships that you find spiritually and morally hurtful. Of course, we are not to withdraw ourselves utterly from unconverted people, or even of very bad people. We are to cultivate oftentimes the acquaintance of unspiritual people, and even of very bad people, in order that we may win them for Christ; but we must always be on our guard in such companionships to bear always in mind to seek to lift them up or else they will be sure to drag us down.

If you find in spite of all your best effort that any companionship is doing harm to your own spiritual life, then give it up. Some people are surrounded with such an atmosphere of unbelief or cynicism or censoriousness or impurity or greed or some other evil thing that it is impossible to associate with them to any large extent without being contaminated. In such a case, the path of wisdom is plain; stop associating with them to any large extent. Stop associating with them at all except in so far as there is some prospect of helping them.

But there are other companionships that mold our lives besides the companionships of living persons. The books that we read are our companions. They exert a tremendous influence for good or for evil. There is nothing that will help us more than a good book, and there is nothing that will hurt us more than a bad book. Among the most helpful books are the biographies of good men. Read again and again the lives of such good and truly great men as Wesley and Finney and Moody. We live in a day in which good biographies abound. Read them. Well-written histories are good companions. No study is more practical and instructive than the study of history, and it is not only instructive but spiritually helpful if we only watch to see the hand of God in history, to see the inevitable triumph of right and the inevitable punishment of wrong in individuals and in nations.

Some few books of fiction are helpful, but here one needs to be very much on his guard. A large portion of modern fiction is positively pernicious morally. Books of fiction that are not positively bad, at least give false views of life and unfit one for life as it really is. Much reading of fiction is mentally injurious. The inveterate novel reader ruins his powers of close and clear thinking. Fiction is so fascinating that it always tends to drive out other reading that is more helpful mentally and morally. We should be on our guard in even reading good literature, that the good does not crowd out the best; that is that the best of man's literature does not crowd out the very best of all – God's Book. God's Book, the Bible, must always have the first place.

Then there is another kind of companionship that has a tremendous influence over our lives, that is the companionship of pictures. The pictures that we see every day of our lives, and the pictures that we see only occasionally, have a tremendous power in the shaping of our lives.

A mother had two dearly loved sons. It was her dream and ambition that these sons should enter the ministry, but both of them went to sea. She could not understand it until a friend one day called her attention to the picture of a magnificent ship in full sail careening through the ocean that hung above the mantel in the dining room. Every day of their lives her boys had gazed upon that picture, had been thrilled by it, and an unconquerable love for the sea and longing for it had thus been created and this had determined their lives.

How many a picture that is a masterpiece of art, but in which there is an evil suggestion, has sent some young men on the road to ruin. Many of our art collections are so polluted with improper pictures that it is not safe for a young man or a young woman to visit them. The evil thought that they suggest may be but for a moment, and yet Satan will know how to bring that picture back again and again and work injury by it. Don't look for a moment at any picture, no matter how praised by art critics, that taints your imagination with evil suggestion. Avoid as you would poison every painting, or engraving, every etching, every photograph that leaves a spot of impurity on your mind, but feast your soul upon the pictures that make you holier, kinder, more sympathetic and more tender.

13

Amusements

*Y*OUNG people need recreation. Our Savior does not frown upon wholesome recreation. He was interested in the games of the children when He was here upon earth. He watched the children at their play (see Matthew 11:16-17), and He watches the children at their play today and delights in their play when it is wholesome and elevating.

In the stress and strain of modern life, older people too need recreation if they are to do their very best work. But there are recreations that are wholesome, and there are amusements that are pernicious. It is impossible to take up amusements one by one, and it is unnecessary. A few principles can be laid down.

1. *Do not indulge in any form of amusement about whose propriety you have any doubts.* Whenever you are in doubt, always give God the benefit of the doubt.

There are plenty of recreations about which there can be no question. "He who doubts is condemned; for whatever is not from faith is sin" (Romans 14:23). Many a young Christian will say, "I am not sure that this amusement is wrong." Are you sure it is right? If not, leave it alone.

2. *Do not indulge in any amusement that you cannot engage in to the glory of God.* "Whether you eat or drink, or whatever you do, do all to the glory of God" (1 Corinthians 10:31). Whenever you are in doubt as to whether you should engage in any amusement, ask yourself, can I do this at this time to the glory of God?

3. *Do not engage in any amusement that will hurt your influence with anybody.* There are amusements, which perhaps are all right in themselves, but which we cannot engage in without losing our influence with someone. Now every true Christian wishes his life to tell with everybody to the utmost. There is so much to be done and so few to do it that every Christian desires every last ounce of power for good that he can have with everybody, and, if any amusement will injure your influence for good with anyone, the price is too great. Do not engage in it.

A young Christian lady had a great desire to lead others to Christ. She made up her mind that she would speak to a young friend of hers about coming to Christ, and while resting between the figures of a dance she said to the young man who was her companion in the dance, "George, are you a Christian?" "No," he said, "I am not, are you?" "Yes," she replied, "I am." "Then," he said, "what are you doing here?" Whether justly or unjustly, the world discounts the professions of those Christians who indulge in certain forms of the world's own amusements. We cannot afford to have our professions thus discounted.

4. *Do not engage in any amusement that you cannot make a matter of prayer*, that you cannot ask God's blessing upon. Pray before your play just as much as you would pray before your work.

5. *Do not go to any place of amusement where you cannot take Christ with you, and where you do not think Christ would feel at home.* Christ went to places of mirth when He was here upon earth. He went to the marriage feast in Cana (see John 2), and contributed to the joy of the occasion, but there are many modern places of amusement where Christ would not be at home. Would the atmosphere of the modern stage be congenial to that holy One whom we call "Lord"? If it would not, don't go.

6. *Don't engage in any amusement that you would not like to be found enjoying if the Lord should come.* He may come at any moment. Blessed is the one, whom, when He comes, He shall find watching and ready, and glad to open to Him immediately (see Luke 12:36, 40). I have a friend who was one day walking down the street thinking upon the return of his Lord. As he thought he was smoking a cigar. The thought came to him, "Would you like to meet Christ now with that cigar in your mouth?" He answered honestly, "No, I would not." He threw that cigar away and never lighted another.

7. *Do not engage in any amusement, no matter how harmless it would be for yourself, that might harm someone else.* Take for example card playing. It is probable that thousands have played cards moderately all their lives and never suffered any direct moral injury from it, but everyone who has studied the matter knows that cards are the gamblers' chosen tools.

He also knows that most, if not all, gamblers took their first lessons in card playing at the quiet family card table. He knows that if a young man goes out into the world knowing how to play cards and indulging at all in this amusement that before long he is going to be put into a place where he is going to be asked to play cards for money, and if he does not consent he will get into serious trouble.

Card playing is a dangerous amusement for the average young man. It is pretty sure to lead to gambling on a larger or a smaller scale, and one of the most crying social evils of our time is the evil of gambling. Some young man may be encouraged to play cards by your playing who will afterwards become a gambler and part of the responsibility will lie at your door.

If I could repeat all the stories that have come to me from broken-hearted men whose lives have been shipwrecked at the gaming table; if I could tell of all the broken-hearted mothers who have come to me – some of them in high position – whose sons have committed suicide at Monte Carlo and other places, ruined by the cards, I think that all thoughtful and true Christians would give them up forever.

For most of us the recreations that are most helpful are those that demand a considerable outlay of physical energy – recreations that take us into the open air, recreations that leave us refreshed in body and invigorated in mind. Physical exercises of the strenuous kind, but not over-exercise, is one of the great safeguards of the moral conduct of boys and young men. There is very little recreation in watching others play the most vigorous game of football, but there is real health for the body and for the soul in a due amount of physical exercise for yourself.

14

Persecution

*O*NE of the discouragements that meets every true Christian before he has gone very far in the Christian life is persecution. God tells us in His Word that "All who desire to live godly in Christ Jesus will suffer persecution" (2 Timothy 3:12). Sooner or later everyone who surrenders absolutely to God and seeks to follow Jesus Christ in everything will find that this verse is true.

We live in a God-hating world and in a compromising age. The world's hatred of God in our day is veiled. It does not express itself in our land in the same way that it expressed itself in Palestine in the days of Jesus Christ, but the world hates God today as much as it ever did, and it hates the one who is loyal to Christ. It may not imprison him or kill him but in some way it will persecute him. Persecution is inevitable for a loyal follower of Jesus Christ. Many a young Christian when he meets with persecution is surprised and discouraged and not a few fall away. Many seem to run well for a few days but like those of whom Jesus spoke, "They have no root in themselves, and so endure only for a time. Afterward, when tribulation or persecution arises for the word's sake, immediately they stumble" (Mark 4:17).

I have seen many an apparently promising Christian life brought to an end in this way. But if persecution is rightly received, it is no longer a hindrance to the Christian life but a help to it. Do not be discouraged when you are persecuted. No matter how fierce and hard the persecution may be, be thankful for it. Jesus says, "Blessed are those who are persecuted for righteousness' sake, for theirs is the kingdom of heaven. Blessed are you when they revile and persecute you, and say all kinds of evil against you falsely for My sake. Rejoice and be exceedingly glad, for great is your reward in heaven, for so they persecuted the prophets who were before you" (Matthew 5:10-12).

It is a great privilege to be persecuted for Christ and for the truth. Peter found this out and wrote to the Christians of his day: "Beloved, do not think it strange concerning the fiery trial which is to try you, as though some strange thing happened to you; but rejoice to the extent that you partake of Christ's sufferings, that when His glory is revealed, you may also be glad with exceeding joy. If you are reproached for the name of Christ, blessed are you, for the Spirit of glory and of God rests upon you. On their part He is blasphemed, but on your part He is glorified" (1 Peter 4:12-14). Be very sure that the persecution is really for Christ's sake and not because of some eccentricity of your own, or because of your stubbornness. There are many who bring upon themselves the displeasure of others because they are stubborn and cranky and then flatter themselves that they are being persecuted for Christ's sake and for righteousness' sake.

Be considerate of the opinions of others and be considerate of the conduct of others. Be sure that you do not push your opinions upon others in an unwarrantable way, or make your conscience a rule of life for other people. But never yield a jot of principle. Stand for what you believe to be the truth. Do it in love, but do it at any cost. And if, when you are standing for conviction and principle, you are disliked for it and slandered for it and treated with all manner of unkindness because of it, do not be sad but rejoice. Do not speak evil of those who speak evil of you, "because Christ also suffered for us, leaving us an example, that you should follow His steps: who, when He was reviled, did not revile in return; when He suffered, He did not threaten, but committed Himself to Him who judges righteously" (1 Peter 2:21, 23).

At this point many a Christian makes a mistake. He stands loyally for the truth, but he receives the persecution that comes for the truth with harshness, he grows bitter, he gets to condemning everyone but himself. There is no blessing in bearing persecution in that way. Persecution should be borne meekly, lovingly, serenely. Don't talk about your own persecutions. Rejoice in them. Thank God for them, and go on obeying God. And don't forget to love and pray for them who persecute you (see Matthew 5:44).

If at any time the persecution seems harder than you can bear, remember how abundant the reward is, "If we endure, we shall also reign with Him. If we deny Him, He also will deny us" (2 Timothy 2:12). Everyone must enter into the kingdom of God through much tribulation (see Acts 14:22), but do not go back on that account. Remember always, however fiercely the fire of persecution may burn, "That the sufferings of this present time are not worthy to be compared with the glory which shall be revealed in us" (Romans 8:18). Remember, too, that "our light affliction, which is but for a moment, is working for us a far more exceeding and eternal weight of glory" (2 Corinthians 4:17).

Keep looking not "at the things which are seen, but at the things which are not seen. For the things which are seen are temporary, but the things which are not seen are eternal" (2 Corinthians 4:18). When the apostles were persecuted, even unto imprisonment and stripes, "they departed from the presence of the council, rejoicing that they were counted worthy to suffer shame for His name. And daily in the temple, and in every house, they did not cease teaching and preaching Jesus as the Christ" (Acts 5:41-42).

The time may come when you think that you are being persecuted more than others, but you do not know what others may have to endure. Even if it were true – that you were being persecuted more than any one else – you ought not to complain but to humbly thank God that He has bestowed upon you such an honor. Keep your eyes fixed upon "Jesus, the author and finisher of our faith, who for the joy that was set before Him endured the cross, despising the shame, and has sat down at the right hand of the throne of God. For consider Him who endured such hostility from sinners against Himself, lest you become weary and discouraged in your souls" (Hebrews 12:2-3).

I was once talking with an old colored man who in the slave days had found his Savior. The cruel master had him flogged again and again for his loyalty to Christ but he said to me, "I simply thought of my Savior dying on the cross in my place, and I rejoiced to suffer persecution for Him."

15

Guidance

I HAVE met a great many who are trying to lead a Christian life who are much troubled over the question of guidance. They wish to do the will of God in all things, but what puzzles them is to tell what the will of God may be in every case. When anyone starts out with the determination to obey God in everything and to be led by the Holy Spirit, Satan seeks to trouble him by perplexing him as to what the will of God is. Satan comes and suggests that something is the will of God that is probably not the will of God at all, and then when he does not do it, Satan says, "There, you disobeyed God." In this way, many a conscientious young Christian gets into a very morbid and unhappy state of mind, fearing that he has disobeyed God and has lost His favor. This is one of the most frequent devices of the devil to keep Christians from being cheerful.

How may we know the will of God?

First of all, let me say that a true Christian life is not a life governed by a whole lot of rules about what one shall eat, and what one shall drink, and what one shall do, and what one shall not do. A life governed by a lot of rules is a life of bondage. One is sure sooner or later to break some of these man-made rules and to get into condemnation. Paul tells us in Romans 8:15, "You did not receive the spirit of bondage again to fear, but you received the Spirit of adoption by whom we cry out, 'Abba, Father.'"

The true Christian life is the life of a trusting, glad, fear-free child; not led by rules, but led by the personal guidance of the Holy Spirit who dwells within us. "As many as are led by the Spirit of God, these are sons of God" (Romans 8:14). If you have received the Holy Spirit, He dwells within you and is ready to lead you at every turn of life.

A life governed by a multitude of rules is a life of bondage and anxiety. A life surrendered to the control of the Holy Spirit is a life of joy and peace and freedom. There is no anxiety in such a life, there is no fear in the presence of God. We trust God and rejoice in His presence just as a true child trusts his earthly father and rejoices in his presence. If we make a mistake at any point, even if we disobey God, we go and tell Him all about it as trustfully as a child and know that He forgives us and that we are restored at once to His full favor (see 1 John 1:9).

But how can we tell the Holy Spirit's guidance that we may obey Him and thus have God's favor at every turn of life? This question is answered in James 1:5-7: "If any of you lacks wisdom, let him ask of God, who gives to all liberally and without reproach, and it will be given to him. But let him ask in faith, with no doubting, for he who doubts is like a wave of the sea driven and tossed by the wind. For let not that man suppose that he will receive anything from the Lord." This is very simple. It includes five points.

1. That you recognize your own ignorance and your own inability to guide your own life – that you lack wisdom.

2. The surrender of your will to God, and a real desire to be led by Him.

3. Definite prayer to Him for guidance.

4. Confident expectation that God will guide you. You "ask in faith, with no doubting."

5. That you follow step by step as He guides.

God may only show you a step at a time. That is enough. All you need to know is the next step. It is here that many make a mistake. They wish God to show them the whole way before they take the first step.

A university student once came to me over the question of guidance. He said, "I cannot find out the will of God. I have been praying but God does not show me His will." This was in the month of July. I said, "About what is it that you are seeking to know the will of God?" "About what I should do next summer." I said, "Do you know what you ought to do tomorrow?" "Yes." "Do you not know what you ought to do next autumn?" "Yes, finish my course. But what I want to know is what I ought to do when my university course is over." He was soon led to see that all he needed to know for the present was what God had already shown him. That when he did that, God would show him the next step.

Do not worry about what you ought to do next week. Do what God shows you you ought to do today. Next week will take care of itself. Indeed, tomorrow will take care of itself. Obey the Spirit of God for today. "Do not worry about tomorrow, for tomorrow will worry about its own things. Sufficient for the day is its own trouble" (Matthew 6:34). It is enough to live a day at a time, if we do our very best for that day.

God's guidance is clear guidance, "God is light and in Him is no darkness at all" (1 John 1:5). Do not be anxious over obscure leadings. Do not let your soul be ruffled by the thought, "Perhaps this obscure leading is what God wants me to do." Obscure leadings are not divine leadings. God's path is as clear as day. Satan's path is full of obscurity and uncertainty and anxiety and questioning. If there comes some leading of which you are not quite sure whether it is the will of God or not, simply go to your heavenly Father and say, "Heavenly Father, I desire to know Your will. I will do Your will if You would only make it clear. But You are light and in You is no darkness at all. If this is Your will make it clear as day and I will do it." Then wait quietly upon God and do not act until He makes it clear, but the moment it is made clear, act at once.

The whole secret of guidance is an absolutely surrendered will, a will that is given up to God and ready to obey Him at any cost. Many of our uncertainties about God's guidance are simply because we are not really willing to do what God is really guiding us to do. We are tempted to say, "I cannot find out what God's will is," when the real trouble is we have found out His will and it is something we do not wish to do and we are trying to make ourselves think that God wants us to do something else.

All supposed leadings of God should be tested by the Word of God. The Bible is God's revealed will. Any leading that contradicts the plain teaching of the Bible is certainly not the leading of the Holy Spirit. The Holy Spirit does not contradict Himself.

A man once came to me and said that God was leading him to marry a certain woman. He said that she was a very devoted Christian woman and they had been greatly drawn towards one another and they felt that God was leading them to be married. But I said to the man, "You already have a wife." "Yes," he said, "but we have never lived happily and we have not lived together for years."

"But," I replied, "that does not alter the case. God in His Word has told us distinctly the duty of the husband to the wife and how wrong it is in His sight for a husband to divorce his wife and marry another." "Yes," said the man, "but the Holy Spirit is leading us to one another." I indignantly replied that "Whatever spirit is leading you to marry one another, it is certainly not the Holy Spirit but the spirit of the evil one. The Holy Spirit never leads anyone to disobey the Word of God."

In seeking to know the guidance of the Spirit, always search the Scriptures, study them prayerfully. Do not make a book of magic out of the Bible. Do not ask God to show you His will and then open your Bible at random and put your finger upon some text and take it out of context without any relation to its real meaning and decide the will of God in that way. This is an irreverent and improper use of Scripture. You may open your Bible at just the right place to find right guidance, but if you do, it will not be by some fanciful interpretation of the passage you find. It will be by taking the passage in its context and interpreting it to mean just what it says as seen in its context. All sorts of mischief has arisen from using the Bible in this perverse way.

I knew an earnest Christian woman once who was somewhat concerned about the predictions made by a false prophet that Chicago was to be destroyed on a certain day. She opened her Bible at random. It opened to the twelfth chapter of Ezekiel, "Son of man, eat your bread with quaking, and drink your water with trembling and anxiety ... Then the cities that are inhabited shall be laid waste, and the land shall become desolate" (Ezekiel 12:18, 20).

This seemed to exactly fit the case and the woman was considerably impressed, but if the verses had been studied in their connection, it would have been evident at once that God was not speaking about Chicago and that they were not applicable to Chicago. It was not an intelligent study of the Word of God and therefore led to a false conclusion.

To sum up, lead a life not led by rules but by the personal guidance of the Holy Spirit. Surrender your will absolutely to God. Whenever you are in doubt as to His guidance, go to Him and ask Him to show you His will, expect Him to do it, follow step by step as He leads. Test all the leadings by the plain and simple teachings of the Bible. Live free from anxiety and worry lest in some unguarded moment you have not done the right thing.

After you have done what you think God led you to do, do not be always going back and wondering whether you did the right thing. You will get into a morbid state if you do. If you really wished to do God's will and sought His guidance, and did what you thought He guided you to do, you may rest assured you did the right thing, no matter what the outcome has been. Satan is bound that we shall not be happy, cheerful Christians if he can prevent it, but God wishes us to be happy, cheerful, bright Christians every day and every hour. He does not wish us to brood but to rejoice (see Philippians 4:4).

A most excellent Christian man came to me one Monday morning in great gloom over the failures of the work of the preceding day. He said to me, "I made wretched work of teaching my Sunday school class yesterday." I said, "Did you honestly seek wisdom from God before you went to your class?" He said, "I did." I said, "Did you expect to receive it?" He said, "I did." "Then," I said, "in the face of God's promise what right have you to doubt that God did give you wisdom?" (see

James 1:5-7). His gloom disappeared and he looked up with a smile and said, "I had no right to doubt."

Let us learn to trust God. Let us remember that if our wills are surrendered to Him He is ever more willing to guide us than we are to be guided. Let us trust that He does guide us at every step and even though what we do does not turn out as we expected, let us never brood over it but trust God. Let us walk in the light of simple trust in God. In this way we shall be glad and peaceful and strong and useful at every turn of life.

Book 2

THE PRACTICE OF THE PRESENCE OF GOD

by

BROTHER LAWRENCE

Contents

Preface

*T*HE *Practice of the Presence of God* is a collection of letters and conversations recorded by Brother Lawrence in his search to experience the Christian life in the presence of the Almighty Lord.

Brother Lawrence was born Nicholas Herman in the region of Lorraine in France, whose letters and conversations are recounted herein testify to the same truth! Written over three centuries ago by himself and compiled by Joseph de Beaufort after his death, his profound insights attest to a wealth of experience gained while on a unique spiritual journey to perfect the art of practicing the presence of God.

May the all who read this book receive from its contents the same revelations of the Christian life, the perseverance to pursue the presence of God and the discipline to remain firmly rooted in it.

Part 1

Conversations

First Conversation

*W*HEN I first met Brother Lawrence on August 3, 1666 he told me that God had shown him immense kindness in his conversion at the age of eighteen.

It was in the winter that he saw a tree stripped of its leaves. Being mindful that the leaves would soon reappear, followed by blossoms and fruit, he received a high view of God's providence and power, which has since been joined to his soul. This realization of God's providence and power had set him apart from the world and gave him such a deep love for God that hasn't subsided on over forty years of serving Him.

In his earlier years Brother Lawrence used to be a valet to M. Fieubert, the treasurer of the monastery. He was a rather awkward fellow who broke everything.

He decided to be received into the monastery, believing that it would serve as punishment for his awkwardness. He subsequently surrendered his life and its many pleasures to God, but instead of punishing him God gave him complete satisfaction.

Brother Lawrence was adamant that we ought to be continually aware of God's presence, by continually conversing with Him. What a shameful thing to choose the things of the world rather than to talk with God. Rather, we should feed and nourish our souls with great expectations in God that are sure to provide us with great joy in being devoted to Him.

He commented on the fact that we as Christians have too weak a faith. We should be ashamed of ourselves for our lack of faith by not allowing it to govern over our lives. But instead we focus our thoughts on trivial devotions, which change daily.

He further suggested that we ought to surrender ourselves to God in a temporal and spiritual sense, and to seek our satisfaction only in obeying His will, whether it leads to suffering or delight. During the dry spells of life by which God tries our love for Him we are given an opportunity to surrender to Him even further. This will only strengthen your faith even more.

The miseries and sins Brother Lawrence bore witness to every day came to him as no surprise. In fact, he was amazed that there wasn't much, much more, considering the malice sinners were capable of. He did his part in praying for them in the knowledge that God could deal with the situation on His own time.

In order to surrender completely to God as He requires, we should constantly guard our souls against the onslaughts of the world, which threaten to interfere in our spiritual relationship with Him. Once we learn to accept God's will and gladly obey it, and succeed in warding off worldly attacks on our souls, we have the freedom to commune with Him as often as we like.

Second Conversation

*B*ROTHER Lawrence remarked that he had always been governed by love and that having committed himself to let God's love shine through all his actions, he found several reasons to be greatly pleased in this endeavor. He took pleasure in the simplest things in life as long as it was rooted in the love of God, seeking Him only and nothing else, not even His gifts.

For a long time Brother Lawrence was troubled by the thought that he is undeserving of God's salvation to such an extent that no one seemed to be able to convince him otherwise. He reasoned that he came to possess the Christian faith owing to his love of God and that his sole purpose was to serve Him only, whether he was certain of his salvation or not. He took comfort in the fact that he did all he could to express his love toward God in word and deed. During this period of uncertainty in his life, Brother Lawrence suffered immensely from inner conflict.

After having been hindered by such thoughts of deep uncertainty about his relationship with God, the uncertainty went away and in its place came freedom and continual joy. Many a time our dear brother deliberately placed his sins between himself and God as a way of stating his unworthiness to receive God's blessing. However, God continued to bestow such blessings in abundance.

He mentioned that getting into the habit of continually talking with God and measuring everything we do according to His will, required some mild form of diligence. But once the habit has gained a firm footing in our lives, we would have no difficulty whatsoever in drawing near to God.

The expectation of having the pleasant days God had given him be replaced by pain and suffering remained at the back of his mind, but he was unperturbed about it. He knew quite well that while he could do nothing of himself, God would not fail to give him the strength he required.

Whenever an opportunity presented itself for him to practice some virtue, he sought advice from God by saying, "Lord, I cannot do this unless You enable me." He would immediately receive more than enough strength for the task at hand.

Whenever he had failed in his duty, he merely confessed it to God, saying, "I can do nothing apart from You. Keep me from falling and rectify my wrongs." After this confession, the matter no longer troubled him.

Brother Lawrence urges us to speak candidly with God, asking Him for help whenever we are in need of it. He further states that God never failed to answer his prayers.

On occasion he was sent into Burgundy to acquire supplies for the monastery. He regarded this to be a very arduous task, because of his lack of business sense and on account of his being lame in one leg. He was unable to walk about the boat without colliding with the casks. He, however, didn't allow these shortcomings to upset him in. He would remind himself that he was executing God's will and found that everything would always turn out well in the end.

Likewise, in performing his duties in the kitchen, to which he had a great dislike, he soon accustomed himself to execute his duties for the greater love of God. He found strength in frequent prayer and eventually grew accustomed to kitchen duty during the fifteen years he served there.

He was very well pleased with his job at that moment, but made it known that he was ready to relinquish his position since he always found pleasure in doing little things for the love of God.

Fully aware of his imperfections, it in no way discouraged him in his daily walk with God. He simply confessed his sins. Following this, he peacefully resumed his usual practice of love and adoration.

Whenever he was troubled by something, he consulted nobody regarding the matter. He was aware that the loving presence of God surrounded him and took comfort in this love no matter what happened. He would then soon find himself once more in God's love.

In his opinion Brother Lawrence felt that negative thoughts spoil all and that our thoughts are where evil originates. We ought to reject such thoughts as soon as we perceive their disrespect for the matter at hand, or our salvation. Only then may we return to our communion with God.

Following his conversion, Brother Lawrence spent his time set aside for prayer rejecting wandering thoughts and falling back into them. All physical punishment and other exercises are useless unless they join us to God through love. Our brother considered this and found it to be the shortest way to go straight to Him by a continual exercise of love, and doing all things for His sake.

There ought to be a great difference between the acts of the understanding and those of the will. The former are of comparatively little value, while the latter are of great value.

Our sole purpose is to love God and delight ourselves in Him.

All possible kinds of self-punishment done outside of God's love can't wipe out a single sin. We ought to expect forgiveness for our sins from the blood of Jesus Christ alone, striving to love Him with all our hearts.

The greatest pains or pleasures of this world could not be compared with what he had experienced of both kinds in a spiritual state. He didn't worry about anything and feared nothing, his only desire to not offend God.

Third Conversation

*B*ROTHER Lawrence told me that the foundation of the spiritual life in him had been a high notion and esteem of God in faith. Once well conceived, his only care was to reject every sinful thought and to perform all his actions for the love of God. There were times when he had not thought of God for a while, but he did not allow it to bother him. After having acknowledged his weakness to God, he returned to Him with even greater trust and joy.

The trust we place in God glorifies His name and draws down great graces. This same trust enabled Brother Lawrence to never worry about any business entrusted to him. When the time came for him to perform his duty, he felt God's guidance showing him precisely how to do it. He had gone about his business in this fashion for some time without any concern, but prior to the above mentioned experience, he had attempted to accomplish everything in his own power, without God's help. Whenever outside business diverted his thoughts from God, God sent a fresh remembrance into his soul, which stirred him up to joyful praise before the Lord. He felt more united to God in his outside, everyday commitments than when he left them for later in the day during his quiet time.

He expected that the worst that could happen to him was to lose his sense of God's presence, which he had enjoyed for such a long time. God's goodness, however, assured our brother that He would not forsake him completely, and that He would strengthen him enough to bear whatever evil He permitted to happen to him. He therefore feared nothing. Complete surrender to God is a sure way to heaven, a way in which we always have sufficient light for our journey.

In the beginning of the spiritual life, we are expected to be faithful in our actions and in denying ourselves. But after that, indescribable joy follows. In difficult times we need only turn to Jesus Christ and seek His grace, with which everything will become easy.

Many people do not advance in their progress of living the Christian life, because they neglect the love of God – the purpose of it all. This is easily spotted in their everyday works and is why we see so little solid virtue in their lives. Neither art nor science is needed to approach God. Only a heart resolutely determined to devote itself to nothing else but Him for His sake, and to love Him above everything else.

Fourth Conversation

*B*ROTHER Lawrence used to speak with me rather frequently and candidly concerning his manner of going to God.

He told me that it is of vital importance to renounce everything which does not lead to God. This will allow us to enter into a continual conversation with Him, with freedom and in simplicity. We need only to recognize God intimately present within us. We may then speak to Him whenever we want, ask His help in knowing His will during uncertain times, and please Him by obeying His will. We are to offer our work to Him before we begin and thank Him afterward.

This conversation with God should also include praising and loving Him incessantly, for His infinite goodness and perfection.

We should ask for His grace with a perfect confidence

while relying on the infinite merits of our Lord. God will never fail to offer us His grace. Our dear Brother Lawrence sinned only when his thoughts had wandered from a sense of God's presence, or when he forgot to ask for His help.

God always shines light on our doubts as long as we have no other desire than to please Him.

Our sanctification does not depend on adjusting our activities as it does on doing them for God's sake rather than for ourselves. It was terrible to see how many people mistake the means for the end, addicting themselves to certain works which they perform very imperfectly as a result of their human shortcomings.

The best method Brother Lawrence had found of communicating with God was simply to go about his business without trying to please anyone else but God.

It is a great delusion to think that our prayer time ought to differ from other times. We are as strictly obliged to let our actions unite us with God as our prayers unite us with Him during our prayer time.

Brother Lawrence's prayer was nothing else but a sense of the presence of God. His soul was resting in God, unaware of everything except the love of God. When the appointed prayer times were past he felt no different, because he still continued praising God with all his might. He lived a life of continual joy as a result.

We ought, once and for all, to completely trust God and surrender of ourselves to Him, confident in the knowledge that He would not deceive us. We should never tire of doing little things for the love of God as He doesn't regard greatness of the work but the love with which it is performed. We should not be discouraged if we fail in the beginning. It will eventually create a habit within us by which we naturally and joyfully continue despite occasional failure.

According to Brother Lawrence the whole substance of religion is faith, hope, and love. Everything besides these three is to be used as a means that we may arrive at our end, lost in the love of God.

All things are possible for one who believes. They are less difficult to one who hopes, they are even easier to one who loves, and still easier to one who practices these three virtues.

The purpose we should strive for in this life is to become the most perfect worshipers of God we can possibly be, as we hope to be through all eternity.

Brother Lawrence added that he had found such an advantage in walking in the presence of God. It was easy for him to recommend doing so to others, but his example was a stronger encouragement than any arguments he could propose.

Part 2

Letters

First Letter

I WOULD like to tell you about the method one of our fellow brothers used to arrive at that habitual sense of God's presence. The account I give you is:

Having found in many books different methods of approaching God, as well as diverse practices of the spiritual life, I thought this would puzzle me more than it would facilitate what I was seeking, which was nothing but how to become wholly God's.

This made me resolve to surrender myself wholly to God and after having done so, I renounced my sins because of my love for Him. I began to live as if there was nothing else in the world except Him. Sometimes I considered myself before Him as a poor criminal. At other times I held Him in my heart as my Father, as my God. I worshiped Him as often as I could, keeping my mind in His holy presence, and recalling it whenever I found myself wandering from Him. I made it my business as best I could to keep my mind from wandering upon anything that could threaten to interrupt my communion with God.

Such has been my common practice ever since I entered into religion. Even though I have strived for perfection in this regard I have not always succeeded. Yet, I have been greatly blessed in my endeavors. These blessings may be attributed to the mere mercy and goodness of God, because we can do nothing without Him. When we are faithful in remaining in His holy presence, putting Him first and following His commands, it brings about a holy freedom within us.

Lastly, by often repeating these acts they become habitual and experiencing the presence of God becomes natural to us. I cannot thank Him enough for His great goodness towards me, for the many favors He has done to such a miserable a sinner as I am. May all things praise Him. Amen.

Second Letter

*I*N a conversation I had with a person of piety some time ago, he told me the spiritual life was a life of grace, which begins with submissive fear, which is increased by the hope of eternal life, and which is consummated by pure love. He further commented that each of these states had different stages by which one arrives at last at that blessed consummation.

I have not followed all these methods. On the contrary, when I entered into religion I took a resolution to submit myself to God and to renounce my sins, because of my love of Him.

During the first years I spent most of my time set apart for devotion, contemplating death, judgment, hell, heaven, and my sins.

Such was my beginning. And yet I must tell you that for the first ten years I suffered much. The apprehension that I was not devoted to God, as I desired to be, my past sins always present in my mind, and the great un-merited favors which God showed me, were the matter and source of my sufferings. During this time I fell often, and rose again promptly.

When I thought of nothing but to end my days in these troubles (which did not at all diminish the trust I had in God, and which served only to increase my faith), I found myself changed at once. And my soul, which till that time was in trouble, felt a profound inward peace.

Since then I have come to walk before God simply, in faith, with humility and with love. I apply myself dil-igently to do nothing and think nothing which may displease Him. I hope that when I have done what I can, He will do with me what He pleases.

As for what passes in me at present, I cannot express it. I have no pain or difficulty about my state, because I have no will but that of God, which I endeavor to accomplish in all things, and to which I am so resigned, that I would not take up a straw from the ground against His order, or from any other motive but purely that of love for Him.

I consider myself as the most wretched of men, full of sores and corruption, and who has committed all sorts of crimes against his King. Touched with a sensible regret I confess to Him all my wickedness, I ask His for-giveness, I abandon myself into His hands, that He may do what He pleases with me. This King, full of mercy and goodness, very far from chastising me, embraces me with love, makes me eat at His table, serves me with

His own hands, gives me the key of His treasures. He converses and delights Himself with me incessantly and treats me in all respects as His favorite. It is thus I consider myself from time to time in His holy presence.

I desire your reverence to reflect rather upon my great wretchedness, of which you are fully informed, than upon the great favors which God does me, all unworthy and ungrateful as I am.

As for my set prayer times, they are only a continuation of the same exercise. Sometimes I consider myself as a stone before a carver, whereof he is to make a statue. I thus present myself before God. I desire Him to make His perfect image in my soul and render me entirely like Himself.

You will, however, oblige me in sending me your opinion, which I hold in high regard, for I have a singular esteem for your reverence, and am yours in our Lord.

Third Letter

*W*E have a God who is infinitely gracious, and knows all our needs and desires. I always thought that He would reduce you to extremity. He will come in His own time, and when you least expect it. Hope in Him more than ever. Thank Him for the favors He does you, particularly for the fortitude and patience which He gives you in your afflictions. It is a plain mark of the care He takes of you. Comfort yourself then with Him, and give thanks for everything.

I admire also the fortitude and bravery of M–. God has given him a good disposition, and a good will, but there is in him still a little of the world, and a great deal of youth. I hope the affliction which God has sent him will prove a wholesome remedy to him, and make him enter into himself. It is an accident very proper to engage him to put all his trust in Him, who accompanies him everywhere. Let him think of Him as often he can, especially in the greatest dangers. A little lifting up of the heart suffices. A little remembrance of God, one act of inward worship, though upon a march, and sword in hand, are prayers which, however short, are nevertheless very acceptable to God. Far from lessening a soldier's courage in occasions of danger, they best serve to fortify it.

Let him then think of God the most he can. Let him accustom himself, by degrees, to this small but holy exercise; nobody perceives it, and nothing is easier than to repeat often in the day these little internal adorations. Recommend to him, if you please, that he think of God as often as possible, in the manner here directed. It is very fit and most necessary for a soldier, who is daily exposed to the dangers of life, and often of his salvation. I hope that God will assist him and all the family, to whom I present my service, being theirs and yours.

Fourth Letter

$\mathcal{I}$ HAVE taken this opportunity to communicate to you the sentiments of one member of our church concerning the admirable effects and continual assistances which he receives from the presence of God. Let you and me both profit by them.

He is so accustomed to the divine presence of God that he receives from it help in all circumstances. For about thirty years, his soul has been filled with joys so continual, and sometimes so great, that he is forced to use means to moderate them, and to keep them from appearing outwardly.

He complains much of our blindness and cries often that we are to be pitied who content ourselves with so little. He says that God has infinite treasure to bestow, and we take up with a little sensible devotion which passes in a moment. Blind as we are, we hinder God, and stop the current of His graces. But when He finds a soul penetrated with a lively faith, He pours into it His graces and favors plentifully. There they flow like a torrent, which, after being forcibly stopped against its ordinary course, when it has found a passage, spreads itself quickly and with abundance.

Yes, we often stop this torrent by the little value we set upon it. But let us stop it no more. Let us enter into ourselves and break down the bank which prevents it. Let us make way for grace. Let us redeem the lost time, for perhaps we have but little left. Death follows us closely; let us be well prepared for it.

Let us enter into ourselves. The time presses. There is no room for delay. Our souls are at stake. I believe you have taken such effectual measures that you will not be surprised. I commend you for it. We must, nevertheless, always work at it, because not to advance in the spiritual life is to go back. But those who have the gale of the Holy Spirit go forward even in sleep. If the vessel of our soul is still tossed with winds and storms, let us awake the Lord, who reposes in it, and He will quickly calm the sea.

I have taken the liberty to impart to you these good sentiments, that you may compare them with your own. They will serve again to kindle and inflame them. Let us then both recall our first fervors. Let us profit by the example and the sentiments of this brother, who is little known of the world, but known of God, and extremely caressed by Him. I will pray for you. I am yours in our Lord.

Fifth Letter

*T*ODAY I received two books and a letter from a sister, who is preparing to commit herself to the service of the Lord.

I will send you one of the books, which discusses the presence of God. I believe that the spiritual life consists of practicing the presence of God and that whoever practices it will soon become spiritual.

The heart must therefore be empty of all other things that would offend God. He wants complete possession of our hearts. He cannot work in our hearts unless He is in complete control.

There is no sweeter and delightful way of living in the world than that of a continual conversation with God. Only those who practice it and experience it are able to understand it. However, I do not advise you to do it from that motive. It is not pleasure which we ought to seek in this exercise. Let us do it from a principle of love, and because of God's will.

If I were a preacher, I would preach about nothing else but the practice of the presence of God. If I were in some kind of leadership position, I would advise the entire world to do it. That is how necessary I think it is.

If we only knew how much we need God's grace and help, we would not lose sight of Him for even a moment. Believe me. Make a firm resolution to never willfully forget Him, and to spend the rest of your life in His holy presence.

Set heartily about this work. If you do it right, you can be assured that you will soon reap the rewards. I will assist you with my prayers. I recommend myself earnestly to yours and those of your church.

Sixth Letter

I'M curious as to why you haven't given me your opinion of the little book I sent you. You must have received it by now. Put it into practice, even in your old age. It is better late than never.

I fail to understand how religious people can be content without the practice of the presence of God. I prefer to retire with Him in the deepest part of my soul as much as I can. While I am in His presence I fear nothing. However, turning even slightly away from Him pains me.

This exercise does not weaken the body. Distancing ourselves from the many little innocent pleasures will comfort us. In fact, God will not permit a soul which desires to be devoted entirely to Him to find such comfort anywhere else but with Him. It makes more sense.

This does not mean that you have to feel compelled

to distance yourself. No, we must serve God in a holy freedom. We must do our business faithfully, without trouble or anxiety, calmly recalling our mind to God whenever we find it wandering from Him.

It is, however, necessary to trust in God completely. Lay aside any other cares and even some forms of devotion, because those devotions are only as a means to an end. Therefore, when practicing the presence of God we are with Him who is our end. It is then useless to return to the means. We may continue loving Him by just remaining in His holy presence. Praise Him, surrender to Him and give Him thanks in every way you feel pressed by your spirit.

I will keep praying for your church. I am yours in our Lord.

Seventh Letter

J SYMPATHIZE with your difficult situation. Perhaps you should consider giving over your worries to God and rather spend the remainder of your life only in worshiping Him. God doesn't ask much of us except to remember Him often, to praise Him, to ask for His grace, to present Him your troubles and to thank Him for the favors He has given us, and still gives us. Lift up your heart to Him, even during your meals. The least little remembrance will always please Him. You don't have to pray aloud. He is nearer to us than we can imagine.

It isn't necessary to stay in church to remain in God's presence. As long as we keep Him in our heart and talk with Him often, we may enjoy loving, gentle conversations with Him. Anyone can have such familiar conversations with God. He knows what we are capable of. Let us begin then. Perhaps He expects but one generous resolution on our part. Have courage. We only have a short time on earth. You are nearly sixty-four and I am almost eighty. Let us live and die with God. Our sufferings will be sweet and pleasant to us, while we are with Him. And without Him the greatest pleasures will be a cruel punishment to us. May He be blessed in everything! Amen.

Offer yourself to worship Him, to beg His grace, to offer Him your heart from time to time, in the midst of your business, even every moment if you can. Don't restrict yourself by following certain rules or special forms of devotion. Rather act with faith in God, with love and humility. I remain your servant in the Lord.

Eighth Letter

*Y*OU are not the only one who is troubled with wandering thoughts. It is natural for the mind to wander, but remember that our God-given will governs all our faculties. We must recall our minds, and carry our thoughts to God. Otherwise, even against our wills, we may be dragged down to the things of the earth.

I believe the remedy for this problem is to confess our faults and to humble ourselves before God. I do not advise you to pray lengthy prayers, because lengthy prayers encourage wandering thoughts.

Present yourself in prayer before God like a beggar at a rich man's gate. Let it be your business to keep your mind in the presence of the Lord. If it happens that your mind wanders, don't get upset. Your will must bring your thoughts back into harmony with God. If you persevere, God will have mercy on you.

Another way to prevent the mind from wandering during prayer time is to not let it wander too far. You should keep it strictly in the presence of God. By doing so, you will find it increasingly easy to keep your mind calm in the time of prayer or at least to prevent it from wandering.

I have told you already in my previous letters of the advantages we may draw from this practice of the presence of God. Let's take it seriously and pray for one another.

Ninth Letter

*T*HE enclosed is an answer to the letter I received from –; please pass it on to her. She seems to be full of good will, but she wants to go faster than grace allows. One doesn't reach spiritual maturity overnight. I highly recommend working with her. We ought to help one another by giving good advice and by setting good examples. Please keep me updated on her spiritual condition so that I may track her progress in growing in the Christian life.

We must keep in mind that our only purpose in this life is to please God. You and I have walked with God for over forty years. But have we really used those years to love and serve God, who, by His mercy, has called us for that very purpose? I am ashamed and confused whenever I reflect on the great favors which God has done and still continues to do for me, and for barely using them to advance in the way of reaching perfection like Christ.

In His mercy God gives us a little more time. Let us start over and repair the lost opportunity. Let us return with a full assurance to our kind Father of mercies, who is always ready to receive us affectionately. Let us generously renounce all that is not of God, because of our love of Him. He deserves infinitely more. Let us think of Him always. Let us put all our trust in Him. When we receive His abundant grace, we will be able to do anything, but without it we can do nothing but sin.

We cannot escape the dangers of life without God's continual help. Let us then pray to Him for it continually. But how can we pray to Him without being with Him?

To be with Him, we must cultivate the holy habit of thinking of Him often. You will tell me that I am always saying the same thing. It is true, for this is the best and easiest method I know, and I don't practice any other. I advise everybody to do the same. We must know before we can love. In order to know God, we must think about Him often. When we come to love Him, we shall then also think of Him often, for our heart will be with our treasure. This is an argument which well deserves your consideration.

Tenth Letter

J HAVE had a good deal of difficulty to bring myself to write to M–, and I do it now purely because you desire me to do so. Would you mind addressing and sending the letter yourself? I am very well pleased with the trust which you have in God. I wish that He may increase it in you more and more. We can never trust such a good and faithful Friend too much. He will never fail us in this world or in the next.

I pray that M– is wise enough to profit from his loss and to put all his confidence in God. Our Lord will soon give him another friend who is more powerful. God deals with our hearts as He pleases. Perhaps M– was too much attached to him he has lost. We ought to love our friends.

Remember what I advised you to do. Think often on God day and night, in everything you do. He is always near you and with you. Never abandon His presence. You would think it rude to desert a friend who came to visit you; why then must God be neglected? Do not then forget Him, but think on Him often. Love Him continually. Live and die with Him. This is the glorious employment of a Christian; in a word, this is our profession. If we don't know it, we must learn it.

I will pray for you and remain yours in our Lord.

Eleventh Letter

I DO not pray that you may be delivered from your pains; but I pray that God would give you strength and patience to carry your burdens as long as He pleases.

Seek from Him the strength to endure as much and as long as He deems necessary. The people of the world don't understand this since they are alone in their suffering, while Christians consider suffering as a favor from God. Those who consider sickness as coming from the hand of God, as the effects of His mercy, and the means which He employs for their salvation, commonly find in it great sweetness and sensible consolation.

I wish you could convince yourself that God is often nearer to us and more effectually present with us in sickness than in health. Don't depend on physicians or put all of your trust in them as your health is ultimately dependent on His will for you. Put all your trust in Him and you will soon see its results in your recovery.

No matter what medication has been prescribed to treat your condition, it will succeed only so far as He permits. When pains come from God, only He can cure them. He often sends diseases of the body to cure those of the soul. Comfort yourself with the sovereign Physician both of soul and body.

I anticipate that you will tell me that I am too relaxed, because I eat and drink at the table of the Lord. You are right in thinking so. But don't you think that it would be a small pain to the greatest criminal in the world to eat at the king's table and be served by him, and notwithstanding such favors to be without assurance of pardon? I believe he would feel exceeding great uneasiness. So I assure you that despite the pleasures I taste at the table of my King, my sins are always present at the back of my mind. It further torments me as I am uncertain of my pardon, though in truth that torment itself is pleasing.

Be happy with the circumstances in which God has placed you. I envy you. Pain and suffering would be a paradise to me with God by my side, and the greatest pleasure would be hell to me without Him. It would comfort me greatly to suffer something for His sake.

It is almost time for me to go and be with God. I urge you to always seek His presence. It is the only support and comfort for your suffering. I shall also pray for Him to be with you.

Twelfth Letter

*I*F we were used to practicing the presence of God, all bodily diseases would be much alleviated thereby. God often allows us to endure some degree of suffering to purify our souls and compel us to continue with Him.

Offer God your worries and suffering, pray to Him for strength to endure them. Above all, get into the habit of spending as much time with God as possible and never let Him out of your thoughts. Keep on loving Him even in your illness. Offer yourself to Him from time to time and, in the height of your sufferings, plead with Him to open you up to His holy will for your life. I shall try to help you by praying for you.

God has many ways of drawing us to Himself. He sometimes hides Himself from us. We only need faith, which will never fail us, to help us. It ought to be the foundation of our confidence, which must be all in God.

I don't know how God will dispose of me. I am always happy while the world and its people are suffering. I, who deserve the strictest punishment, have an everlasting joy so great that I can barely contain it.

I wouldn't hesitate in asking God to let me take your suffering on myself, but knowing myself I am afraid that if He leaves me alone for even one moment I would be the most wretched man alive. And I still don't know how He can leave me alone, because faith gives me as strong a conviction as sense can, that He never forsakes us unless we have first forsaken Him. Let us fear to leave Him. Let us always seek His presence. Let us live and die in His presence.

Are you praying for me, as I am praying for you?

Thirteenth Letter

*J*T pains me to see your suffering drawn out so long. It gives me some relief to know that your suffering is evidence of God's love for you. You must try to view your suffering against this fact which, in turn, will ease it. In your case it is my opinion that you should stay away from human remedies and submit yourself entirely to the providence of God. Perhaps He is just waiting for you to submit to Him and affirm your perfect trust in Him to cure you.

I told you in my previous letter that God sometimes allows bodily diseases to cure the distempers of the soul. Take heart. Don't ask God to ease your suffering, but to give you strength to endure, because of your love for Him for as long as He wishes.

Such prayers are indeed not part of human nature, but most acceptable to God and sweet to those who love Him. Love sweetens suffering and when one loves God, one suffers for His sake with joy and courage.

I beg with you to comfort yourself with Him, the only Physician of all our ailments. He is the Father of the afflicted, always ready to help us. He loves us infinitely more than we can imagine. Therefore, love Him only and stop looking for consolation elsewhere. I hope you will soon receive it.

I am with you always in prayer and remain yours in our Lord.

Fourteenth Letter

I GIVE thanks to our Lord for having eased your suffering a little, according to your desire. I have often come near to death, though I was never so much satisfied as then. I did not pray for any relief, but I prayed for strength to suffer with courage, humility and love.

How sweet is it to suffer with God! However great the sufferings may be, receive them with love. It is paradise to suffer and be with Him so that if in this life we would enjoy the peace of paradise, we must familiarize ourselves to a familiar, humble, affectionate conversation with Him. We must keep our spirits from wandering from Him upon any occasion. We must make our hearts spiritual temples wherein to love Him continually. We must watch continually over ourselves so that we don't do, say or think anything that may displease Him.

When our thoughts are fixed on God, our suffering will become full of consolation.

I know that to arrive at this state, the beginning is very difficult. We must act purely in faith. But though it is difficult, we know also that we can do all things with the grace of God, which He never refuses to them who ask it earnestly.

Knock, persevere in knocking, and I guarantee that He will open to you in due time and grant you all that which He has deferred during many years.

Pray to Him for me, as I pray to Him for you. I hope to see Him quickly.

Fifteenth Letter

*G*OD knows best what we need and everything He does is for our good. If we knew how much He loves us, we would always be ready to receive equally and with indifference from His hand the sweet and the bitter. When we see our worst sufferings in the hand of God who dispenses them, when we know that it is our loving Father who distresses us, our sufferings lose their bitterness.

Let everything we do be aimed at knowing God. The more one knows Him, the more one desires to know Him. Because knowledge is commonly seen as the measure of love, the deeper and more extensive our knowledge shall be, the greater will be our love. And if our love of God were great we would love Him equally in pains and pleasures.

Let us seek God often by faith. Because He is within

us we don't need to look for Him elsewhere. Let us begin to be devoted to Him in all earnest. Let us cast everything else out of our hearts. If we do what we can on our parts we shall soon see that change brought about in us which we aspire after.

I cannot thank Him enough for the consolation He has blessed you with. I hope from His mercy the favor to see Him within a few days. Let us pray for one another.

[Brother Lawrence died a few days after writing this last letter.]

Book 3

THE CHRISTIAN'S SECRET OF A HAPPY LIFE

by

HANNAH WHITALL SMITH

Contents

Part 3
Results

Preface

*T*HIS is not a theological book. I frankly confess I have not been trained in theological
schools, and do not understand their methods or their
terms. But the Lord has taught me experimentally and
practically certain lessons out of His Word, which have
greatly helped me in my Christian life, and have made it
a very happy one.

And I want to tell my secret, in the best way I can,
in order that some others may be helped into a happy
life also. I do not seek to change the theological views
of a single individual. I dare say most of my readers
know far more about theology than I do myself, and
perhaps may discover abundance of what will seem to
be theological mistakes. But let me ask that these may
be overlooked, and that my reader will try, instead, to
get at the experimental point of that which I have tried

to say, and if that is practical and helpful, forgive the blundering way in which it is expressed.

I have tried to reach the absolute truth which lies at the foundation of all "creeds" and "views," and to bring the soul into those personal relations with God which must exist alike in every form of religion, let the expression of them differ as they may.

I have committed my book to the Lord, and have asked Him to counteract all in it that is wrong, and to let only that which is true find entrance into any heart. It is sent out in tender sympathy and yearning love for all the struggling, weary ones in the church of Christ, and its message goes right from my heart to theirs. I have given the best I have, and could do no more. May the blessed Holy Spirit use it to teach some of my readers the true secret of a happy life!

HANNAH WHITALL SMITH,
GERMANTOWN, PENNSYLVANIA

Part 1

The Life

1

Introduction:
God's Side vs. Man's Side

*I*N introducing this subject of the life and walk of faith, I desire, at the very outset, to clear away one misunderstanding which very commonly arises in reference to the teaching of it, and which effectually hinders a clear apprehension of such teaching. This misunderstanding comes from the fact that the two sides of the subject are rarely kept in view at the same time. People see distinctly the way in which one side is presented, and, dwelling exclusively upon this, without even a thought of any other, it is no wonder that distorted views of the whole matter are the legitimate consequence.

Now there are two very decided and distinct sides to this subject, and, like all other subjects, it cannot be fully understood unless both of these sides are kept constantly in view. I refer, of course, to God's side and man's side; or, in other words, to God's part in the work of sanctification, and man's part. These are very distinct and even contrastive, but are not contradictory; though, to a cursory observer, they sometimes look so.

This was very strikingly illustrated to me not long ago. There were two teachers of this higher Christian life holding meetings in the same place, at alternate hours. One spoke only of God's part in the work, and the other dwelt exclusively upon man's part. They were both in perfect sympathy with one another, and realized fully that they were each teaching different sides of the same great truth; and this also was understood by a large proportion of their hearers. But with some of the hearers it was different, and one lady said to me, in the greatest perplexity, "I cannot understand it at all. Here are two preachers undertaking to teach just the same truth, and yet to me they seem flatly to contradict one another." And I felt at the time that she expressed a puzzle which really causes a great deal of difficulty in the minds of many honest inquirers after this truth.

Suppose two friends go to see some celebrated building, and return home to describe it. One has seen only the north side, and the other only the south. The first says, "The building was built in such a manner, and has such and such stories and ornaments." "Oh, no!" says the other, interrupting him, "you are altogether mistaken; I saw the building, and it was built in quite a different manner, and its ornaments and stories were so and so." A lively dispute would probably follow upon the truth of the respective descriptions, until the two friends discover that they have been describing different sides of the building, and then all is reconciled at once.

I would like to state as clearly as I can what I judge to be the two distinct sides in this matter; and to show how the looking at one without seeing the other, will be sure to create wrong impressions and views of the truth.

To state it in brief, I would just say that man's part is to trust and God's part is to work; and it can be seen at a glance how contrastive these two parts are, and yet not necessarily contradictory. I mean this. There is a certain work to be accomplished. We are to be delivered from the power of sin, and are to be made perfect in every good work to do the will of God. "Beholding as in a glass the glory of the Lord," we are to be actually "changed into the same image from glory to glory, even as by the Spirit of the Lord." We are to be transformed by the renewing of our minds that we may prove what is that good and acceptable and perfect will of God (see Romans 12:12).

A real work is to be wrought in us and upon us. Besetting sins are to be conquered. Evil habits are to be overcome. Wrong dispositions and feelings are to be rooted out, and holy tempers and emotions are to be begotten. A positive transformation is to take place. So at least the Bible teaches. Now somebody must do this. Either we must do it for ourselves, or another must do it for us. We have most of us tried to do it for ourselves at first, and have grievously failed; then we discover from the Scriptures and from our own experience that it is a work we are utterly unable to do for ourselves, but that the Lord Jesus Christ has come on purpose to do it, and that He will do it for all who put themselves wholly into His hand, and trust Him to do it.

Now under these circumstances, what is the part of the believer, and what is the part of the Lord? Plainly the believer can do nothing but trust; while the Lord, in whom he trusts, actually does the work entrusted to Him. Trusting and doing are certainly contrastive things, and often contradictory; but are they contradictory in this case? Manifestly not, because it is two different parties that are concerned. If we should say of one party in a transaction that he trusted his case to another, and yet attended to it himself, we should state a contradiction and an impossibility. But when we say of two parties in a transaction that one trusts the other to do something, and that that other goes to work and does it, we are making a statement that is perfectly simple and harmonious. When we say, therefore, that in this higher life, man's part is to trust, and that God does the thing entrusted to Him, we do not surely present any very difficult or puzzling problem.

The preacher who is speaking on man's part in this matter cannot speak of anything but surrender and trust, because this is positively all the man can do. We all agree about this. And yet such preachers are constantly criticized as though, in saying this, they had meant to imply there was no other part, and that therefore nothing but trusting is done. And the cry goes out that this doctrine of faith does away with all realities, that souls are just told to trust, and that is the end of it, and they sit down thenceforward in a sort of religious easy-chair, dreaming away a life fruitless of any actual results.

All this misapprehension arises, of course, from the fact that either the preacher has neglected to state, or the hearer has failed to hear, the other side of the matter; which is that when we trust the Lord works, and that a great deal is done, not by us, but by Him. Actual results are reached by our trusting, because our Lord undertakes the thing trusted to Him, and accomplishes it. We do not do anything, but He does it; and it is all the more effectually done because of this. The puzzle as to the preaching of faith disappears entirely as soon as this is clearly seen.

On the other hand, the preacher who dwells on God's side of the question is criticized on a totally different ground. He does not speak of trust, for the Lord's part is not to trust, but to work. The Lord does the thing entrusted to Him. He disciplines and trains the soul by inward exercises and outward providences. He brings to bear all the resources of His wisdom and love upon the refining and purifying of that soul. He makes everything in the life and circumstances of such a one subservient to the one great purpose of making him grow in grace, and of conforming him, day by day and hour by hour, to the image of Christ. He carries him through a process of transformation, longer or shorter, as his peculiar case may require, making actual and experimental the results for which the soul has trusted. We have dared, for instance, according to the command in Romans 6:11, by faith to reckon ourselves "dead unto sin." The Lord makes this a reality, and leads us to victory over self, by the daily and hourly discipline of His providences. Our reckoning is available only because God thus makes it real. And yet the preacher who dwells upon this practical side of the matter, and tells of God's processes for making faith's reckonings experimental realities, is accused of contradicting the preaching of faith altogether, and of declaring only a process of gradual sanctification by works, and of setting before the soul an impossible and hopeless task.

Now, sanctification is both a sudden step of faith, and also a gradual process of works. It is a step as far as we are concerned; it is a process as to God's part. By a step of faith we get into Christ; by a process we are made to grow up unto Him in all things. By a step of faith we put ourselves into the hands of the Divine Potter; by a gradual process He makes us into a vessel unto His own honor, sanctified and useful for Him, and prepared for every good work (see 2 Timothy 2:21).

To illustrate all this: suppose I were to be describing to a person who was entirely ignorant of the subject, the way in which a lump of clay is made into a beautiful vessel. I tell him first the part of the clay in the matter, and all I can say about this is that the clay is put into the potter's hands, and then lies passive there, submitting itself to all the turnings and overturnings of the potter's hands upon it. There is really nothing else to be said about the clay's part. But could my hearer argue from this that nothing else is done, because I say that this is all the clay can do? If he is an intelligent hearer, he will not dream of doing so, but will say, "I understand. This is what the clay must do; but what must the potter do?" "Ah," I answer, "now we come to the important part. The potter takes the clay thus abandoned to his working, and begins to mold and fashion it according to his own will. He kneads and works it, he tears it apart and presses it together again, he wets it and then suffers it to dry. Sometimes he works at it for hours together, sometimes he lays it aside for days and does not touch it. And then, when by all these processes he has made it perfectly pliable in his hands, he proceeds to make it up into the vessel he has purposed. He turns it upon the wheel, planes it and smooths it, and dries it in the sun, bakes it in the oven, and finally turns it out of his workshop, a vessel to his honor and fit for his use" (see 2 Timothy 2:21).

Will my hearer be likely now to say that I am contradicting myself; that a little while ago I had said the clay had nothing to do but lie passive in the potter's hands, and that now I am putting upon it a great work which it is not able to perform; and that to make itself into such a vessel is an impossible and hopeless undertaking? Surely not. For he will see that, while before I was speaking of the clay's part in the matter, I am now speaking of the potter's part, and that these two are necessarily contrastive, but not in the least contradictory, and that the clay is not expected to do the potter's work, but only to yield itself up to his working.

Nothing, it seems to me, could be clearer than the perfect harmony between these two apparently contradictory sorts of teaching on this subject. What can be said about man's part in this great work, but that he must continually surrender himself and continually trust?

But when we come to God's side of the question, what is there that may not be said as to the manifold and wonderful ways in which He accomplishes the work entrusted to Him? It is here that the growing comes in. The lump of clay would never grow into a beautiful vessel if it stayed in the clay-pit for thousands of years. But once put into the hands of a skilful potter, and, under his fashioning, it grows rapidly into a vessel to his honor. And so the soul, abandoned to the working of the heavenly Potter, is changed rapidly from glory to glory into the image of the Lord by His Spirit.

Having, therefore, taken the step of faith by which you have put yourself wholly and absolutely into His hands, you must now expect Him to begin to work. His way of accomplishing that which you have entrusted to Him may be different from your way. But He knows, and you must be satisfied.

I knew a lady who had entered into this life of faith with a great outpouring of the Spirit, and a wonderful flood of light and joy. She supposed, of course, this was a preparation for some great service, and expected to be put forth immediately into the Lord's harvest field. Instead of this, almost at once her husband lost all his money, and she was shut up in her own house to attend to all sorts of domestic duties, with no time or strength left for any gospel work at all. She accepted the discipline, and yielded herself up as heartily to sweep, and dust, and bake, and sew, as she would have done to preach, or pray, or write for the Lord. And the result was that through this very training He made her into a vessel "sanctified and useful for the Master, prepared for every good work" (2 Timothy 2:21).

Another lady, who had entered this life of faith under similar circumstances of wondrous blessing, and who also expected to be sent out to do some great work, was shut up with two peevish invalid nieces, to nurse, and humor, and amuse them all day long. Unlike the first lady, this one did not accept the training, but chafed and fretted, and finally rebelled, lost all her blessing, and went back into a state of sad coldness and misery. She had understood her part of trusting to begin with, but not understanding the divine process of accomplishing that for which she had trusted, she took herself out of the hands of the heavenly Potter, and the vessel was marred on the wheel.

I believe many a vessel has been similarly marred by a want of understanding these things. The maturity of Christian experience cannot be reached in a moment, but is the result of the work of God's Holy Spirit, who, by His energizing and transforming power, causes us to grow up into Christ in all things. And we cannot hope to reach this maturity in any other way than by yielding ourselves up utterly and willingly to His mighty working. But the sanctification the Scriptures urge as a present experience upon all believers does not consist in maturity of growth, but in purity of heart, and this may be as complete in the babe in Christ as in the veteran believer.

The lump of clay, from the moment it comes under the transforming hand of the potter, is, during each day and each hour of the process, just what the potter wants it to be at that hour or on that day, and therefore pleases him. But it is very far from being matured into the vessel he intends in the future to make it.

The little babe may be all that a babe could be, or ought to be, and may therefore perfectly please its mother, and yet it is very far from being what that mother would wish it to be when the years of maturity shall come. The apple in June is a perfect apple for June. It is the best apple that June can produce. But it is very different from the apple in October, which is a perfected apple. God's works are perfect in every stage of their growth. Man's works are never perfect until they are in every respect complete.

All that we claim then in this life of sanctification is that by a step of faith we put ourselves into the hands of the Lord, for Him to work in us all the good pleasure of His will; and that by a continuous exercise of faith we keep ourselves there. This is our part in the matter. And when we do it, and while we do it, we are, in the scriptural sense, truly pleasing to God, although it may require years of training and discipline to mature us into a vessel that shall be in all respects to His honor, and fitted to every good work.

Our part is the trusting; it is His to accomplish the results. And when we do our part, He never fails to do His, for no one ever trusted in the Lord and was confounded. Do not be afraid, then, that if you trust, or tell others to trust, the matter will end there.

Trust is only the beginning and the continual foundation; when we trust, the Lord works, and His work is the important part of the whole matter. And this explains that apparent paradox which puzzles so many. They say, "In one breath you tell us to do nothing but trust, and in the next you tell us to do impossible things. How can you reconcile such contradictory statements?"

They are to be reconciled just as we reconcile the statements concerning a saw in a carpenter's shop, when we say at one moment that the saw has sawn asunder a log, and the next moment declare that the carpenter has done it. The saw is the instrument used, the power that uses it is the carpenter's.

And so we, yielding ourselves unto God, and our members as instruments of righteousness unto Him, find that He works in us to will and to do of His good pleasure; and we can say with Paul, "I labored more abundantly than they all, yet not I, but the grace of God which was with me" (1 Corinthians 15:10).

For we are to be His workmanship, not our own (see Ephesians 2:10). And in fact, when we come to look at it, only God, who created us at first, can re-create us, for He alone understands the "work of His own hands." All efforts after self-creating result in the marring of the vessel, and no soul can ever reach its highest fulfillment except through the working of Him who "works out everything in conformity with the purpose of His will" (Ephesians 1:11 NIV).

In this book I shall of course dwell mostly upon man's side in the matter, as I am writing for man, and in the hope of teaching believers how to fulfill their part of the great work. But I wish it to be distinctly understood all through, that unless I believed with all my heart in God's effectual working on His side, not one word of this book would ever have been written.

2

The Secret to a Happy Christian Life

*W*HEN I approach this subject of the true Christian life, that life which is hid with Christ in God, so many thoughts struggle for utterance that I am almost speechless. Where shall I begin? What is the most important thing to say? How shall I make people read and believe? The subject is so glorious, and human words seem so powerless! But something I am impelled to say. The secret must be told. For it is one concerning that victory which overcomes the world, that promised deliverance from all our enemies, for which every child of God longs and prays, but which seems so often and so generally to elude their grasp. May God grant me so to tell it that every believer to whom this book shall come may have his eyes opened to see the truth as it is in Jesus, and may be enabled to enter into possession of this glorious life for himself.

I am sure that every converted soul longs for victory and rest, and nearly every one feels instinctively, at times, that they are his birthright. Can you not remember, some of you, the shout of triumph your souls gave when you first became acquainted with the Lord Jesus, and had a glimpse of His mighty saving power? How sure you were of victory then! How easy it seemed, to be more than conquerors, through Him that loved you. Under the leadership of a Captain who had never been foiled in battle, how could you dream of defeat?

And yet, to many of you, how different has been your real experience. The victories have been but few and fleeting, the defeats many and disastrous. You have not lived as you feel children of God ought to live. There has been a resting in a clear understanding of doctrinal truth, without pressing after the power and life thereof. There has been a rejoicing in the knowledge of things testified of in the Scriptures, without a living realization of the things themselves, consciously felt in the soul.

Christ is believed in, talked about, and served, but He is not known as the soul's actual and very life, abiding there forever, and revealing Himself there continually in His beauty. You have found Jesus as your Savior and your Master, and you have tried to serve Him and advance the cause of His kingdom. You have carefully studied the holy Scriptures and have gathered much precious truth from them, which you have endeavored faithfully to practice.

But notwithstanding all your knowledge and all your activities in the service of the Lord, your souls are secretly starving, and you cry out again and again for that bread and water of life which you saw promised in the Scriptures to all believers. In the very depths of your hearts you know that your experience is not a scriptural experience; that, as an old writer says, your religion is "but a talk to what the early Christians enjoyed, possessed, and lived in." Your souls have sunk within you, as day after day, and year after year, your early visions of triumph have seemed to grow more and more dim, and you have been forced to settle down to the conviction that the best you can expect from your religion is a life of alternate failure and victory; one hour sinning, and the next repenting; and beginning again, only to fail again, and again to repent.

But is this all? Had the Lord Jesus only this in His mind when He laid down His precious life to deliver you from your sore and cruel bondage to sin? Did He propose to Himself only this partial deliverance? Did He intend to leave you thus struggling along under a weary consciousness of defeat and discouragement? Did He fear that a continuous victory would dishonor Him, and bring reproach on His name? When all those declarations were made concerning His coming, and the work He was to accomplish, did they mean only this that you have experienced? Was there a hidden reserve in each promise that was meant to deprive it of its complete fulfillment? Did "rescue us from the hand of our enemies" mean only a few of them (Luke 1:74 NIV)?

Did "God always leads us in triumph" (2 Corinthians 2:14) mean only sometimes; or being "more than conquerors through Him who loved us" (Romans 8:37) mean constant defeat and failure? No, no, a thousand times no! God is able to save unto the uttermost, and He means to do it. His promise, confirmed by His oath, was "to grant us that we, being delivered from the hand of our enemies, might serve Him without fear, in holiness and righteousness before Him all the days of our life" (Luke 1:74-75). It is a mighty work to do, but our Deliverer is able to do it. He came to destroy the works of the devil, and dare we dream for a moment that He is not able or not willing to accomplish His own purposes?

At the very outset, then, settle down on this one thing, that the Lord is able to save you fully, now, in this life, from the power and dominion of sin, and to deliver you altogether out of the hands of your enemies. If you do not think He is, search your Bible, and collect together every announcement or declaration concerning the purposes and object of His death on the cross. You will be astonished to find how full they are. Everywhere and always His work is said to be to deliver us from our sins, from our bondage, from our defilement; and not a hint is given anywhere that this deliverance was to be only the limited and partial one with which the church so continually tries to be satisfied.

Let me give you a few texts on this subject. When the angel of the Lord appeared unto Joseph in a dream, and announced the coming birth of the Savior, he said, "And you shall call His name JESUS, for He will save His people from their sins" (Matthew 1:21).

When Zacharias was "filled with the Holy Spirit" (Luke 1:67) at the birth of his son, and "prophesied," he declared that God had visited His people in order to fulfill the promise and the oath He had made them, which was "to grant us that we, being delivered from the hand of our enemies, might serve Him without fear, in holiness and righteousness before Him all the days of our life" (Luke 1:74-75).

When Peter was preaching in the porch of the temple to the wondering Jews, he said, "To you first, God, having raised up His Servant Jesus, sent Him to bless you, in turning away every one of you from your iniquities" (Acts 3:26).

When Paul was telling the Ephesian church the wondrous truth that Christ had loved them so much as to give Himself for them, he went on to declare that His purpose in thus doing so was, "that He might sanctify and cleanse her [the church] with the washing of water by the word, that He might present her to Himself a glorious church, not having spot or wrinkle or any such thing, but that she should be holy and without blemish" (Ephesians 5:26-27).

When Paul was seeking to instruct Titus, his own son after the common faith, concerning the grace of God, he declared that the object of that grace was to teach us that "denying ungodliness and worldly lusts, we should live soberly, righteously, and godly in the present age" (Titus 2:12); and adds, as the reason of this, that Christ "gave Himself for us to redeem us from all wickedness and to purify for Himself a people that are His very own, eager to do what is good" (Titus 2:14 NIV).

When Peter was urging upon the Christian, to whom he was writing, a holy and Christ-like walk, he tells them that "to this you were called, because Christ also suffered for us, leaving us an example, that you should follow His steps: 'Who committed no sin, nor was deceit found in His mouth'" (1 Peter 2:21-22); and adds, "who Himself bore our sins in His own body on the tree, that we, having died to sins, might live for righteousness – by whose stripes you were healed" (1 Peter 2:24).

When Paul was contrasting in the Ephesians the walk suitable for a Christian, with the walk of an unbeliever, he sets before them the truth in Jesus as being this, "that you put off, concerning your former conduct, the old man which grows corrupt according to the deceitful lusts, and be renewed in the spirit of your mind, and that you put on the new man which was created according to God, in true righteousness and holiness" (Ephesians 4:22-24).

And when, in Romans 6, he was answering forever the question as to continuing in sin, and showing how utterly foreign it was to the whole spirit and aim of the salvation of Jesus, he brings up the fact of our judicial death and resurrection with Christ as an unanswerable argument for our practical deliverance from it, and says, "By no means! We are those who have died to sin; how can we live in it any longer? Or don't you know that all of us who were baptized into Christ Jesus were baptized into His death? We were therefore buried with Him through baptism into death in order that, just as Christ was raised from the dead through the glory of the Father, we too may live a new life" (Romans 6:2-4 NIV). He adds, "For we know that our old self was crucified with Him so that the body ruled by sin might be done away with, that we should no longer be slaves to sin" (Romans 6:6 NIV).

Dear Christians, will you receive the testimony of Scripture on this matter? The same questions that troubled the church in Paul's day are troubling it now: first, "Shall we continue in sin that grace may abound?" (Romans 6:1). And second, "Do we then make void the law through faith?" (Romans 3:31). Shall not our answer to these be Paul's emphatic "by no means"? His triumphant assertions are that instead of making it void, "we establish the law"; and that "what the law was powerless to do because it was weakened by the flesh, God did by sending His own Son in the likeness of sinful flesh to be a sin offering. And so He condemned sin in the flesh, in order that the righteous requirement of the law might be fully met in us, who do not live according to the flesh but according to the Spirit" (Romans 8:3-4 NIV).

Can we suppose for a moment that the holy God, who hates sin in the sinner, is willing to tolerate it in the Christian, and that He has even arranged the plan of salvation in such a way as to make it impossible for those who are saved from the guilt of sin to find deliverance from its power?

As Dr Chalmers well says, "Sin is that scandal which must be rooted out from the great spiritual household over which the Divinity rejoices ... Strange administration, indeed, for sin to be so hateful to God as to lay all who had incurred it under death, and yet when readmitted into life that sin should be permitted; and that what was before the object of destroying vengeance, should now become the object of an upheld and protected toleration.

"Now that the penalty is taken off, think you that it is possible the unchangeable God has so given up His antipathy to sin, as that man, ruined and redeemed man, may now perseveringly indulge under the new arrangement in that which under the old destroyed him? Does not the God who loved righteousness and hated iniquity six thousand years ago, bear the same love to righteousness and hatred to iniquity still? ...

"I now breathe the air of loving-kindness from heaven, and can walk before God in peace and graciousness; shall I again attempt the incompatible alliance of two principles so adverse as that of an approving God and a persevering sinner? How shall we, recovered from so awful a catastrophe, continue that which first involved us in it? The cross of Christ, by the same mighty and decisive stroke wherewith it moved the curse of sin away from us, also surely moves away the power and the love of it from over us."

And not Dr Chalmers only, but many other holy men of his generation and of our own, as well as of generations long past, have united in declaring that the redemption accomplished for us by our Lord Jesus Christ on the cross at Calvary is a redemption from the power of sin as well as from its guilt, and that He is able to save to the uttermost all who come unto God by Him.

A quaint old divine of the seventeenth century says: "There is nothing so contrary to God as sin, and God will not suffer sin always to rule His masterpiece, man. When we consider the infiniteness of God's power for destroying that which is contrary to Him, who can believe that the devil must always stand and prevail? I believe it is inconsistent and disagreeable with true faith for people to be Christians, and yet to believe that Christ, the eternal Son of God, to whom all power in heaven and earth is given, will suffer sin and the devil to have dominion over them.

"But you will say no man by all the power he has can redeem himself, and no man can live without sin. We will say 'Amen' to it. But if men tell us that when God's power comes to help us and to redeem us out of sin it cannot be effected, then this doctrine we cannot away with; nor I hope you neither.

"Would you approve of it, if I should tell you that God puts forth His power to do such a thing, but the devil hinders Him? That it is impossible for God to do it because the devil does not like it? That it is impossible that any one should be free from sin because the devil has got such a power in them that God cannot cast him out? This is lamentable doctrine, yet has not this been preached? It does in plain terms say, though God does interpose His power, it is impossible, because the devil has so rooted sin in the nature of man. Is not man God's creature, and cannot He make him new, and cast sin out of him? If you say sin is deeply rooted in man, I say so, too. But Christ Jesus has entered so deeply into the root of the nature of man that He has received power to destroy the devil and his works, and to recover and redeem man into righteousness and holiness. Or else it is false that 'He is able to save completely those who come to God through Him' (Hebrews 7:25 NIV). We must throw away the Bible if we say that it is impossible for God to deliver man out of sin.

"We know," he continues, "when our friends are in captivity, as in Turkey, or elsewhere, we pay our money for their redemption; but we will not pay our money if they be kept in their fetters still. Would not any one think himself cheated to pay so much money for their redemption, and the bargain be made so that he shall be said to be redeemed, and be called a redeemed captive, but he must wear his fetters still?

"This is for bodies, but now I am speaking of souls. Christ must be made to me redemption, and rescue me from captivity. Am I a prisoner anywhere? Yes, 'Very truly I tell you, everyone who sins is a slave to sin' (John 8:34 NIV). If you have sinned, you are a slave, a captive that must be redeemed out of captivity. Who will pay a price for me? I am poor; I have nothing; I cannot redeem myself; who will pay a price for me? There is One come who has paid a price for me. That is well; that is good news, then I hope I shall come out of my captivity. His name is Jesus, He is the Redeemer. So, then, I do expect the benefit of my redemption, and that I shall go out of my captivity. No, say they, you must abide in sin as long as you live. What! Must we never be delivered? Must this crooked heart and perverse will always remain? Must I be a believer, and yet have no faith that reaches to sanctification and holy living? Is there no mastery to be had, no getting victory over sin? Must it prevail over me as long as I live? What sort of a Redeemer, then, is this, or what benefit have I in this life, of my redemption?"

Similar extracts might be quoted from Marshall, Romaine, and many others, to show that this doctrine is no new one in the church, however much it may have been lost sight of by the present generation of believers. It is the same old story that has filled with songs of triumph the daily lives of many saints of God throughout all ages; and is now afresh being sounded forth to the unspeakable joy of weary and burdened souls.

Do not reject it, then, dear reader, until you have prayerfully searched the Scriptures to see whether these things be indeed so. Ask God to open the eyes of your understanding by His Spirit, that you may know "what is the exceeding greatness of His power toward us who believe, according to the working of His mighty power which He worked in Christ when He raised Him from the dead and seated Him at His right hand in the heavenly places" (Ephesians 1:19-20). And when you have begun to have some faint glimpses of this power, learn to look away utterly from your own weakness, and, putting your case into His hands, trust Him to deliver you. In Psalm 8:6, we are told that God made man to have dominion over the works of His hands. The fulfillment of this is declared in 2 Corinthians 2:14, where the apostle cries, "Thanks be to God who always leads us in triumph in Christ."

If the maker of a machine should declare that he had made it to accomplish a certain purpose, and if upon trial it should be found incapable of accomplishing that purpose, we would all say of that maker that he was a fraud. Surely then we will not dare to think that it is impossible for the creature whom God has made, to accomplish the declared object for which he was created. Especially when the Scriptures are so full of the assertions that Christ has made it possible.

The only thing that can hinder is the creature's own failure to work in harmony with the plans of his Creator, and if this want of harmony can be removed, then God can work. Christ came to bring about an atonement between God and man, which should make it possible for God thus to work in man to will and to do of His good pleasure. Therefore we may be of good courage; for the work Christ has undertaken He is surely able and willing to perform. Let us then "follow in the footsteps of the faith that our father Abraham had," who "did not waver through unbelief regarding the promise of God, but was strengthened in his faith and gave glory to God, being fully persuaded that God had power to do what He had promised" (Romans 4:12, 20-21 NIV).

3

The Characteristics of a
Higher Christian Life

*I*N my last chapter I tried to settle the question as to the scripturalness of the experience sometimes called the Higher Christian Life, but which to my own mind is best described in the words, the "life is hidden with Christ in God."

I shall now, therefore, consider it as a settled point that the Scriptures do set before the believer in the Lord Jesus a life of abiding rest and of continual victory, which is very far beyond the ordinary line of Christian experience; and that in the Bible we have presented to us a Savior able to save us from the power of our sins, as really as He saves us from their guilt.

The point to be next considered is, as to what this hidden life consists in, and how it differs from every other sort of Christian experience. And as to this, it is simply letting the Lord carry our burdens and manage our affairs for us, instead of trying to do it ourselves.

Most Christians are like a man who was toiling along the road, bending under a heavy burden, when a wagon overtook him, and the driver kindly offered to help him on his journey. He joyfully accepted the offer, but when seated, continued to bend beneath his burden, which he still kept on his shoulders.

"Why do you not lay down your burden?" asked the kindhearted driver. "Oh!" replied the man, "I feel that it is almost too much to ask you to carry me, and I could not think of letting you carry my burden too." And so Christians, who have given themselves into the care and keeping of the Lord Jesus, still continue to bend beneath the weight of their burden, and often go weary and heavy-laden throughout the whole length of their journey.

When I speak of burdens, I mean everything that troubles us, whether spiritual or temporal. I mean, first of all, ourselves. The greatest burden we have to carry in life is the self. The most difficult thing we have to manage is the self. Our own daily living, our frames and feelings, our specific weaknesses and temptations, and our peculiar temperaments, our inward affairs of every kind, these are the things that perplex and worry us more than anything else, and that bring us often into bondage and darkness.

In laying off your burdens, therefore, the first one you must get rid of is yourself. You must hand yourself and all your inward experiences, your temptations, your temperament, your frames and feelings, all over into the care and keeping of your God, and leave them there. He made you, and therefore He understands you and knows how to manage you, and you must trust Him to do it. Say to Him, "Here, Lord, I abandon myself to You. I have tried in every way I could think of to manage myself, and to make myself what I know I ought to be, but have always failed. Now I give it up to You. Take entire possession of me. Work in me all the good pleasure of Your will. Mold and fashion me into such a vessel as seems good to You. I leave myself in Your hands, and I believe You will, according to Your promise, make me into a vessel unto Your honor, 'sanctified and useful for the Master, prepared for every good work'" (2 Timothy 2:21). And here you must rest, trusting yourself thus to Him continually and absolutely.

Next, you must lay off every other burden – your health, your reputation, your Christian work, your houses, your children, your business, your servants; everything, in short, that concerns you, whether inward or outward.

Christians always commit the keeping of their souls for eternity to the Lord, because they know, without a shadow of a doubt, that they cannot keep these themselves. But the things of this present life they take into their own keeping, and try to carry on their own shoulders, with the perhaps unconfessed feeling that it is a great deal to ask of the Lord to carry them, and they cannot think of asking Him to carry their burdens too.

I knew a Christian lady who had a very heavy temporal burden. It took away her sleep and her appetite, and there was danger of her health breaking down under it. One day, when it seemed especially heavy, she noticed lying on the table near her a little tract called "Hannah's Faith." Attracted by the title, she picked it up and began to read it, little knowing, however, that it was to create a revolution in her whole experience.

The story was of a poor woman who had been carried triumphantly through a life of unusual sorrow. She was giving the history of her life to a kind visitor on one occasion, and at the close the visitor said, feelingly, "O Hannah, I do not see how you could bear so much sorrow!" "I did not bear it," was the quick reply, "the Lord bore it for me."

"Yes," said the visitor, "that is the right way. You must take your troubles to the Lord." "Yes," replied Hannah, "but we must do more than that, we must leave them there. Most people," she continued, "take their burdens to Him, but they bring them away with them again, and are just as worried and unhappy as ever. But I take mine, and I leave them with Him, and come away and forget them. And if the worry comes back, I take it to Him again; I do this over and over, until at last I just forget that I have any worries, and am at perfect rest."

My friend was very much struck with this plan and resolved to try it. The circumstances of her life she could not alter, but she took them to the Lord, and handed them over into His management; and then she believed that He took them, and she left all the responsibility and the worry and anxiety with Him. As often as the anxieties returned she took them back; and the result was that, although the circumstances remained unchanged, her soul was kept in perfect peace in the midst of them. She felt that she had found out a blessed secret, and from that time she tried never again to carry her own burdens, nor to manage anything for herself.

The secret she found so effectual in her outward affairs she found to be still more effectual in her inward ones, which were in truth even more utterly unmanageable. She abandoned her whole self to the Lord, with all that she was and all that she had, and, believing that He took that which she had committed to Him, she ceased to fret and worry, and her life became all sunshine in the gladness of belonging to Him.

This was the Higher Christian Life! It was a very simple secret she found out. Only this: that it was possible to obey God's commandment contained in those words, "Do not be anxious about anything, but in every situation, by prayer and petition, with thanksgiving, present your requests to God" (Philippians 4:6 NIV); and that, in obeying it, the result would inevitably be, according to the promise, that "the peace of God, which transcends all understanding, will guard your hearts and your minds in Christ Jesus" (Philippians 4:7 NIV).

There are many other things to be said about this life hid with Christ in God, many details as to what the Lord Jesus does for those who thus abandon themselves to Him. But the gist of the whole matter is here stated, and the soul that has got hold of this secret has found the key that will unlock the whole treasure-house of God.

And now I do trust that I have made you hunger for this blessed life. Would you not like to get rid of your burdens? Do you not long to hand over the management of your unmanageable self into the hands of One who is able to manage you? Are you not tired and weary, and does not the rest I speak of look sweet to you?

Do you recollect the delicious sense of rest with which you have sometimes gone to bed at night, after a day of great exertion and weariness? How delightful was the sensation of relaxing every muscle, and letting your body go in a perfect abandonment of ease and comfort. The strain of the day had ceased for a few hours at least, and the work of the day had been thrown off. You no longer had to hold up an aching head or a weary back. You trusted yourself to the bed in an absolute confidence, and it held you up, without effort, or strain, or even thought on your part. You rested.

But suppose you had doubted the strength or the stability of your bed, and had dreaded each moment to find it giving away beneath you and landing you on the floor; could you have rested then? Would not every muscle have been strained in a fruitless effort to hold yourself up, and would not the weariness have been greater than not to have gone to bed at all?

Let this analogy teach you what it means to rest in the Lord. Let your souls lie down upon His sweet will, as your bodies lie down in your beds at night. Relax every strain and lay off every burden. Let yourselves go in perfect abandonment of ease and comfort, sure that when He holds you up you are perfectly safe. Your part is simply to rest. His part is to sustain you, and He cannot fail.

Or take another analogy, which our Lord Himself has abundantly sanctioned, that of the child-life. For "Jesus called a little child to Him, set him in the midst of them, and said, 'Assuredly, I say to you, unless you are converted and become as little children, you will by no means enter the kingdom of heaven'" (Matthew 18:2-3).

Now, what are the characteristics of a little child and how does he live? He lives by faith, and his chief characteristic is thoughtlessness. His life is one long trust from year's end to year's end. He trusts his parents, he trusts his caretakers, he trusts his teachers, he even trusts people often who are utterly unworthy of trust, because of the confidingness of his nature.

And his trust is abundantly answered. He provides nothing for himself, and yet everything is provided. He takes no thought for tomorrow, and forms no plans, and yet all his life is planned out for him, and he finds his paths made ready, opening out to him as he comes to them day by day, and hour by hour.

He goes in and out of his father's house with an unspeakable ease and abandonment, enjoying all the good things it contains, without having spent a penny in procuring them. Pestilence may walk through the streets of his city, but he regards it not. Famine and fire and war may rage around him, but under his father's tender care he abides in utter unconcern and perfect rest. He lives in the present moment, and receives his life without question as it comes to him day by day from his father's hands.

I was visiting once in a wealthy house, where there was one only adopted child, upon whom was lavished all the love and tenderness and care that human hearts could bestow or human means procure. And as I watched that child running in and out day by day, free and light-hearted, with the happy carelessness of childhood, I thought what a picture it was of our wonderful position as children in the house of our heavenly Father.

I said to myself, "If nothing could so grieve and wound the loving hearts around her, as to see this little child beginning to be worried or anxious about herself in any way, about whether her food and clothes would be provided for her, or how she was to get her education or her future support, how much more must the great, loving heart of our God and Father be grieved and wounded at seeing His children taking so much anxious care and thought!" And I understood why it was that our Lord had said to us so emphatically, "Do not worry about your life" (Matthew 6:25).

Who is the best cared for in every household? Is it not the little children? And does not the least of all, the helpless baby, receive the largest share? As a late writer has said, the baby "toils not, neither does he spin; and yet he is fed, and clothed, and loved, and rejoiced in," and none so much as he.

This life of faith, then, about which I am writing, consists in just this, being a child in the Father's house. And when this is said, enough is said to transform every weary, burdened life into one of blessedness and rest.

Let the ways of childish confidence and freedom from care, which so please you and win your hearts in your own little ones, teach you what should be your ways with God; and leaving yourselves in His hands, learn to be literally "careful for nothing"; and you shall find it to be a fact that "the peace of God, which transcends all understanding, will guard your hearts and your minds in Christ Jesus" (Philippians 4:7 NIV).

Notice the word "nothing" in the above passage, as covering all possible grounds for anxiety, both inward and outward. We are continually tempted to think it is our duty to be anxious about some things.

Perhaps our thought will be, "Oh, yes, it is quite right to give up all anxiety in a general way; and in spiritual matters of course anxiety is wrong; but there are things about which it would be a sin not to be anxious; about our children, for instance, or those we love, or about our church affairs and the cause of truth, or about our business matters. It would show a great want of right feeling not to be anxious about such things as these."

Or else our thoughts take the other tack, and we say to ourselves, "Yes, it is quite right to commit our loved ones and all our outward affairs to the Lord, but when it comes to our inward lives, our religious experiences, our temptations, our besetting sins, our growth in grace, and all such things, these we ought to be anxious about; for if we are not, they will be sure to be neglected."

To such suggestions, and to all similar ones, the answer is found in our text, "Be anxious for nothing"

(Philippians 4:6). In Matthew 6:25-34, our Lord illustrates this being without anxiety by telling us to behold the fowls of the air and the lilies of the field, as examples of the sort of life He would have us live. As the birds rejoice in the care of their God and are fed, and as the lilies grow in His sunlight, so must we, without anxiety, and without fear.

4

Surrendering to Christ

*H*AVING tried to settle the question as to the scripturalness of the experience of this life of full trust, and having also shown a little of what it is; the next point is as to how it is to be reached and realized.

And first, I would say that this blessed life must not be looked upon in any sense as an attainment but as an obtainment. We cannot earn it, we cannot climb up to it, we cannot win it; we can do nothing but ask for it and receive it. It is the gift of God in Christ Jesus.

And where a thing is a gift, the only course left for the receiver is to take it and thank the giver. We never say of a gift, "See what I have attained," and boast of our skill and wisdom in having attained it; but we say, "See what has been given me," and boast of the love and wealth and generosity of the giver. And everything in our salvation is a gift. From beginning to end, God is the giver and we are the receivers; and it is not to those who do great things, but to those who "receive God's abundant provision of grace and of the gift of righteousness" (Romans 5:17 NIV), that the richest promises are made.

In order, therefore, to enter into a realized experience of this interior life, the soul must be in a receptive attitude, fully recognizing the fact that it is to be God's gift in Christ Jesus, and that it cannot be gained by any efforts or works of our own. This will simplify the matter exceedingly; and the only thing left to be considered then will be to discover upon whom God bestows this gift, and how they are to receive it. And to this I would answer in short, that He bestows it only upon the fully consecrated soul, and that it is to be received by faith.

Consecration is the first thing. Not in any legal sense, not in order to purchase or deserve the blessing, but to remove the difficulties out of the way and make it possible for God to bestow it. In order for a lump of clay to be made into a beautiful vessel, it must be entirely abandoned to the potter, and must lie passive in his hands. And in order for a soul to be made into a vessel unto God's honor, "sanctified and useful for the Master, prepared for every good work" (2 Timothy 2:21), it must be entirely abandoned to Him, and must lie passive in His hands. This is manifest at the first glance.

I was once trying to explain to a physician, who had charge of a large hospital, what consecration meant, and its necessity, but he seemed unable to understand. At last I said to him, "Suppose, in going your rounds among your patients, you should meet with one man who entreated you earnestly to take his case under your special care in order to cure him, but who should at the same time refuse to tell you all the symptoms, or to take all your prescribed remedies; and should say to you, 'I am quite willing to follow your directions as to certain things, because they commend themselves to my mind as good, but in other matters I prefer judging for myself and following my own directions.' What would you do in such a case?" I asked.

"Do!" he replied with indignation. "Do! I would soon leave such a man as that to his own care. For of course," he added, "I could do nothing for him, unless he would put his whole case into my hands without any reserves, and would obey my directions implicitly."

"It is necessary then," I said, "for doctors to be obeyed, if they are to have any chance to cure their patients?" "Implicitly obeyed!" was his emphatic reply. "And that is consecration," I continued. "God must have the whole case put into His hands without any reserves, and His directions must be implicitly followed." "I see it," he exclaimed, "I see it! And I will do it. God shall have His own way with me from henceforth."

Perhaps to some minds the word "abandonment" might express this idea better. But whatever word we use, we mean an entire surrender of the whole being to God; spirit, soul, and body placed under His absolute control, for Him to do with us just what He pleases. We mean that the language of our soul, under all circumstances, and in view of every act, is to be, "Your will be done" (Matthew 6:10, Luke 11:2). We mean the giving up of all liberty of choice. We mean a life of inevitable obedience.

To a soul ignorant of God, this may look hard. But to those who know Him, it is the happiest and most restful of lives. He is our Father, and He loves us, and He knows just what is best, and therefore, of course, His will is the most blessed thing that can come to us under all circumstances. I do not understand how it is that Satan has succeeded in blinding the eyes of the church to this fact. But it really would seem as if God's own children were more afraid of His will than of anything else in life; His lovely, lovable will, which only means loving-kindnesses and tender mercies, and blessings unspeakable to their souls. I wish I could only show to every one the unfathomable sweetness of the will of God.

Heaven is a place of infinite bliss because His will is perfectly done there, and our lives share in this bliss just in proportion as His will is perfectly done in them. He loves us, loves us, I say, and the will of love is always blessing for its loved one. Some of us know what it is to love, and we know that could we only have our way, our beloved ones would be overwhelmed with blessings. All that is good, and sweet, and lovely in life would be poured out upon them from our lavish hands, had we but the power to carry out our will for them. And if this is the way of love with us, how much more must it be so with our God, who is love itself. Could we but for one moment get a glimpse into the mighty depths of

His love, our hearts would spring out to meet His will, and embrace it as our richest treasure; and we would abandon ourselves to it with an enthusiasm of gratitude and joy, that such a wondrous privilege could be ours.

A great many Christians actually seem to think that all their Father in heaven wants is a chance to make them miserable, and to take away all their blessings, and they imagine, poor souls, that if they hold on to things in their own will, they can hinder Him from doing this. I am ashamed to write the words, and yet we must face a fact which is making wretched hundreds of lives.

A Christian lady who had this feeling was once expressing to a friend how impossible she found it to say, "Your will be done," and how afraid she should be to do it. She was the mother of one little boy, who was the heir to a great fortune, and the idol of her heart. After she had stated her difficulties fully, her friend said, "Suppose your little Charley should come running to you tomorrow and say, 'Mother, I have made up my mind to let you have your own way with me from this time forward. I am always going to obey you, and I want you to do just whatever you think best with me. I know you love me, and I am going to trust myself to your love.'

"How would you feel towards him? Would you say to yourself, 'Ah, now I shall have a chance to make Charley miserable. I will take away all his pleasures, and fill his life with every hard and disagreeable thing I can find. I will compel him to do just the things that are the most difficult for him to do, and will give him all sorts of impossible commands'?" "Oh, no, no, no!" exclaimed the indignant mother. "You know I would not. You know I would hug him to my heart and cover him with kisses, and would hasten to fill his life with all that was sweetest and best." "And are you more tender and more loving than God?" asked her friend. "Ah, no," was the reply, "I see my mistake, and I will not be afraid of saying 'Your will be done,' to my heavenly Father any more than I would want my Charley to be afraid of saying it to me."

Better and sweeter than health, or friends, or money, or fame, or ease, or prosperity, is the adorable will of our God. It gilds the darkest hours with a divine halo, and sheds brightest sunshine on the gloomiest paths. He always reigns who has made it his kingdom; and nothing can go amiss to him.

Surely, then, it is nothing but a glorious privilege that is opening before you when I tell you that the first step you must take in order to enter into the life hid with Christ in God is that of entire consecration. I cannot have you look at it as a hard and stern demand. You must do it gladly, thankfully, enthusiastically. You must go in on what I call the privileged side of consecration; and I can assure you, from a blessed experience, that you will find it the happiest place you have ever entered yet.

Faith is the next thing. Faith is an absolutely necessary element in the reception of any gift; for let our friends give a thing to us ever so fully, it is not really ours until we believe it has been given and claim it as our own. Above all, this is true in gifts which are purely mental or spiritual. Love may be lavished upon us by another without stint or measure, but until we believe that we are loved, it never really becomes ours.

I suppose most Christians understand this principle in reference to the matter of their forgiveness. They know that the forgiveness of sins through Jesus might have been preached to them forever, but it would never have become theirs consciously until they believed this preaching, and claimed the forgiveness as their own. But when it comes to living the Christian life, they lose sight of this principle, and think that, having been saved by faith, they are now to live by works and efforts; and instead of continuing to receive, they are now to begin to do.

This makes our declaration that the life hid with Christ in God is to be entered by faith, seem perfectly unintelligible to them. And yet it is plainly declared that "as you therefore have received Christ Jesus the Lord, so walk in Him" (Colossians 2:6). We received Him by faith, and by faith alone; therefore we are to walk in Him by faith, and by faith alone. And the faith by which we enter into this hidden life is just the same as the faith by which we were translated out of the kingdom of darkness into the kingdom of God's dear Son, only it lays hold of a different thing. Then we believed that Jesus was our Savior from the guilt of sin, and according to our faith it was unto us.

Now we must believe that He is our Savior from the power of sin, and according to our faith it shall be unto us. Then we trusted Him for our justification, and it became ours; now we must trust Him for our sanctification, and it shall become ours also. Then we took Him as a Savior in the future from the penalties of our sins; now we must take Him as a Savior in the present from the bondage of our sins. Then He was our Redeemer, now He is to be our Life. Then He lifted us out of the pit, now He is to seat us in heavenly places with Himself.

I mean all this of course experimentally and practically. Theologically and judicially I know that every believer has everything the minute he is converted. But experimentally nothing is his until by faith he claims it. "Every place that the sole of your foot will tread upon I have given you" (Joshua 1:3). God "has blessed us in the heavenly realms with every spiritual blessing in Christ" (Ephesians 1:3 NIV), but until we set the foot of faith upon them they do not practically become ours. "According to your faith" (Matthew 9:29) is always the limit and the rule.

But this faith of which I am speaking must be a present faith. No faith that is exercised in the future tense amounts to anything. A man may believe forever that his sins will be forgiven at some future time, and he will never find peace. He has to come to the now belief, and say by faith, "My sins are now forgiven," before he can live the new life. And, similarly, no faith which looks for a future deliverance from the power of sin will ever lead a soul into the life we are describing. The enemy delights in this future faith, for he knows it is powerless to accomplish any practical results. But he trembles and flees when the soul of the believer dares to claim a present deliverance, and to reckon itself now to be free from his power.

To sum up, then: in order to enter into this blessed interior life of rest and triumph, you have two steps to take: first, entire abandonment; and second, absolute faith. No matter what may be the complications of your peculiar experience, no matter what your difficulties or your surroundings or your associations, these two steps, definitely taken and unwaveringly persevered in, will certainly bring you out sooner or later into the green pastures and still waters of this Higher Christian Life.

You may be sure of this. And if you will let every other consideration go, and simply devote your attention to these two points, and be very clear and definite about them, your progress will be rapid and your soul will reach its desired haven far sooner than you think possible.

Shall I repeat the steps, that there may be no mistake? You are a child of God, and long to please Him. You love your precious Savior, and are sick and weary of the sin that grieves Him. You long to be delivered from its power. Everything you have hitherto tried has failed to deliver you, and now in your despair you are asking if it can indeed be, as these happy people say, that the Lord is able and willing to deliver you.

Surely you know in your very soul that He is; that to save you out of the hand of all your enemies is in fact just the very thing He came to do. Then trust Him. Commit your case to Him in absolute abandonment, and believe that He undertakes it; and at once, knowing what He is and what He has said, claim that He does even now fully save.

Just as you believed at first that He delivered you from the guilt of sin because He said so, believe now that He delivers you from the power of sin because He says so. Let your faith now lay hold of a new power in Christ. You have trusted Him as your dying Savior, now trust Him as your living Savior. Just as much as He came to deliver you from future punishment, did He also come to deliver you from present bondage. Just as truly as He came to bear your sins for you, has He come to live His life in you. You are as utterly powerless in the one case as in the other. You could as easily have got yourself rid of your own sins, as you could now accomplish for yourself practical righteousness. Christ, and Christ only, must do both for you, and your part in both cases is simply to give the thing to Him to do, and then believe that He does it.

A lady, now very eminent in this life of trust, when she was seeking in great darkness and perplexity to enter in, said to the friend who was trying to help her, "You all say, 'Abandon yourself, and trust, abandon yourself, and trust,' but I do not know how. I wish you would just do it out loud, so that I may see how you do it."

Shall I do it out loud for you?

"Lord Jesus, I believe that You are able and willing to deliver me from all the care and unrest and bondage of my Christian life. I believe that You died to set me free, not only in the future, but now and here. I believe You are stronger than Satan, and that You can keep me, even me, in my extreme of weakness, from falling into his snares or yielding obedience to his commands.

And, Lord, I am going to trust You to keep me. I have tried keeping myself, and have failed, and failed most grievously. I am absolutely helpless; so now I will trust You. I will give myself to You; I keep back no reserves. Body, soul, and spirit, I present myself to You, a worthless lump of clay, to be made into anything You love and Your wisdom shall choose.

"And now, I am Yours. I believe You do accept that which I present to You; I believe that this poor, weak, foolish heart has been taken possession of by You, and You have even at this very moment begun to work in me to will and to do of Your good pleasure. I trust You utterly, and I trust You now!"

Are you afraid to take this step? Does it seem too sudden, too much like a leap in the dark? Do you not know that the steps of faith always "fall on the seeming void, but find the rock beneath" (John Greenleaf Whittier)?

A man, having to descend a well by a rope, found, to his horror, when he was a great way down, that it was too short. He had reached the end, and yet was, he estimated, about thirty feet from the bottom of the well. He knew not what to do. He had not the strength or skill to climb up the rope, and to let go was to be dashed to pieces.

His arms began to fail, and at last he decided that as he could not hold on much longer, he might as well let go and meet his fate at once. He resigned himself to destruction, and loosened his grasp. He fell! To the bottom of the well it was – just three inches!

If ever your feet are to touch the "rock beneath," you must let go of every holding-place and drop into God; for there is no other way. And to do it now may save you months and even years of strain and weariness.

In all the old castles of England there used to be a place called the keep. It was always the strongest and best protected place in the castle, and in it were hidden all who were weak and helpless and unable to defend themselves in times of danger. Had you been a timid, helpless woman in such a castle during a time of siege, would it have seemed to you a leap in the dark to have hidden yourself there? Would you have been afraid to do it? And shall we be afraid to hide ourselves in the keeping power of our Divine Keeper, who neither slumbers nor sleeps, and who has promised to preserve our going out and our coming in, from this time forth and even forever more?

Part 2

Difficulties

5

Consecration:
Faith before Emotions

*I*T is very important that Christians should not be ignorant of the devices of the enemy; for he stands ready to oppose every onward step of the soul's progress. And especially is he busy when he sees a believer awakened to a hunger and thirst after righteousness, and seeking to reach out to apprehend all the fullness that is in the Lord Jesus Christ for him.

One of the first difficulties he throws in the way of such a one is concerning consecration. The seeker after holiness is told that he must consecrate himself; and he endeavors to do so. But at once he meets with a difficulty. He has done it, as he thinks, and yet does not feel differently from before; nothing seems changed, as he has been led to expect it would be, and he is completely baffled, and asks the question almost despairingly, "How am I to know when I am consecrated?"

The one grand temptation which has met such a soul at this juncture is the temptation which never fails to assert itself on every possible occasion, and generally with marked success, and that is in reference to feeling. The soul cannot believe it is consecrated until it feels that it is; and because it does not feel that God has taken it in hand, it cannot believe that He has. As usual, it puts feeling first and faith second. Now, God's invariable rule is faith first and feeling second, in everything; and it is striving against the inevitable when we seek to make it different.

The way to meet this temptation, then, in reference to consecration, is simply to take God's side in the matter, and to put faith before feeling. Give yourself to the Lord definitely and fully, according to your present light, asking the Holy Spirit to show you all that is contrary to God, either in your heart or life. If He shows you anything, give it to the Lord immediately, and say in reference to it, "Thy will be done." If He shows you nothing, then you must believe that there is nothing, and must conclude that you have given Him all. Then you must believe that He takes you. You positively must not wait to feel either that you have given yourself or that He has taken you. You must simply believe it, and reckon it to be the case.

If you were to give an estate to a friend, you would have to give it, and he would have to receive it by faith. An estate is not a thing that can be picked up and handed over to another; the gift of it and its reception are altogether a mental transaction and therefore one of faith.

Now, if you should give an estate one day to a friend, and then should go away and wonder whether you really had given it, and whether he had actually taken it and considered it his own, and should feel it necessary to go the next day and renew the gift; and if on the third day you should still feel a similar uncertainty about it, and should again go and renew the gift, and on the fourth day go through a like process, and so on, day after day for months and years, what would your friend think, and what at last would be the condition of your own mind in reference to it? Your friend certainly would begin to doubt whether you ever had intended to give it to him at all; and you yourself would be in such hopeless perplexity about it that you would not know whether the estate was yours, or his, or whose it was.

Now, is not this very much the way in which you have been acting towards God in this matter of consecration? You have given yourself to Him over and over daily, perhaps for months, but you have invariably come away from your seasons of consecration wondering whether you really have given yourself after all, and whether He has taken you; and because you have not felt any differently, you have concluded at last, after many painful tossings, that the thing has not been done. Do you know, dear believer, that this sort of perplexity will last forever, unless you cut it short by faith? You must come to the point of reckoning the matter to be an accomplished and settled thing, and leaving it there, before you can possibly expect any change of feeling.

The very law of offerings to the Lord settles this as a primary fact, that everything which is given to Him becomes by that very act something holy, set apart from all other things, and cannot without sacrilege be put to any other uses. "Nevertheless no devoted offering that a man may devote to the LORD of all that he has, both man and beast, or the field of his possession, shall be sold or redeemed; every devoted offering is most holy to the LORD" (Leviticus 27:28).

Having once given it to the Lord, the devoted thing henceforth was reckoned by all Israel as being the Lord's, and no one dared to stretch forth a hand to retake it. The giver might have made his offering very grudgingly and half-heartedly, but having made it, the matter was taken out of his hands altogether, and the devoted thing by God's own law became "most holy to the Lord."

It was not the intention of the giver that made it holy, but the holiness of the receiver. "The altar that sanctifies the gift" (Matthew 23:19). And an offering, once laid upon the altar, from that moment belonged to the Lord.

I can imagine someone who had deposited a gift beginning to search his heart as to his sincerity and honesty in doing it, and coming back to the priest to say that he was afraid after all he had not given it right, or had not been perfectly sincere in giving it. I feel sure that the priest would have silenced him at once with saying, "As to how you gave your offering, or what were your motives in giving it, I do not know. The facts are that you did give it, and that it is the Lord's, for every devoted thing is most holy unto Him. It is too late to recall the transaction now."

And not only the priest but all Israel would have been aghast at the man who, having once given his offering, should have reached out his hand to take it back. And yet, day after day, earnest-hearted Christians who would have shuddered at such an act of sacrilege on the part of a Jew, are guilty in their own experience of a similar act, by giving themselves to the Lord in solemn consecration, and then through unbelief taking back that which they have given.

Because God is not visibly present to the eye, it is difficult to feel that a transaction with Him is real. I suppose if, when we made our acts of consecration, we could actually see Him present with us, we should feel it to be a very real thing, and would realize that we had given our word to Him and could not dare to take it back, no matter how much we might wish to do so.

Such a transaction would have to us the binding power that a spoken promise to an earthly friend always has to a man of honor. And what we need is to see that God's presence is a certain fact always, and that every act of our soul is done right before Him, and that a word spoken in prayer is as really spoken to Him, as if our eyes could see Him and our hands could touch Him. Then we shall cease to have such vague conceptions of our relations with Him, and shall feel the binding force of every word we say in His presence.

I know some will say here, "Ah, yes; but if He would only speak to me, and say that He took me when I gave myself to Him, I would have no trouble then in believing it." No, of course you would not; but He does not generally say this until the soul has first proved its loyalty by believing what He has already said. It is he who believes who has the witness, not he who doubts. And by His very command to us to present ourselves to Him a living sacrifice, He has pledged Himself to receive us. I cannot conceive of an honorable man asking another to give him a thing which, after all, he was doubtful about taking; still less can I conceive of a loving parent acting so towards a darling child.

"My son, give me your heart" (Proverbs 23:26) is a sure warrant for knowing that the moment the heart is given, it will be taken by the One who has commanded the gift. We may, no, we must, feel the utmost confidence then that when we surrender ourselves to the Lord, according to His own command, He does then and there receive us, and from that moment we are His. A real transaction has taken place, which cannot be violated without dishonor on our part, and which we know will not be violated by Him.

In Deuteronomy 26:17-19, we see God's way of working under these circumstances: "Today you have proclaimed the LORD to be your God, and that you will walk in His ways and keep His statutes, His commandments, and His judgments, and that you will obey His voice. Also today the LORD has proclaimed you to be His special people, just as He promised you, that you should keep all His commandments, and that He will set you high above all nations which He has made, in praise, in name, and in honor, and that you may be a holy people to the LORD your God, just as He has spoken."

When we avouch the Lord to be our God, and that we will walk in His ways and keep His commandments, He avouches us to be His, and that we shall keep all His commandments. And from that moment He takes possession of us. This has always been His principle of working, and it continues to be so. "Every devoted offering is most holy to the LORD" (Leviticus 27:28). This seems to me so plain as scarcely to admit of a question.

But if the soul still feels in doubt or difficulty, let me refer you to a New Testament declaration which approaches the subject from a different side, but which settles it, I think, quite as definitely. It is in 1 John 5:14-15, and reads: "This is the confidence that we have in Him, that if we ask anything according to His will, He hears us. And if we know that He hears us, whatever we ask, we know that we have the petitions that we have asked of Him."

Is it according to His will that you should be entirely consecrated to Him? There can be, of course, but one answer to this, for He has commanded it. Is it not also according to His will that He should work in you to will and to do of His good pleasure? This question also can have but one answer, for He has declared it to be His purpose. You know, then, that these things are according to His will, therefore on God's own word you are obliged to know that He hears you; and knowing this much, you are compelled to go further and know that you have the petitions that you have desired of Him. That you have, I say, not will have or may have, but have now in actual possession. It is thus that we "obtain promises" by faith. It is thus that we have "access by faith" into the grace that is given us in our Lord Jesus Christ. It is thus, and thus only, that we come to know our hearts are "purified by faith," and are enabled to live by faith, to stand by faith, to walk by faith.

I desire to make this subject so plain and practical that no one need have any further difficulty about it, and therefore I will repeat again just what must be the acts of your soul in order to bring you out of this difficulty about consecration.

I suppose that you have trusted the Lord Jesus for the forgiveness of your sins, and know something of what it is to belong to the family of God, and to be made an heir of God through faith in Christ. And now you feel springing up in your soul the longing to be conformed to the image of your Lord. In order for this, you know there must be an entire surrender of yourself to Him, that He may work in you all the good pleasure of His will; and you have tried over and over to do it, but hitherto without any apparent success.

At this point it is that I desire to help you. What you must do now is to come once more to Him in a surrender of your whole self to His will, as complete as you know how to make it. You must ask Him to reveal to you by His Spirit any hidden rebellion; and if He reveals nothing, then you must believe that there is nothing, and that the surrender is complete. This must, then, be considered a settled matter. You have abandoned yourself to the Lord, and from henceforth you do not in any sense belong to yourself; you must never even so much as listen to a suggestion to the contrary.

If the temptation comes to wonder whether you really have completely surrendered yourself, meet it with an assertion that you have. Do not even argue the matter. Repel any such idea instantly and with decision. You meant it then, you mean it now, you have really done it. Your emotions may clamor against the surrender, but your will must hold firm. It is your purpose God looks at, not your feelings about that purpose, and your purpose, or will, is therefore the only thing you need attend to.

The surrender, then, having been made, never to be questioned or recalled, the next point is to believe that God takes that which you have surrendered, and to reckon that it is His. Not that it will be at some future time, but is now; and that He has begun to work in you to will, and to do, of His good pleasure. And here you must rest. There is nothing more for you to do, for you are the Lord's now, absolutely and entirely in His hands, and He has undertaken the whole care and management and forming of you; and will, according to His word, be "working in you what is well pleasing in His sight" (Hebrews 13:21).

But you must hold steadily here. If you begin to question your surrender, or God's acceptance of it, then your wavering faith will produce a wavering experience, and He cannot work. But while you trust He works, and the result of His working always is to change you into the image of Christ, from glory to glory, by His mighty Spirit.

Do you, then, now at this moment, surrender yourself wholly to Him? You answer, "Yes." Then, my dear friend, begin at once to reckon that you are His; that He has taken you, and that He is working in you to will and to do of His good pleasure. And keep on reckoning this. You will find it a great help to put your reckoning into words, and to say over and over to yourself and to your God, "Lord, I am Yours; I do yield myself up to You entirely, and I believe that You take me. I leave myself with You. Work in me all the good pleasure of Your will, and I will only lie still in Your hands, and trust You."

Make this a daily definite act of your will, and many times a day recur to it, as being your continual attitude before Him. Confess it to yourself. Confess it to your God. Confess it to your friends. Avouch the Lord to be your God continually and unwaveringly, and declare your purpose of walking in His ways and keeping His statutes; and you will find in practical experience that He has avouched you to be His peculiar people and that you shall keep all His commandments, and that you will be "a holy people to the LORD your God" (Deuteronomy 7:6).

6

Understanding Faith

*T*HE next step after consecration, in the soul's progress out of the wilderness of Christian experience, into the land that flows with milk and honey, is that of faith. And here, as in the first step, the enemy is very skilful in making difficulties and interposing obstacles.

The child of God, having had his eyes opened to see the fullness there is in Jesus for him, and having been made to long to appropriate that fullness to himself, is met with the assertion on the part of every teacher to whom he applies, that this fullness is only to be received by faith.

But the subject of faith is involved in such a hopeless mystery in his mind that this assertion, instead of throwing light upon the way of entrance, only seems to make it more difficult and involved than ever.

"Of course it is to be by faith," he says, "for I know that everything in the Christian life is by faith. But then, that is just what makes it so hard, for I have no faith, and I do not even know what it is, nor how to get it." And, baffled at the very outset by this insuperable difficulty, he is plunged into darkness, and almost despair.

This trouble all arises from the fact that the subject of faith is very generally misunderstood; for in reality faith is the plainest and most simple thing in the world, and the most easy of attainment.

Your idea of faith, I suppose, has been something like this. You have looked upon it as in some way a sort of thing, either a religious exercise of soul, or an inward gracious disposition of heart; something tangible, in fact, which, when you have got it, you can look at and rejoice over, and use as a passport to God's favor, or a coin with which to purchase His gifts. And you have been praying for faith, expecting all the while to get something like this, and never having received any such thing, you are insisting upon it that you have no faith. Now faith, in fact, is not in the least this sort of thing. It is nothing at all tangible. It is simply believing God, and, like sight, it is nothing apart from its object. You might as well shut your eyes and look inside to see whether you have sight, as to look inside to discover whether you have faith. You see something, and thus know that you have sight; you believe something, and thus know that you have faith. For, as sight is only seeing, so faith is only believing. And as the only necessary thing about seeing is that you see the thing as it is, so the only necessary thing about believing is that you believe the thing as it is. The virtue does not lie in your believing, but in the thing you believe. If you believe the truth, you are saved; if you believe a lie, you are lost. The believing in both cases is the same; the things believed in are exactly opposite, and it is this which makes the mighty difference. Your salvation comes, not because your faith saves you, but because it links you to the Savior who saves; and your believing is really nothing but the link.

I do beg of you to recognize, then, the extreme simplicity of faith; that it is nothing more nor less than just believing God when He says He either has done something for us, or will do it; and then trusting Him to do it. It is so simple that it is hard to explain.

If any one asks me what it means to trust another to do a piece of work for me, I can only answer that it means letting that other one do it, and feeling it perfectly unnecessary for me to do it myself. Every one of us has trusted very important pieces of work to others in this way, and has felt perfect rest in thus trusting, because of the confidence we have had in those who have undertaken to do it. How constantly do mothers trust their most precious infants to the care of nurses, and feel no shadow of anxiety? How continually we are all of us trusting our health and our lives, without a thought of fear, to cooks and coachmen, engine drivers, railway conductors, and all sorts of paid servants, who have us completely at their mercy, and could plunge us into misery or death in a moment, if they chose to do so, or even if they failed in the necessary carefulness? All this we do, and make no fuss about it. Upon the slightest acquaintance, often, we thus put our trust in people, requiring only the general knowledge of human nature, and the common rules of human interaction; and we never feel as if we were doing anything in the least remarkable.

You have done all this yourself, dear reader, and are doing it continually. You would not be able to live in this world and go through the customary routine of life a single day, if you could not trust your fellowmen. And it never enters into your head to say you cannot. But yet you do not hesitate to say, continually, that you cannot trust your God!

I wish you would just now try to imagine yourself acting in your human relations as you do in your spiritual relations. Suppose you should begin tomorrow with the notion in your head that you could not trust anybody, because you had no faith. When you sat down to breakfast you would say, "I cannot eat anything on this table, for I have no faith, and I cannot believe the cook has not put poison in the coffee, or that the butcher has not sent home diseased meat." So you would go, starving, away.

Then when you went out to your daily avocations, you would say, "I cannot ride in the railway train, for I have no faith, and therefore I cannot trust the engineer, nor the conductor, nor the builders of the carriages, nor the managers of the road." So you would be compelled to walk everywhere, and grow unutterably weary in the effort, besides being actually unable to reach many of the places you could have reached in the train. Then, when your friends met you with any statements, or your business agent with any accounts, you would say, "I am very sorry that I cannot believe you, but I have no faith, and never can believe anybody." If you opened a newspaper you would be forced to lay it down again, saying, "I really cannot believe a word this paper says, for I have no faith; I do not believe there is any such person as the queen, for I never saw her; nor any such country as Ireland, for I was never there. And I have no faith, so of course I cannot believe anything that I have not actually felt and touched myself. It is a great trial, but I cannot help it, for I have no faith."

Just picture such a day as this, and see how disastrous it would be to yourself, and what utter folly it would appear to any one who should watch you through the whole of it. Realize how your friends would feel insulted, and how your servants would refuse to serve you another day. And then ask yourself the question, if this want of faith in your fellow-men would be so dreadful, and such utter folly, what must it be when you tell God that you have no power to trust Him nor to believe His word; that "it is a great trial, but you cannot help it, for you have no faith"?

Is it possible that you can trust your fellow-men and cannot trust your God? That you can receive the "witness of men," and cannot receive the "witness of God"? That you can believe man's records, and cannot believe God's record? That you can commit your dearest earthly interests to your weak, failing fellow-creatures without a fear, and are afraid to commit your spiritual interests to the blessed Savior who shed His blood for the very purpose of saving you, and who is declared to be "able to save to the uttermost" (Hebrews 7:25)?

Surely, surely, dear believer, you, whose very name of believer implies that you can believe, will never again dare to excuse yourself on the plea of having no faith. For when you say this, you mean of course that you have no faith in God, since you are not asked to have faith in yourself, and you would be in a very wrong condition of soul if you had. Let me beg of you then, when you think or say these things, always to complete the sentence and say, "I have no faith in God, I cannot believe God"; and this I am sure will soon become so dreadful to you that you will not dare to continue it.

But you say, "I cannot believe without the Holy Spirit." Very well. Will you conclude that your want of faith is because of the failure of the blessed Spirit to do His work? For if it is, then surely you are not to blame, and need feel no condemnation; and all exhortations to you to believe are useless.

But, no! Do you not see that, in taking up this position of having no faith and being unable to believe, you are not only "making God a liar," but you are also manifesting an utter want of confidence in the Holy Spirit? For He is always ready to help our infirmities. We never have to wait for Him, He is always waiting for us. And I, for my part, have such absolute confidence in the blessed Holy Ghost, and in His being always ready to do His work, that I dare to say to every one of you that you can believe now, at this very moment, and that if you do not, it is not the Spirit's fault, but your own.

Put your will then over on to the believing side. Say, "Lord, I will believe, I do believe," and continue to say it. Insist upon believing, in the face of every suggestion of doubt with which you may be tempted. Out of your very unbelief, throw yourself headlong on to the word and promises of God, and dare to abandon yourself to the keeping and saving power of the Lord Jesus. If you have ever trusted a precious interest in the hands of any earthly friend, I conjure you, trust yourself now and all your spiritual interests in the hands of your heavenly Friend, and never, never, *never* allow yourself to doubt again.

And remember, there are two things which are more incompatible than even oil and water, and these two are trust and worry. Would you call it trust if you should give something into the hands of a friend to attend to for you, and then should spend your nights and days in anxious thought and worry as to whether it would be rightly and successfully done? And can you call it trust when you have given the saving and keeping of your soul into the hands of the Lord, if, day after day and night after night, you are spending hours of anxious thought and questionings about the matter? When a believer really trusts anything, he ceases to worry about that thing which he has trusted. And when he worries, it is a plain proof that he does not trust. Tested by this rule, how little real trust there is in the church of Christ! No wonder our Lord asked the pathetic question, "When the Son of Man comes, will He really find faith on the earth?" (Luke 18:8). He will find plenty of activity, a great deal of earnestness, and doubtless many consecrated hearts; but shall He find faith, the one thing He values more than all the rest?

It is a solemn question, and I would that every Christian heart ponder it well. In our past experiences we may well have shared in the unbelief of the world; but let us, every one who knows our blessed Lord and His unspeakable trustworthiness, set to our seal that He is true, by our generous abandonment of trust in Him.

I remember, very early in my Christian life, having every tender and loyal impulse within me stirred to its depths by an appeal I met with in a volume of old sermons to all who loved the Lord Jesus, that they should show to others how worthy He was of being trusted, by the steadfastness of their own faith in Him. And I remember my soul cried out with an eager longing that I might be called to walk in paths so dark that an utter abandonment of trust might be my blessed and glorious privilege.

"You have not passed this way before" (Joshua 3:4) it may be; but today it is your happy privilege to prove, as never before, your loyal confidence in the Lord by starting out with Him on a life and walk of faith, lived moment by moment in absolute and childlike trust in Him.

You have trusted Him in a few things, and He has not failed you. Trust Him now for everything, and see if He does not do for you exceeding abundantly above all that you could ever have asked or thought; not according to your power or capacity, but according to His own mighty power that will work in you all the good pleasure of His most blessed will.

You find no difficulty in trusting the Lord with the management of the universe and all the outward creation, and can your case be any more complex or difficult than these that you need to be anxious or troubled about his management of it. Away with such unworthy doubts! Take your stand on the power and trustworthiness of your God, and see how quickly all difficulties will vanish before a steadfast determination to believe. Trust in the dark, trust in the light, trust at night, and trust in the morning, and you will find that the faith, which may begin by a mighty effort, will end sooner or later by becoming the easy and natural habit of the soul.

All things are possible to God, and "everything is possible for one who believes" (Mark 9:23 NIV). Faith has, in times past, "subdued kingdoms, worked righteousness, obtained promises, stopped the mouths of lions, quenched the violence of fire, escaped the edge of the sword, out of weakness were made strong, became valiant in battle, turned to flight the armies of the aliens" (Hebrews 11:33-34); and faith can do it again. For our Lord Himself says unto us, "If you have faith as a mustard seed, you will say to this mountain, 'Move from here to there,' and it will move; and nothing will be impossible for you" (Matthew 17:20).

If you are a child of God at all, you must have at least

as much faith as a grain of mustard, and therefore you dare not say again that you cannot trust because you have no faith. Say rather, "I can trust my Lord, and I will trust Him, and not all the powers of earth or hell shall be able to make me doubt my wonderful, glorious, faithful Redeemer!"

In the greatest event of this century, the emancipation of our slaves, there is a wonderful illustration of the way of faith. The slaves received their freedom by faith, just as we must receive ours. The good news was carried to them that the government had proclaimed their freedom. As a matter of fact they were free the moment the Proclamation was issued, but as a matter of experience they did not come into actual possession of their freedom until they had heard the good news and had believed it. The fact had to come first, but the believing was necessary before the fact became available, and the feeling would follow last of all. This is the divine order always, and the order of common-sense as well: a) The fact; b) the faith; and c) the feeling. But man reverses this order and says, "a) The feeling. b) The faith. c) The fact."

Had the slaves followed man's order regarding their emancipation, and refused to believe until they had first felt it, they might have remained in slavery a long while. I have heard of one instance where this was the case. In a remote Southern town, a woman found, about two or three years after the war was over, some slaves who had not yet taken possession of their freedom. An assertion of hers, that the North had set them free, aroused the attention of an elderly colored woman, who asked her eagerly, "O missus, is we free?"

"Of course you are," replied the lady.

"O missus, is you sure?" urged the woman, with intense eagerness.

"Certainly, I am sure," answered the lady. "Why, is it possible you did not know it?"

"Well," said the woman, "we heered tell as how we was free, and we asked master, and he 'lowed we wasn't, and so we was afraid to go. And then we heered tell again, and we went to the cunnel, and he 'lowed we'd better stay with ole massa. And so we's just been off and on. Sometimes we'd hope we was free, and then again we'd think we wasn't. But now, missus, if you is sure we is free, won't you tell me all about it?"

Seeing that this was a case of real need, the lady took the pains to explain the whole thing to the poor woman; all about the war, and the Northern army, and Abraham Lincoln, and his Proclamation of Emancipation, and the present freedom.

The poor slave listened with the most intense eagerness. She heard the good news. She believed it. And when the story was ended, she walked out of the room with an air of the utmost independence, saying as she went, "I's free! I's ain't a going to stay with ole massa any longer!"

She had at last received her freedom, and she had received it by faith. The government had declared her to be free long before, but this had not availed her, because she had never yet believed in this declaration.

The good news had not profited her, not being "mixed with faith" in the one who heard it. But now she believed, and believing, she dared to reckon herself to be free. And this, not because of any change in herself or her surroundings, not because of any feelings of emotions of her own heart, but because she had confidence in the word of another, who had come to her proclaiming the good news of her freedom.

Need I make the application? In a hundred different messages God has declared to us our freedom, and over and over He urges us to reckon ourselves free. Let your faith then lay hold of His proclamation, and assert it to be true. Declare to yourself, to your friends, and in the secret of your soul to God, that you are free. Refuse to listen for a moment to the lying assertions of your old master, that you are still his slave. Let nothing discourage you, no inward feelings nor outward signs. Hold on to your reckoning in the face of all opposition, and I can promise you, on the authority of our Lord, that according to your faith it shall be unto you.

Of all the worships we can bring our God, none is so sweet to Him as this utter self-abandoning trust, and none brings Him so much glory. Therefore in every dark hour remember that "though now for a little while, if need be, you have been grieved by various trials" (1 Peter 1:6), it is in order that "the genuineness of your faith, being much more precious than gold that perishes, though it is tested by fire, may be found to praise, honor, and glory at the revelation of Jesus Christ" (1 Peter 1:7).

7

God's Will vs. Man's Will

*W*HEN the child of God has, by the way of entire abandonment and absolute trust, stepped out of himself into Christ, and has begun to know something of the blessedness of the life hid with Christ in God, there is one form of difficulty which is very likely to start up in his path.

After the first emotions of peace and rest have somewhat subsided, or if, as is sometimes the case, they have never seemed to come at all, he begins to feel such an utter unreality in the things he has been passing through, that he seems to himself like a hypocrite when he says or even thinks they are real. It seems to him that his belief does not go below the surface, that it is a mere lip-belief, and therefore of no account, and that his surrender is not a surrender of the heart, and therefore cannot be acceptable to God. He is afraid to say he is altogether the Lord's, for fear he will be telling an untruth, and yet he cannot bring himself to say he is not, because he longs for it so intensely. The difficulty is real and very disheartening.

But there is nothing here which will not be very easily overcome when the Christian thoroughly understands the principles of the new life, and has learned how to live in it. The common thought is that this life hid with Christ in God is to be lived in the emotions, and consequently all the attention of the soul is directed towards them, and as they are satisfactory or otherwise, the soul rests or is troubled. Now the truth is that this life is not to be lived in the emotions at all, but in the will, and therefore the varying states of emotion do not in the least disturb or affect the reality of the life, if only the will is kept steadfastly abiding in its centre, God's will.

To make this plain, I must enlarge a little. Fenelon says somewhere that "pure religion resides in the will alone." By this he means that as the will is the governing power in the man's nature, if the will is set straight, all the rest of the nature must come into harmony. By the will I do not mean the wish of the man, nor even his purpose, but the choice, the deciding power, the king, to which all that is in the man must yield obedience.

It is sometimes thought that the emotions are the governing power in our nature. But, as a matter of practical experience, I think all of us know that there is something within us, behind our emotions, and behind our wishes, an independent self, that after all decides everything and controls everything. Our emotions belong to us, and are suffered and enjoyed by us, but they are not ourselves; and if God is to take possession of us, it must be into this central will or personality that He shall enter. If, then, He is reigning there by the power of His Spirit, all the rest of our nature must come under His sway; and as the will is, so is the man.

The practical bearing of this truth upon the difficulty I am considering is very great. For the decisions of our will are often so directly opposed to the decisions of our emotions that, if we are in the habit of considering our emotions as the test, we shall be very apt to feel like hypocrites in declaring those things to be real which our will alone has decided. But the moment we see that the will is king, we shall utterly disregard anything that clamors against it, and shall claim as real its decisions, let the emotions rebel as they may.

I am aware that this is a difficult subject to deal with, but it is so exceedingly practical in its bearing upon the life of faith, that I beg of you, dear reader, not to turn from it until you have mastered it.

Perhaps an illustration will help you. A young man of great intelligence, seeking to enter into this new life, was utterly discouraged at finding himself the slave to an inveterate habit of doubting. To his emotions nothing seemed true, nothing seemed real; and the more he struggled the more unreal it all became. He was told this secret concerning the will, that if he would only put his will over on to the believing side; if he would choose to believe; if, in short, he would, in the ego of his nature, say, "I will believe! I do believe!" he need not trouble about his emotions, for they would find themselves compelled, sooner or later, to come into harmony.

"What!" he said, "do you mean to tell me that I can choose to believe in that way, when nothing seems true to me; and will that kind of believing be real?" "Yes," was the answer, "your part is only this, to put your will over on God's side in this matter of believing; and when you do this, God immediately takes possession of it, and works in you to will of His good pleasure, and you will soon find that He has brought all the rest of your nature into subjection to Himself." "Well," was the answer, "I can do this. I cannot control my emotions, but I can control my will, and the new life begins to look possible to me, if it is only my will that needs to be set straight in the matter. I can give my will to God, and I do!"

From that moment, disregarding all the pitiful clamoring of his emotions, which continually accused him of being a wretched hypocrite, this young man held on steadily to the decision of his will, answering every accusation with the continued assertion that he chose to believe, he meant to believe, he did believe; until at the end of a few days he found himself triumphant, with every emotion and every thought brought into captivity to the mighty power of the blessed Spirit of God, who had taken possession of the will thus put into His hands. He had held fast the profession of his faith without wavering, although it had seemed to him that, as to real faith itself, he had none to hold fast. At times it had drained all the willpower he possessed to his lips, to say that he believed, so contrary was it to all the evidence of his senses or of his emotions. But he had caught the idea that his will was, after all, himself, and that if he kept that on God's side, he was doing all he could do, and that God alone could change his emotions or control his being. The result has been one of the grandest Christian lives I know of, in its marvelous simplicity, directness, and power over sin.

The secret lies just here. That our will, which is the spring of all our actions, is in our natural state under the control of self, and self has been working it in us to our utter ruin and misery. Now God calls us to yield ourselves up unto Him, as those who are alive from the dead, and He will work in us to will and to do of His good pleasure. And the moment we yield ourselves, He of course takes possession of us, and works in us "what is well pleasing in His sight, through Jesus Christ" (Hebrews 13:21), giving us the mind that was in Christ, and transforming us into His image (see Romans 12:1-2).

Let us take another illustration. A lady, who had entered into this life hid with Christ, was confronted by a great prospective trial. Every emotion she had within her rose up in rebellion against it, and had she considered her emotions to be her king, she would have been in utter despair. But she had learned this secret of the will, and knowing that, at the bottom, she herself did really choose the will of God for her portion, she did not pay the slightest attention to her emotions, but persisted in meeting every thought concerning the trial, with the words, repeated over and over, "Your will be done! Your will be done!" asserting in the face of all her rebelling feelings that she did submit her will to God's, that she chose to submit, and that His will should be and was her delight! The result was that in an incredibly short space of time every thought was brought into captivity; and she began to find even her very emotions rejoicing in the will of God.

Again, there was a lady who had a besetting sin, which in her emotions she dearly loved, but which in her will she hated. Having believed herself to be necessarily under the control of her emotions, she had therefore thought she was unable to conquer it, unless her emotions should first be changed. But she learned this secret concerning the will, and going to her knees she said, "Lord, You see that with one part of my nature I love this sin, but in my real central self I hate it. And now I put my will over on Your side. I will not do it any more. Do deliver me."

Immediately God took possession of the will thus surrendered to Himself, and began to work in her, so that His will in the matter gained the mastery over her emotions, and she found herself delivered, not by the power of an outward commandment, but by the inward power of the Spirit of God working in her that was well pleasing in His sight.

And now, dear Christian, let me show you how to apply this principle to your difficulties. Cease to consider your emotions, for they are only the servants; and regard simply your will, which is the real king in your being. Is that given up to God? Is that put into His hands? Does your will decide to believe? Does your will choose to obey? If this is the case, then you are in the Lord's hands, and you decide to believe, and you choose to obey; for your will is yourself. And the thing is done. The transaction with God is as real, where only your will acts, as when every emotion coincides. It does not seem as real to you; but in God's sight it is real.

And when you have got hold of this secret, and have discovered that you need not attend to your emotions, but simply to the state of your will, as Scripture commands, to yield yourself to God, to present yourself a living sacrifice to Him, to abide in Christ, to walk in the light, they will become possible; for you are conscious that, in all these, your will can act, and can take God's side: whereas, if it had been your emotions that must do it, you would sink down in despair, knowing them to be utterly uncontrollable.

When, then, this feeling of unreality or hypocrisy comes, do not be troubled by it. It is only in your emotions, and is not worth a moment's thought. Only see to it that your will is in God's hands; that your inward self is abandoned to His working; that your choice, your decision, is on His side; and there leave it.

Your surging emotions, like a tossing vessel, which, by degrees, yields to the steady pull of the cable, finding themselves attached to the mighty power of God by the choice of your will, must inevitably come into captivity, and give in their allegiance to Him; and you will verify the truth of the saying that, "If any man will do His will, he shall know of the doctrine."

The will is like a wise mother in a nursery; the feelings are like a set of clamoring, crying children. The mother decides upon a certain course of action, which she believes to be right and best. The children clamor against it, and declare it shall not be. But the mother, knowing that she is mistress and not they, pursues her course calmly, unmoved by their clamors, and takes no notice of them except in trying to soothe and quiet them.

The result is that the children are sooner or later compelled to yield, and fall in with the mother's decision. Thus order and harmony are preserved. But if that mother should for a moment let in the thought that the children were the mistresses instead of herself, confusion would reign unchecked. Such instances have been known in family life! And in how many souls at this very moment is there nothing but confusion, simply because the feelings are allowed to govern, instead of the will!

Remember, then, that the real thing in your experience is what your will decides, and not the verdict of your emotions; and that you are far more in danger of hypocrisy and untruth in yielding to the assertions of your feelings than in holding fast to the decision of your will. So that, if your will is on God's side, you are no hypocrite at this moment in claiming as your own the blessed reality of belonging altogether to Him, even though your emotions may all declare the contrary.

I am convinced that, throughout the Bible, the expressions concerning the "heart" do not mean the emotions, that which we now understand by the word "heart"; but they mean the will, the personality of the man, the man's own central self; and that the object of God's dealings with man is that this "I" may be yielded up to Him, and this central life abandoned to His entire control. It is not the feelings of the man God wants, but the man himself.

Have you given Him yourself, dear reader? Have you abandoned your will to His working? Do you consent to surrender the very center of your being into His hands? Then, let the outposts of your nature clamor as they may; it is your right to say, even now, with the apostle, "I have been crucified with Christ and I no longer live, but Christ lives in me. The life I now live in the body, I live by faith in the Son of God, who loved me and gave Himself for me" (Galatians 2:20 NIV).

8

The Omnipresence of God

*O*NE of the greatest obstacles to living unwaveringly this life of entire surrender is the difficulty of
seeing God in everything. People say, "I can easily submit to things which come from God; but I cannot submit to man, and most of my trials and crosses come
through human instrumentality." Or they say, "It is all
well enough to talk of trusting; but when I commit a
matter to God, man is sure to come in and disarrange it
all; and while I have no difficulty in trusting God, I do see
serious difficulties in the way of trusting men."

This is no imaginary trouble, but it is of vital importance, and if it cannot be met, it does really make
the life of faith an impossible and visionary theory. For
nearly everything in life comes to us through human
instrumentalities, and most of our trials are the result
of somebody's failure, or ignorance, or carelessness, or

sin. We know God cannot be the author of these things, and yet unless He is the agent in the matter, how can we say to Him about it, "Your will be done"?

Besides, what good is there in trusting our affairs to God if, after all, man is to be allowed to come in and disarrange them; and how is it possible to live by faith, if human agencies, in whom it would be wrong and foolish to trust, are to have a predominant influence in molding our lives?

Moreover, things in which we can see God's hand always have a sweetness in them which consoles while it wounds. But the trials inflicted by man are full of bitterness.

What is needed, then, is to see God in everything, and to receive everything directly from His hands, with no intervention of second causes. And it is just to this that we must be brought, before we can know an abiding experience of entire abandonment and perfect trust. Our abandonment must be to God, not to man, and our trust must be in Him, not in any arm of flesh, or we shall fail at the first trial.

The question here confronts us at once, "But is God in everything, and have we any warrant from the Scripture for receiving everything from His hands, without regarding the second causes which may have been instrumental in bringing it about?" I answer to this, unhesitatingly, "Yes." To the children of God everything comes directly from their Father's hand, no matter who or what may have been the apparent agents. There are no "second causes" for them.

The whole teaching of the Bible asserts and implies this. Not one sparrow falls to the ground without our Father knowing of it (see Matthew 10:29). The very hairs of our head are all numbered (see Matthew 10:30). We are not to be careful about anything, because our Father cares for us. We are not to avenge ourselves, because our Father has charged Himself with our defense (see Romans 12:19). We are not to fear, for the Lord is on our side (see Hebrews 13:6). No one can be against us, because He is for us (see Romans 8:31). We shall not want, for He is our Shepherd (see Psalm 23:1). When we pass through the rivers they shall not overflow us, and when we walk through the fire we shall not be burned, because He will be with us (see Isaiah 43:2).

He shuts the mouths of lions, that they cannot hurt us (see Daniel 6:22). "He delivers and rescues" (Daniel 6:27). "He changes the times and the seasons; He removes kings and raises up kings" (Daniel 2:21). A man's heart is in His hand, and, "like the rivers of water; He turns it wherever He wishes" (Proverbs 21:1). "The LORD brings the counsel of the nations to nothing; He makes the plans of the peoples of no effect" (Psalm 33:10), so that none is able to withstand Him. "You rule the raging of the sea; when its waves rise, You still them" (Psalm 89:9). "The LORD does whatever pleases Him, in the heavens and on the earth, in the seas and all their depths" (Psalm 135:6 NIV).

"If you see the oppression of the poor, and the violent perversion of justice and righteousness in a province, do not marvel at the matter; for high official watches over high official, and higher officials are over them" (Ecclesiastes 5:8). "Indeed these are the mere edges of His ways, and how small a whisper we hear of Him! But the thunder of His power who can understand?" (Job 26:14). "Do you not know? Have you not heard? The LORD is the everlasting God, the Creator of the ends of the earth. He will not grow tired or weary, and His understanding no one can fathom" (Isaiah 40:28 NIV).

And this: "God is our refuge and strength, a very present help in trouble. Therefore we will not fear, even though the earth be removed, and though the mountains be carried into the midst of the sea; though its waters roar and be troubled, though the mountains shake with its swelling" (Psalm 46:1-3).

"I will say of the LORD, 'He is my refuge and my fortress; my God, in Him I will trust.' Surely He shall deliver you from the snare of the fowler and from the perilous pestilence. He shall cover you with His feathers, and under His wings you shall take refuge; His truth shall be your shield and buckler. You shall not be afraid of the terror by night, nor of the arrow that flies by day, nor of the pestilence that walks in darkness, nor of the destruction that lays waste at noonday. A thousand may fall at your side, and ten thousand at your right hand; but it shall not come near you. Because you have made the LORD, who is my refuge, even the Most High, your dwelling place, no evil shall befall you, nor shall any plague come near your dwelling; for He shall give His angels charge over you, to keep you in all your ways" (Psalm 91:2-7, 9-11).

To my own mind, these Scriptures, and many others like them, settle forever the question as to the power of second causes in the life of the children of God. They are all under the control of our Father, and nothing can touch us except with His knowledge and by His permission. It may be the sin of man that originates the action, and therefore the thing itself cannot be said to be the will of God, but by the time it reaches us, it has become God's will for us, and must be accepted as directly from His hands. No man or company of men, no power in earth or heaven, can touch that soul which is abiding in Christ, without first passing through Him, and receiving the seal of His permission. If God be for us, it matters not who may be against us; nothing can disturb or harm us, except He shall see that it is best for us, and shall stand aside to let it pass.

An earthly parent's care for his helpless child is a feeble illustration of this. If the child is in its father's arms, nothing can touch it without that father's consent, unless he is too weak to prevent it. And even if this should be the case, he suffers the harm first in his own person, before he allows it to reach his child. And if an earthly parent would thus care for his little helpless one, how much more will our heavenly Father, whose love is infinitely greater, and whose strength and wisdom can never be baffled (see Matthew 7:11)!

I am afraid there are some, even of God's own children, who scarcely think that He is equal to themselves in tenderness, and love, and thoughtful care; and who in their secret thoughts charge Him with a neglect and indifference of which they would feel themselves incapable. The truth is that His care is infinitely superior to any possibilities of human care; and that He who counts the very hairs of our head, and suffers not a sparrow to fall without Him, takes note of the minutest matters that can affect the lives of His children, and regulates them all according to His own sweet will, let their origin be what they may.

The instances of this are numberless. Take Joseph. What could have seemed more utterly contrary to the will of God than his being sold into slavery? And yet Joseph, in speaking of it, said, "But as for you, you meant evil against me; but God meant it for good" (Genesis 50:20) and "Now, do not therefore be grieved or angry with yourselves because you sold me here; for God sent me before you to preserve life" (Genesis 45:5).

To the eye of sense it was surely Joseph's wicked brothers who had sent him into Egypt; and yet Joseph, looking at it with the eye of faith, could say, "God sent me." It had been undoubtedly a grievous sin in his brothers, but, by the time it had reached Joseph, it had become God's will for him, and was in truth, though at first it did not look so, the greatest blessing of his whole life. And thus we see how the Lord can make even the wrath of man to praise Him, and how all things, even the sins of others, shall work together for good to them who love Him.

I learned this lesson practically and experimentally long before I knew the scriptural truth concerning it. I was attending a prayer-meeting, held for the promotion of scriptural holiness, when a strange lady rose to speak, and I looked at her, wondering who she could be, little thinking she was to bring a message to my soul which would teach me such a grand lesson. She said she had had great difficulty in living the life of faith, on account of the second causes that seemed to her to control nearly everything that concerned her. Her perplexity became so great that at last she began to ask God to teach her the truth about it, whether He really was in everything or not.

After praying this for a few days, she had what she described as a vision. She thought she was in a perfectly dark place, and that there advanced towards her from a distance a body of light, which gradually surrounded and enveloped her and everything around her. As it approached, a voice seemed to say, "This is the presence of God; this is the presence of God." While surrounded with this presence, all the great and awful things in life seemed to pass before her, fighting armies, wicked men, raging beasts, storms and pestilences, sin and suffering of every kind.

She shrank back at first in terror, but she soon saw that the presence of God so surrounded and enveloped each one of these that not a lion could reach out its paw, nor a bullet fly through the air, except as His presence moved out of the way to permit it. And she saw that, let there be ever so thin a sheet, as it were, of this glorious presence between herself and the most terrible violence, not a hair of her head could be ruffled, nor anything touch her, unless the presence divided to let the evil through. Then all the small and annoying things of life passed before her, and equally she saw that these all were so enveloped in this presence of God that not a cross look, not a harsh word, nor petty trial of any kind, could reach her unless His presence moved out of the way to let them through.

Her difficulty vanished. Her question was answered forever. God was in everything; and to her henceforth there were no second causes. She saw that her life came to her day by day and hour by hour directly from His hand, let the agencies which should seem to control it be what they might. And never again had she found any difficulty in an abiding consent to His will and an unwavering trust in His care.

If we look at the seen things, we shall not be able to understand the secret of this. But the children of God are called to look, "not on what is seen, but on what is unseen, since what is seen is temporary, but what is unseen is eternal" (2 Corinthians 4:18 NIV). Could we but see with our bodily eyes His unseen forces surrounding us on every side, we would walk through this world in an impregnable fortress, which nothing could ever overthrow or penetrate, for "the angel of the LORD encamps all around those who fear Him, and delivers them" (Psalm 34:7).

We have a striking illustration of this in the history of Elisha. The king of Syria was warring against Israel, but his evil designs were continually frustrated by the prophet; and at last he sent his army to the prophet's own city for the express purpose of taking him captive (see 2 Kings 6). We read, "He sent horses and chariots and a great army there, and they came by night and surrounded the city" (2 Kings 6:14). This was the seen thing. And the servant of the prophet, whose eyes had not yet been opened to see the unseen things, was alarmed.

And we read, "And when the servant of the man of God arose early and went out, there was an army, surrounding the city with horses and chariots. And his servant said to him, 'Alas, my master! What shall we do?'" (2 Kings 6:15). But his master could see the unseen things, and he replied, "Do not fear, for those who are with us are more than those who are with them" (2 Kings 6:16). And then Elisha prayed, saying, "'LORD, I pray, open his eyes that he may see.' Then the LORD opened the eyes of the young man, and he saw. And behold, the mountain was full of horses and chariots of fire all around Elisha" (2 Kings 6:17).

The presence of God is the fortress of His people. Nothing can withstand it. At His presence the wicked perish; the earth trembles; the hills melt like wax; the cities are broken down; "the heavens also dropped rain at the presence of God; Sinai itself was moved at the presence of God" (Psalm 68:8). And in the secret of this presence He has promised to hide His people from the pride of man, and from the strife of tongues. "My Presence will go with you," He says, "and I will give you rest" (Exodus 33:14).

I wish it were only possible to make every Christian see this truth as plainly as I see it; for I am convinced it is the only clue to a completely restful life. Nothing else will enable a soul to live only in the present moment, as we are commanded to do, and to take no thought for tomorrow. Nothing else will take all the risks and "supposes" out of a Christian's heart, and enable him to say, "Surely goodness and mercy shall follow me all the days of my life" (Psalm 23:6).

I once heard of a poor woman who earned a precarious living by daily labor, but who was a joyous, triumphant Christian. "Ah! Nancy," said a gloomy Christian lady to her one day, who almost disapproved of her constant cheerfulness, and yet envied it, "it is all well enough to be happy now; but I should think the thoughts of your future would sober you. Only suppose, for instance, that you should have a spell of sickness and be unable to work; or suppose your present employers should move away, and no one else should give you anything to do; or suppose ..." "Stop!" cried Nancy, "I never supposes. De Lord is my Shepherd, and I knows I shall not want. And, honey," she added to her gloomy friend, "it's all dem supposes as is makin' you so misable. You'd better give dem all up, and just trust de Lord."

There is one text that will take all the "supposes" out of a believer's life, if only it is received and acted out in a childlike faith: "'I will never leave you nor forsake you.' So we may boldly say: 'The LORD is my helper; I will not fear. What can man do to me?'" (Hebrews 13:5-6). What if dangers of all sorts shall threaten you from every side, and the malice or foolishness or ignorance of men shall combine to do you harm? You may face every possible contingency with these triumphant words, "The Lord is my helper, and I will not fear what man shall do unto me." If the Lord is your helper, how can you fear what man may do unto you? There is no man in this world, nor company of men, that can touch you, unless your God, in whom you trust, shall please to let them.

"He will not let your foot slip – He who watches over you will not slumber; indeed, He who watches over Israel will neither slumber nor sleep. The LORD watches over you – the LORD is your shade at your right hand; the sun will not harm you by day, nor the moon by night. The LORD will keep you from all harm – He will watch over your life; the LORD will watch over your coming and going both now and forevermore" (Psalm 121:3-8 NIV).

Nothing else but this seeing God in everything will make us loving and patient with those who annoy and trouble us. They will be to us then only the instruments for accomplishing His tender and wise purposes towards us, and we shall even find ourselves at last inwardly thanking them for the blessings they bring us.

Nothing else will completely put an end to all murmuring or rebelling thoughts. Christians often feel a liberty to murmur against man, when they would not dare to murmur against God. But this way of receiving things would make it impossible ever to murmur. If our Father permits a trial to come, it must be because that trial is the sweetest and best thing that could happen to us, and we must accept it with thanks from His dear hand. The trial itself may be hard to flesh and blood, and I do not mean that we can like or enjoy the suffering of it. But we can and must love the will of God in the trial, for His will is always sweet, whether it be in joy or in sorrow.

Our trials may be our chariots. We long for some victory over sin and self, and we ask God to grant it to us. His answer comes in the form of a trial which He means shall be the chariot to bear us to the longed-for triumph. We may either let it roll over us and crush us, or we may mount into it and ride triumphantly onward.

Joseph's chariots, which bore him on to the place of his exaltation, were the trials of being sold into slavery, and being cast unjustly into prison. Our chariots may be much more insignificant things than these; they may be nothing but irritating people or uncomfortable circumstances. But whatever they are, God means them to be our cars of triumph, which shall bear us onward to the victories we have prayed for. If we are impatient in our dispositions and long to be made patient, our chariot will probably be a trying person to live in the house with us, whose ways or words will rasp our very souls. If we accept the trial as from God, and bow our necks to the yoke, we shall find it just the discipline that will most effectually produce in us the very grace of patience for which we have asked.

God does not order the wrong thing, but He uses it for our blessing; just as He used the cruelty of Joseph's wicked brethren, and the false accusations of Pharaoh's wife. In short, this way of seeing our Father in everything makes life one long thanksgiving, and gives a rest of heart, and more than that, a gaiety of spirit that is unspeakable. Someone says, "God's will on earth is always joy, always tranquility." And since He must have His own way concerning His children, into what wonderful green pastures of inward rest, and beside what blessedly still waters of inward refreshment, is the soul led that learns this secret.

If the will of God is our will, and if He always has His way, then we always have our way also, and we reign in a perpetual kingdom. He who sides with God cannot fail to win in every encounter; and whether the result shall be joy or sorrow, failure or success, death or life, we may, under all circumstances, join in the apostle's shout of victory, "Thanks be to God who always leads us in triumph in Christ" (2 Corinthians 2:14).

9

Spiritual Growth

*W*HEN the believer has been brought to the point of entire surrender and perfect trust, and finds himself dwelling and walking in a life of happy communion and perfect peace, the question naturally arises, "Is this the end?" I answer emphatically, "No, it is only the beginning."

And yet this is so little understood, that one of the greatest objections made against the advocates of this life of faith is that they do not believe in growth in grace. They are supposed to teach that the soul arrives at a state of perfection beyond which there is no advance, and that all the exhortations in the Scripture which point towards growth and development are rendered void by this teaching.

As exactly the opposite of this is true, I have thought it important next to consider this subject carefully, that

I may, if possible, fully answer such objections, and may also show what is the scriptural place to grow in, and how the soul is to grow.

The text which is most frequently quoted is 2 Peter 3:18: "But grow in the grace and knowledge of our Lord and Savior Jesus Christ." Now this text exactly expresses what we believe to be God's will for us, and what also we believe He has made it possible for us to experience. We accept, in their very fullest meaning, all the commands and promises concerning our being no more children, and our growing up into Christ in all things, "until we all reach unity in the faith and in the knowledge of the Son of God and become mature, attaining to the whole measure of the fullness of Christ" (Ephesians 4:13 NIV).

We rejoice that we need not continue always to be babes, needing milk; but that we may, by reason of use and development become such as have need of strong meat, skilful in the word of righteousness, and able to discern both good and evil. And none would grieve more than we at the thought of any finality in the Christian life beyond which there could be no advance.

But then we believe in growth that does really produce maturity, and in a development that, as a fact, does bring forth ripe fruit. We expect to reach the aim set before us, and if we do not, we feel sure there must be some fault in our growing. No parent would be satisfied with the growth of his child, if, day after day, and year after year, it remained the same helpless babe it was in the first months of its life; and no farmer would feel comfortable under such growing of his grain as should stop short at the blade, and never produce the ear, nor the full corn in the ear. Growth, to be real, must be progressive, and the days and weeks and months must see a development and increase of maturity in the thing growing. But is this the case with a large part of that which is called growth in grace? Does not the very Christian who is the most strenuous in his longings and in his efforts after it, too often find that at the end of the year he is not as far on in his Christian experience as at the beginning, and that his zeal, and his devotedness, and his separation from the world are not as whole-souled or complete as when his Christian life first began?

I was once urging upon a company of Christians the privileges and rest of an immediate and definite step into the land of promise, when a lady of great intelligence interrupted me, with what she evidently felt to be a complete rebuttal of all I had been saying, exclaiming, "Ah! But, my dear friend, I believe in growing in grace." "How long have you been growing?" I asked. "About twenty-five years," was her answer. "And how much more unworldly and devoted to the Lord are you now than when you began your Christian life?" I continued. "Alas!" was the answer, "I fear I am not nearly so much so." And with this answer her eyes were opened to see that at all events her way of growing had not been successful, but quite the reverse.

The trouble with her, and every other such case, is simply this: they are trying to grow into grace, instead of in it. They are like a rosebush which the gardener should plant in the hard, stony path, with a view to its growing into the flower-bed, and which would of course dwindle and wither in consequence, instead of flourishing and maturing. The children of Israel wandering in the wilderness are a perfect picture of this sort of growing. They were traveling about for forty years, taking many weary steps, and finding but little rest from their wanderings, and yet, at the end of it all, were no nearer the Promised Land than they were at the beginning. When they started on their wanderings at Kadesh Barnea, they were at the borders of the land, and a few steps would have taken them into it.

When they ended their wanderings in the Plains of Moab, they were also at its borders; only with this great difference, that now there was a river to cross, which at first there would not have been. All their wanderings and fighting in the wilderness had not put them in possession of one inch of the Promised Land. In order to get possession of this land it was necessary first to be in it; and in order to grow in grace, it is necessary first to be planted in grace. But when once in the land, their conquest was very rapid; and when once planted in grace, the growth of the soul in one month will exceed that of years in any other soil.

For grace is a most fruitful soil, and the plants that grow therein are plants of a marvelous growth. They are tended by a Divine Husbandman, and are warmed by the Sun of Righteousness, and watered by the dew from heaven. Surely it is no wonder that they bring forth fruit, "some a hundredfold, some sixty, some thirty" (Matthew 13:8).

But, it will be asked, what is meant by growing in grace? It is difficult to answer this question because so few people have any conception of what the grace of God really is. To say that it is free, unmerited favor only expresses a little of its meaning. It is the wondrous, boundless love of God, poured out upon us without stint or measure, not according to our deserving, but according to His infinite heart of love, which passes knowledge, so unfathomable are its heights and depths.

I sometimes think we give a totally different meaning to the word "love" when it is associated with God, than that we so well understand in its human application. But if ever human love was tender and self-sacrificing and devoted; if ever it could bear and forbear; if ever it could suffer gladly for its loved ones; if ever it was willing to pour itself out in a lavish abandonment for the comfort or pleasure of its objects, then infinitely more is divine love tender and self-sacrificing and devoted, and glad to bear and forbear, and to suffer, and to lavish its best of gifts and blessings upon the objects of its love.

Put together all the tenderest love you know of, dear reader, the deepest you have ever felt, and the strongest that has ever been poured out upon you, and heap upon it all the love of all the loving human hearts in the world, and then multiply it by infinity, and you will begin perhaps to have some faint glimpses of what the love of God in Christ Jesus is. And this is grace. And to be planted in grace is to live in the very heart of this love, to be enveloped by it, to be steeped in it, to revel in it, to know nothing else but love only and love always, to grow day by day in the knowledge of it, and in faith in it, to entrust everything to its care, and to have no shadow of a doubt but that it will surely order all things well.

To grow in grace is opposed to all self-dependence, to all self-effort, to all legality of every kind. It is to put our growing, as well as everything else, into the hands of the Lord, and leave it with Him. It is to be so satisfied with our Husbandman, and with His skill and wisdom, that not a question will cross our minds as to His modes of treatment or His plan of cultivation. It is to grow as the lilies grow, or as the babes grow, without a care and without anxiety; to grow by the power of an inward life principle that cannot help but grow; to grow because we live and therefore must grow; to grow because He who has planted us has planted a growing thing, and has made us to grow.

Surely this is what our Lord meant when He said "Consider the lilies of the field, how they grow: they neither toil nor spin; and yet I say to you that even Solomon in all his glory was not arrayed like one of these" (Matthew 6:28-29). Or when He says, "Can any one of you by worrying add a single hour to your life?" (Matthew 6:27 NIV). There is no effort in the growing of a child or of a lily. They do not toil nor spin, they do not stretch nor strain, they do not make any effort of any kind to grow; they are not conscious even that they are growing; but by an inward life principle, and through the nurturing care of God's providence, and the fostering of a caretaker or gardener, by the heat of the sun and the falling of the rain, they grow and grow.

And the result is sure. Even Solomon, our Lord says, in all his glory, was not arrayed like one of these. Solomon's array cost much toiling and spinning, and gold and silver in abundance, but the lily's array costs none of these. And though we may toil and spin to make for ourselves beautiful spiritual garments, and may strain and stretch in our efforts after spiritual growth, we shall accomplish nothing; for no man by worrying can add one cubit to his stature; and no array of ours can ever equal the beautiful dress with which the great Husbandman clothes the plants that grow in His garden of grace and under His fostering care.

If I could but make each one of my readers realize how utterly helpless we are in this matter of growing, I am convinced a large part of the strain would be taken out of many lives at once. Imagine a child possessed of the monomania that he would not grow unless he made some personal effort after it, and who should insist upon a combination of rope and pulleys whereby to stretch himself up to the desired height. He might, it is true, spend his days and years in a weary strain, but after all there would be no change in the inexorable fact, "Which of you by worrying can add one cubit to his stature?"; and his years of labor would be only wasted, if they did not really hinder the longed-for end.

Imagine a lily trying to clothe itself in beautiful colors and graceful lines, stretching its leaves and stems to make them grow, and seeking to manage the clouds and the sunshine, that its needs might be all judiciously supplied!

And yet in this picture we have, I conceive, only too true a picture of what many Christians are trying to do; who, knowing they ought to grow, and feeling within them an instinct that longs for growth, think to accomplish it by toiling, and spinning, and stretching, and straining, and pass their lives in such a round of self-effort as is a weariness to contemplate.

Grow, dear friends, but grow, I beseech you, in God's way, which is the only effectual way. See to it that you are planted in grace, and then let the Divine Husbandman cultivate you in His own way and by His own means. Put yourselves out in the sunshine of His presence, and let the dew of heaven come down upon you, and see what will come of it. Leaves and flowers and fruit must surely come in their season, for your Husbandman is a skilful one, and He never fails in His harvesting.

Only see to it that you interpose no hindrance to the shining of the Sun of Righteousness or the falling of the dew from heaven. A very thin covering may serve to keep off the heat or the moisture, and the plant may wither even in their midst; and the slightest barrier between your soul and Christ may cause you to dwindle and fade as a plant in a cellar or under a bushel. Keep the sky clear. Open wide every avenue of your being to receive the blessed influences our Divine Husbandman may bring to bear upon you. Bask in the sunshine of His love. Drink in of the waters of His goodness. Keep your face upturned to Him. Look, and your soul shall live.

You need make no efforts to grow; but let your efforts instead be all concentrated on this, that you abide in the Vine. The Husbandman who has the care of the vine will care for its branches also, and will so prune and purge and water and tend them that they will grow and bring forth fruit, and their fruit shall remain; and, like the lily, they shall find themselves arrayed in apparel so glorious that that of Solomon will be as nothing to it.

What if you seem to yourselves to be planted at this moment in a desert soil where nothing can grow! Put yourself absolutely into the hands of the great Husbandman, and He will at once make that desert blossom as the rose, and will cause springs and fountains of water to start up out of its sandy wastes; for the promise is sure, that the man who trusts in the Lord "will be like a tree planted by the water that sends out its roots by the stream. It does not fear when heat comes; its leaves are always green. It has no worries in a year of drought and never fails to bear fruit" (Jeremiah 17:8 NIV).

It is the great prerogative of our Divine Husbandman that He is able to turn any soil, whatever it may be like, into the soil of grace, the moment we put our growing into His hands. He does not need to transplant us into a different field, but right where we are, with just the circumstances that surround us, He makes His sun to shine and His dew to fall upon us, and transforms the very things that were before our greatest hindrances into the chiefest and most blessed means of our growth. I care not what the circumstances may be, His wonder-working power can accomplish this. And we must trust Him with it all. Surely He is a Husbandman we can trust.

And if He sends storms, or winds, or rains, or sunshine, all must be accepted at His hands with the most unwavering confidence that He who has undertaken to cultivate us, and to bring us to maturity, knows the very best way of accomplishing His end, and regulates the elements, which are all at His disposal, expressly with a view to our most rapid growth.

Let me entreat of you, then, to give up all your efforts after growing, and simply to let yourselves grow. Leave it all to the Husbandman, whose care it is, and who alone is able to manage it. No difficulties in your case can baffle Him. No dwarfing of your growth in years that are past, no apparent dryness of your inward springs of life, no crookedness or deformity in any of your past development, can in the least mar the perfect work that He will accomplish, if you will only put yourselves absolutely into His hands, and let Him have His own way with you. His own gracious promise to His backsliding children assures you of this.

"I will heal their backsliding, I will love them freely, for My anger has turned away from him. I will be like the dew to Israel; He shall grow like the lily, and lengthen his roots like Lebanon. His branches shall spread; His beauty shall be like an olive tree, and his fragrance like Lebanon. Those who dwell under his shadow shall return; they shall be revived like grain, and grow like a vine. Their scent shall be like the wine of Lebanon" (Hosea 14:4-7). And again He says, "Do not be afraid, you beasts of the field; for the open pastures are springing up, and the tree bears its fruit; the fig tree and the vine yield their strength. The threshing floors shall be full of wheat, and the vats shall overflow with new wine and oil. So I will restore to you the years that the swarming locust has eaten. You shall eat in plenty and be satisfied, and praise the name of the LORD your God, who has dealt wondrously with you; and My people shall never be put to shame" (Joel 2:22, 24-26).

Oh, that you could but know just what your Lord meant when He said, "Consider the lilies of the field, how they grow: they neither toil nor spin" (Matthew 6:28). Surely these words give us a picture of a life and of a growth far different from the ordinary life and growth of Christians; a life of rest, and a growth without effort; and yet a life and a growth crowned with glorious results. And to every soul that will thus become a lily in the garden of the Lord, and will grow as the lilies grow, the same glorious array will be surely given as is given them; and they will know the fulfillment of that wonderful mystical passage concerning their Beloved, that "He feeds his flock among the lilies" (Song of Solomon 2:16).

This is the sort of growth in grace in which we who have entered into the life of full trust believe: a growth which brings the desired results, which blossoms out into flower and fruit, and becomes "like a tree planted by the rivers of water, that brings forth its fruit in its season, whose leaf also shall not wither; and whatever he does shall prosper" (Psalm 1:3). And we rejoice to know that there are growing up now in the Lord's heritage many such plants, who, as the lilies behold the face of the sun and grow thereby, are "beholding as in a mirror the glory of the Lord, are being transformed into the same image from glory to glory, just as by the Spirit of the Lord" (2 Corinthians 3:18).

Should you ask such, how it is that they grow so rapidly and with such success, their answer would be that they are not concerned about their growing, and are hardly conscious that they do grow; that their Lord has told them to abide in Him, and has promised that if they do thus abide, they shall certainly bring forth much fruit; and that they are concerned only about the abiding, which is their part, and leave the cultivating and the growing and the training and pruning to their good Husbandman, who alone is able to manage these things or bring them about.

You will find that such souls are not engaged in watching self, but in "looking unto Jesus" (Hebrews 12:2). They do not toil nor spin for their spiritual garments, but leave themselves in the hands of the Lord to be arrayed as it may please Him. Self-effort and self-dependence are at an end with them. Their interest in self is gone, transferred over into the hands of another. Self has become really nothing, and Christ alone is all in all to such as these. And the blessed result is, that not even Solomon, in all his glory, was arrayed like these shall be.

Let us look at this subject practically. We all know that growing is not a thing of effort, but is the result of an inward life, a principle of growth. All the stretching and pulling in the world could not make a dead oak grow. But a live oak grows without stretching. It is plain, therefore, that the essential thing is to get within you the growing life, and then you cannot help but grow. And this life is the life hid with Christ in God, the wonderful divine life of an indwelling Holy Ghost. Be filled with this, dear believer, and, whether you are conscious of it or not, you must grow, you cannot help growing.

Do not trouble about your growing, but see to it that you have the growing life. Abide in the Vine. Let the life from Him flow through all your spiritual veins. Interpose no barrier to His mighty life-giving power, working in you all the good pleasure of His will. Yield yourself up utterly to His sweet control.

Put your growing into His hands, as completely as you have put all your other affairs. Suffer Him to manage it as He will. Do not concern yourself about it, nor even think of it. Trust Him absolutely, and always. Accept each moment's dispensation as it comes to you, from His dear hands, as being the needed sunshine or dew for that moment's growth. Say a continual "Yes" to your Father's will.

Before you have perhaps tried, as so many do, to be both the lily and the gardener, both the vineyard and the husbandman. You have taken upon your shoulders the burdens and responsibilities that belong only to the Divine Husbandman, and which He alone is able to bear. Henceforth consent to take your rightful place and to be only what you really are.

Say to yourself, if I am the garden only, and not the gardener, if I am the vine only, and not the husbandman, it is surely essential to my right growth and well being that I should keep the place and act the part of the garden, and should not usurp the gardener's place, nor try to act the gardener's part.

Do not seek then to choose your own soil, nor the laying out of your borders; do not plant your own seeds, nor dig about, nor prune, nor watch over your own vines. Be content with what the Divine Husbandman arranges for you, and with the care He gives.

Let Him choose the sorts of plant and fruit He sees best to cultivate, and grow a potato as gladly as a rose, if such be His will, and homely everyday virtues as willingly as exalted fervors. Be satisfied with the seasons He sends, with the sunshine and rain He gives, with the rapidity or slowness of your growth, in short, with all His dealings and processes, no matter how little we may comprehend them.

There is infinite repose in this. As the viole rests in its little nook, receiving contentedly its daily portion satisfied to let rains fall, and suns rise, and the earth to whirl, without one anxious pang, so must we repose in the present as God gives it to us, accepting contentedly our daily portion, and with no anxiety as to all that may be whirling around us, in His great creative and re-demptive plan.

10

Serving God

*T*HERE is, perhaps, no part of Christian experience where a greater change is known upon entering into the life hid with Christ in God, than in the matter of service. In all the lower forms of Christian life, service is apt to have more or less of bondage in it; that is, it is one purely as a matter of duty, and often as a trial and a cross.

Certain things, which at the first may have been a joy and delight, become weary tasks, performed faithfully, perhaps, but with much secret disinclination, and many confessed or unconfessed wishes that they need not be done at all, or at least that they need not be done so often. The soul finds itself saying, instead of the "May I" of love, the "Must I" of duty. The yoke, which was at first easy, begins to gall, and the burden feels heavy instead of light.

One dear Christian expressed it once to me in this way. "When I was first converted," she said, "I was so full of joy and love that I was only too glad and thankful to be allowed to do anything for my Lord, and I eagerly entered every open door. But after a while, as my early joy faded away, and my love burned less fervently, I began to wish I had not been quite so eager; for I found myself involved in lines of service which were gradually becoming very distasteful and burdensome to me.

I could not very well give them up, since I had begun them, without exciting great remark, and yet I longed to do so increasingly. I was expected to visit the sick, and pray beside their beds. I was expected to attend prayer-meetings, and speak at them. I was expected to be always ready for every effort in Christian work, and the sense of these expectations bowed me down continually.

"At last it became so unspeakably burdensome to me to live the sort of Christian life I had entered upon, and was expected by all around me to live, that I felt as if any kind of manual labor would have been easier, and I would have preferred, infinitely, scrubbing all day on my hands and knees, to being compelled to go through the treadmill of my daily Christian work. I envied," she said, "the servants in the kitchen, and the women at the washtubs."

This may seem to some like a strong statement, but does it not present a vivid picture of some of your own experiences, dear Christian? Have you never gone to your work as a slave to his daily task, knowing it to be your duty, and that therefore you must do it, but rebounding like an india-rubber ball back into your real interests and pleasures the moment your work was over?

Of course you have known this was the wrong way to feel, and have been ashamed of it from the bottom of your heart, but still you have seen no way to help it. You have not loved your work, and, could you have done so with an easy conscience, you would have been glad to have given it up altogether.

Or, if this does not describe your case, perhaps another picture will. You do love your work in the abstract; but, in the doing of it, you find so many cares and responsibilities connected with it, so many misgivings and doubts as to your own capacity or fitness, that it becomes a very heavy burden, and you go to it bowed down and weary, before the labor has even begun. Then also you are continually distressing yourself about the results of your work, and greatly troubled if they are not just what you would like, and this of itself is a constant burden.

Now from all these forms of bondage the soul is entirely delivered that enters fully into the blessed life of faith. In the first place, service of any sort becomes delightful to it, because, having surrendered its will into the keeping of the Lord, He works in it to will and to do of His good pleasure, and the soul finds itself really wanting to do the things God wants it to do. It is always very pleasant to do the things we want to do, let them be ever so difficult of accomplishment, or involve ever so much of bodily weariness. If a man's will is really set on a thing, he regards with a sublime indifference the obstacles that lie in the way of his reaching it, and laughs to himself at the idea of any opposition or difficulties hindering him.

How many men have gone gladly and thankfully to the ends of the world in search of worldly fortunes, or to fulfill worldly ambitions, and have scorned the thoughts of any cross connected with it!

How many mothers have congratulated themselves and rejoiced over the honor done their sons in being promoted to some place of power and usefulness in their country's service, although it has involved perhaps years of separation, and a life of hardship for their dear ones?

And yet these same men and these very mothers would have felt and said that they were taking up crosses too heavy almost to be borne, had the service of Christ required the same sacrifice of home, and friends, and worldly ease. It is altogether the way we look at things, whether we think they are crosses or not. And I am ashamed to think that any Christian should ever put on a long face and shed tears over doing a thing for Christ, which a worldly man would be only too glad to do for money.

What we need in the Christian life is to get believers to want to do God's will, as much as other people want to do their own will. And this is the idea of the Gospel. It is what God intended for us; and it is what He has promised. In describing the new covenant in Hebrews

8:6-13, He says it shall no more be the old covenant made on Sinai; that is, a law given from the outside, controlling a man by force, but it shall be a law written within constraining a man by love. "I will put My laws," He says, "in their mind and write them on their hearts" (Hebrews 8:10 NIV).

This can mean nothing but that we shall love His law, for anything written on our hearts we must love. And putting it into our minds is surely the same as God working in us "to will and to do for His good pleasure" (Philippians 2:13), and means that we shall will what God wills, and shall obey His sweet commands, not because it is our duty to do so, but because we ourselves want to do what He wants us to do. Nothing could possibly be conceived more effectual than this.

How often have we thought when dealing with our children, "Oh, if I could only get inside of them and make them want to do just what I want, how easy it would be to manage them then!"

And how often practically in experience we have found that, to deal with cross-grained people, we must carefully avoid suggesting our wishes to them, but must in some way induce them to suggest them themselves, sure that then there will be no opposition to contend with. And we, who are by nature a stiff-necked people, always rebel more or less against a law from outside of us, while we joyfully embrace the same law springing up within.

God's plan for us therefore is to get possession of the inside of a man, to take the control and management of his will, and to work it for him; and then obedience is easy and a delight, and service becomes perfect freedom, until the Christian is forced to exclaim, "This happy service! Who could dream earth had such liberty?"

What you need to do then, dear Christian, if you are in bondage, is to put your will over completely into the hands of your Lord, surrendering to Him the entire control of it. Say, "Yes, Lord, YES!" to everything; and trust Him so to work in you to will, as to bring your whole wishes and affections into conformity with His own sweet and lovable and most lovely will.

I have seen this done over and over, in cases where it looked beforehand an utterly impossible thing. In one case, where a lady had been for years rebelling fearfully against a thing which she knew was right, but which she hated, I saw her, out of the depths of despair and without any feeling, give her will in that matter up into the hands of her Lord, and begin to say to Him, "Your will be done; Your will be done!" And in one short hour that very thing began to look sweet and precious to her.

It is wonderful what miracles God works in wills that are utterly surrendered to Him. He turns hard things into easy, and bitter things into sweet. It is not that He puts easy things in the place of the hard, but He actually changes the hard thing into an easy one. And this is salvation. It is grand. Do try it, you who are going about your daily Christian living as to a hard and weary task, and see if your Divine Master will not transform the very life you live now as a bondage, into the most delicious liberty!

Or again, if you do love His will in the abstract, but find the doing of it hard and burdensome, from this also there is deliverance in the wonderful life of faith. For in this life no burdens are carried, nor anxieties felt. The Lord is our burden-bearer, and upon Him we must lay off every care. He says, in effect, be careful for nothing, but just make your requests known to Him, and He will attend to them all. Be careful for nothing, He says (see Philippians 4:6), not even your service. Above all, I should think, our service, because we know ourselves to be so utterly helpless in this, that even if we were careful, it would not amount to anything.

What have we to do with thinking whether we are fit or not! The Master Workman surely has a right to use any tool He pleases for His own work, and it is plainly not the business of the tool to decide whether it is the right one to be used or not. He knows, and if He chooses to use us, of course we must be fit. And in truth, if we only knew it, our chiefest fitness is in our utter help-lessness. His strength can only be made perfect in our weakness. I can give you a convincing illustration of this.

I was once visiting an institution for the handicapped, looking at the children going through dumbbell exer-cises. Now we all know that it is a very difficult thing for the handicapped to manage their movements. They have strength enough, generally, but no skill to use this strength, and as a consequence cannot do much. And in these dumbbell exercises this deficiency was very apparent. They made all sorts of awkward movements. Now and then, by a happy chance, they would make a movement in harmony with the music and the teacher's directions, but for the most part all was out of harmony.

One little girl, however, I noticed, made perfect movements. Not a jar nor a break disturbed the harmony of her exercises. And the reason was not that she had more strength than the others, but that she had no strength at all. She could not so much as close her hands over the dumb-bells, nor lift her arms, and the master had to stand behind her and do it all. She yielded up her members as instruments to him, and his strength was made perfect in her weakness. He knew how to go through those exercises, for he himself had planned them, and therefore when he did it, it was done right. She did nothing but yield herself up utterly into his hands, and he did it all. The yielding was her part, the responsibility was all his. It was not her skill that was needed to make harmonious movements, but only his.

The question was not of her capacity, but of his. Her utter weakness was her greatest strength. And if this is a picture of our Christian life, it is no wonder that Paul could say, "Most gladly I will rather boast in my infirmities, that the power of Christ may rest upon me" (2 Corinthians 12:9). Who would not glory in being so utterly weak and helpless that the Lord Jesus Christ should find no hindrance to the perfect working of His mighty power through us and in us?

Then, too, if the work is His, the responsibility is His, and we have no room left for worrying about it. Everything in reference to it is known to Him, and He can manage it all. Why not leave it all with Him then, and consent to be treated like a child and guided where to go. It is a fact that the most effectual workers I know are those who do not feel the least care or anxiety about their work, but who commit it all to their dear Master, and, asking Him to guide them moment by moment in reference to it, trust Him implicitly for each moment's needed supplies of wisdom and of strength. To see such, you would almost think perhaps that they were too free from care, where such mighty interests are at stake. But when you have learned God's secret of trusting, and see the beauty and the power of that life which is yielded up to His working, you will cease to condemn, and will begin to wonder how any of God's workers can dare to carry burdens, or assume responsibilities which He alone is able to bear.

There are one or two other bonds of service from which this life of trust delivers us. We find out that we are not responsible for all the work in the world. The commands cease to be general, and become personal and individual. The Master does not map out a general course of action for us and leave us to get along through it by our own wisdom and skill as best we may, but He leads us step by step, giving us each hour the special guidance needed for that hour.

His blessed Spirit dwelling in us, brings to our re-membrance at the time the necessary command; so that we do not need to take any thought ahead but simply to take each step as it is made known to us, following our Lord whithersoever He leads us. "The steps of a good man are ordered by the LORD" (Psalm

37:23) – not his way only, but each separate step in that way. Many Christians make the mistake of expecting to receive God's commands all in a lump, as it were. They think because He tells them to give a tract to one person in a railway train, for instance, that He means them always to give tracts to everybody, and they burden themselves with an impossible command.

There was a young Christian once, who, because the Lord had sent her to speak a message to one soul whom she met in a walk, took it as a general command for always, and thought she must speak to every one she met about their souls. This was, of course, impossible, and as a consequence she was soon in hopeless bondage about it. She became absolutely afraid to go outside of her own door, and lived in perpetual condemnation.

At last she disclosed her distress to a friend who was instructed in the ways of God with His servants, and this friend told her she was making a great mistake; that the Lord had His own special work for each special workman, and that the servants in a well-regulated household might as well each one take it upon himself to try and do the work of all the rest, as for the Lord's servants to think they were each one under obligation to do everything.

He told her just to put herself under the Lord's personal guidance as to her work, and trust Him to point out to her each particular person to whom He would have her speak, assuring her that He never puts forth His own sheep without going before them, and making a way for them Himself.

She followed this advice, and laid the burden of her work on the Lord, and the result was a happy pathway of daily guidance, in which she was led into much blessed work for her Master, but was able to do it all without a care or a burden, because He led her out and prepared the way before her.

Putting ourselves into God's hands in this way, seems to me just like making the junction between the machinery and the steam engine. The power is not in the machinery, but in the steam; disconnected from the engine, the machinery is perfectly useless; but let the connection be made, and the machinery goes easily and without effort, because of the mighty power there is behind it. Thus the Christian life becomes an easy, natural life when it is the development of the divine working within.

Most Christians live on a strain, because their wills are not fully in harmony with the will of God, the connection is not perfectly made at every point, and it requires an effort to move the machinery. But once the connection is fully made, and the law of the Spirit of life in Christ Jesus can work in us with all its mighty power, we are then indeed made free from the law of sin and death, and shall know the glorious liberty of the children of God. We shall lead frictionless lives.

Another form of bondage as to service, from which the life of faith delivers the soul, is in reference to the after-reflections which always follow any Christian work. These self-reflections are of two sorts. Either the soul congratulates itself upon its success, and is lifted up; or it is distressed over its failure, and is utterly cast down. One of these is sure to come, and of the two I think the first is the more to be dreaded, although the last causes at the time the greater suffering. But in the life of trust, neither will trouble us; for, having committed ourselves and our work to the Lord, we will be satisfied to leave it to Him, and will not think about ourselves in the matter at all.

Years ago I came across this sentence in an old book: "Never indulge, at the close of an action, in any self-reflective acts of any kind, whether of self-congratulation or of self-despair. Forget the things that are behind, the moment they are past, leaving them with God." It has been of unspeakable value to me. When the temptation comes, as it always does, to indulge in these reflections, either of one sort or the other, I turn from them at once, and positively refuse to think about my work at all, leaving it with the Lord to overrule the mistakes, and to bless it as He chooses.

To sum it all up then, what is needed for happy and effectual service is simply to put your work into the Lord's hands, and leave it there. Do not take it to Him in prayer, saying, "Lord, guide me; Lord, give me wisdom; Lord, arrange for me," and then arise from your knees, and take the burden all back, and try to guide and arrange for yourself. Leave it with the Lord, and remember that what you trust to Him, you must not worry over nor feel anxious about.

Trust and worry cannot go together. If your work is a burden, it is because you are not trusting it to Him.

But if you do trust it to Him, you will surely find that the yoke He puts upon you is easy, and the burden He gives you to carry is light, and even in the midst of a life of ceaseless activity you shall find rest to your soul.

But some may say that this teaching would make us into mere puppets. I answer no, it would simply make us into servants. It is required of a servant, not that he shall plan, or arrange, or decide, or supply the necessary material, but simply and only that he shall obey. It is for the Master to do all the rest. The servant is not responsible, either, for results.

The Master alone knows what results He wished to have produced, and therefore He alone can judge of them. Intelligent service will, of course, include some degree of intelligent sympathy with the thoughts and plans of the Master, but after all there cannot be a full comprehension, and the responsibility cannot be transferred from the Master's shoulders to the servant's.

In our case, where our outlook is so limited and our ignorance so great, we can do very little more than be in harmony with the will of our Divine Master, without expecting to comprehend it very fully, and we must leave all the results with Him. What looks to us like failure on the seen side is often, on the unseen side, the most glorious success; and if we allow ourselves to lament and worry, we shall often be doing the foolish and useless thing of weeping where we ought to be singing and rejoicing.

Far better is it to refuse utterly to indulge in any self-reflective acts at all; to refuse, in fact, to think about self in any way, whether for good or evil. We are not our own property, nor our own business. We belong to God, and are His instruments and His business; and since He always attends to His own business, He will of course attend to us.

I heard once of a slave who was on board a vessel in a violent storm, and who was whistling contentedly while every one else was in an agony of terror. At last someone asked him if he was not afraid he would be drowned. He replied with a broad grin, "Well, missus, s'pose I is. I don't b'long to myself, and it will only be massa's loss any how."

Something of this spirit would deliver us from many of our perplexities and sufferings in service. And with a band of servants thus abandoned to our Master's use and to His care, what might He not accomplish? Truly one such servant would "one chase a thousand, and two put ten thousand to flight" (Deuteronomy 32:30); and nothing would be impossible to them. For it is nothing for the Lord "to help, whether with many or with those who have no power" (2 Chronicles 14:11).

May God raise up such an army speedily! And may you, my dear reader, enroll your name in this army today and, yielding yourself unto God as one who is alive from the dead, may every one of your members be also yielded unto Him as instruments of righteousness, to be used by Him as He pleases.

11

God's Guidance

*Y*OU have now begun, dear reader, the life of faith. You have given yourself to the Lord to be His wholly and altogether, and He has taken you and has begun to mold and fashion you into a vessel unto His honor. Your one most earnest desire is to be very pliable in His hands, and to follow Him wherever He may lead you, and you are trusting Him to work in you to will and to do of His good pleasure (see Philippians 2:13). But you find a great difficulty here. You have not learned yet to know the voice of the Good Shepherd, and are therefore in great doubt and perplexity as to what really is His will concerning you.

Perhaps there are certain paths into which God seems to be calling you, of which your friends utterly disapprove. And these friends, it may be, are older than yourself in the Christian life, and seem to you also to be much further advanced. You can scarcely bear to differ from them or distress them; and you feel also very diffident of yielding to any seeming impressions of duty of which they do not approve. And yet you cannot get rid of these impressions, and you are plunged into great doubt and uneasiness.

There is a way out of all these difficulties, to the fully surrendered soul. I would repeat, fully surrendered, because if there is any reserve of will upon any point, it becomes almost impossible to find out the mind of God in reference to that point; and therefore the first thing is to be sure that you really do purpose to obey the Lord in every respect. If, however, this is the case, and your soul only needs to know the will of God in order to consent to it, then you surely cannot doubt His willingness to make His will known, and to guide you in the right paths.

There are many very clear promises in reference to this. Take, for instance, John 10:3-4: "He calls His own sheep by name and leads them out. And when He brings out His own sheep, He goes before them; and the sheep follow Him, for they know His voice." Or, John 14:26: "But the Helper, the Holy Spirit, whom the Father will send in My name, He will teach you all things, and bring to your remembrance all things that I said to you." Or, James 1:5: "If any of you lacks wisdom, let him ask of God, who gives to all liberally and without reproach, and it will be given to him." With such passages as these, and many more like them, we must believe that divine guidance is promised to us, and our faith must confidently look for and expect it. This is essential, for in James 1:6-7 we are told, "Let him ask in faith, with no doubting, for he who doubts is like a wave of the sea driven and tossed by the wind. For let not that man suppose that he will receive anything from the Lord."

Settle this point then first of all, that divine guidance has been promised, and that you are sure to have it if you ask for it; and let no suggestion of doubt turn you from this.

Next, you must remember that our God has all knowledge and all wisdom, and that therefore it is very possible He may guide you into paths wherein He knows great blessings are awaiting you, but which to the short-sighted human eyes around you seem sure to result in confusion and loss. You must recognize the fact that God's thoughts are not as man's thoughts, nor His ways as man's ways; and that He who knows the end of things from the beginning alone can judge of what the results of any course of action may be. You must therefore realize that His very love for you may perhaps lead you to run counter to the loving wishes of even your dearest friends.

You must learn from Luke 14:26-33 and similar passages that in order not to be saved only, but to be a disciple or follower of your Lord, you may perhaps be called upon to forsake all that you have, and to turn your backs on even father or mother, or brother or sister, or husband or wife, or it may be your own life also. Unless the possibility of this is clearly recognized, the soul would be very likely to get into difficulty, because it often happens that the child of God who enters upon this life of obedience is sooner or later led into paths which meet with the disapproval of those he best loves; and unless he is prepared for this, and can trust the Lord through it all, he will scarcely know what to do.

All this, it will of course be understood, is perfectly in harmony with those duties of honor and love which we owe to one another in the various relations of life. The nearer we are to Christ, the more we shall be enabled to exemplify the meekness and gentleness of our Lord, and the more tender will be our consideration for those who are our natural guardians and counselors. The Master's guidance will always manifest itself by the Master's Spirit, and where, in obedience to Him, we are led to act contrary to the advice or wishes of our friends, we shall prove that this is our motive, by the love and patience which will mark our conduct.

But this point having been settled, we come now to the question as to how God's guidance is to come to us, and how we shall be able to know His voice.

There are four special ways in which God speaks: by the voice of Scripture, the voice of the inward impressions of the Holy Spirit, the voice of our own higher judgment, and the voice of providential circumstances.

Where these four harmonize, it is safe to say that God speaks. For I lay it down as a foundation principle, which no one can gainsay, that of course His voice will always be in harmony with itself, no matter in how many different ways He may speak. The voices may be many, the message can be but one. If God tells me in one voice to do or to leave undone anything, He cannot possibly tell me the opposite in another voice. If there is a contradiction in the voices, the speaker cannot be the same. Therefore, my rule for distinguishing the voice of God would be to bring it to the test of this harmony.

If I have an impression, therefore, I must see if it is in accordance with Scripture, and whether it commends itself to my own higher judgment, and also whether, as we Quakers say, "way opens" for its carrying out. If either one of these tests fail, it is not safe to proceed; but I must wait in quiet trust until the Lord shows me the point of harmony, which He surely will, sooner or later, if it is His voice that has spoken.

For we must not overlook the fact that there are other voices that speak to the soul. There is the loud and clamoring voice of self that is always seeking to be heard. And there are the voices, too, of evil and deceiving spirits, who lie in wait to entrap every traveler entering these higher regions of the spiritual life. In the same epistle which tells us that we are seated in "heavenly realms in Christ Jesus" (Ephesians 2:6 NIV), we are also told that we shall have to fight there with spiritual enemies (see Ephesians 6:12). These spiritual enemies, whoever or whatever they may be, must necessarily communicate with us by means of our spiritual faculties, and their voices, therefore, will be, as the voice of God is, an inward impression made upon our spirits.

Therefore, just as the Holy Spirit may tell us, by impressions, what is the will of God concerning us, so also will these spiritual enemies tell us, by impressions, what is their will concerning us, though not of course giving it their name.

It is very plain, therefore, that we must have some test or standard by which to try these inward impressions, in order that we may know whose voice it is that is speaking. And that test will always be the harmony to which I have referred. Sometimes, under a mistaken idea of exalting the Divine Spirit, earnest and honest Christians have ignored and even violated the teachings of Scripture, have disregarded the plain pointings of Providence, and have outraged their own higher judgment. God, who sees the sincerity of their hearts, can and does pity and forgive, but the consequences as to this life are often very sad.

Our first test, therefore, of the divine authority of any voice which may seem to speak to us, must be its harmony in moral character with the mind and will of God, as revealed to us in the Gospel of Christ. Whatever is contrary to this cannot be divine, because God cannot contradict Himself.

Until we have found and obeyed God's will in reference to any subject, as it is revealed in the Bible, we cannot expect a separate direct personal revelation. A great many fatal mistakes are made in this matter of guidance, by the overlooking of this simple rule. Where our Father has written out for us plain directions about anything, He will not, of course, make a special revelation to us concerning it. No man, for instance, needs or could expect any direct revelation to tell him not to steal, because God has already in the Scriptures plainly declared His will about it. This seems such an obvious thing that I would not speak of it, but that I have frequently met with Christians who have altogether overlooked it, and have gone off into fanaticism as the result.

The Scriptures are far more explicit even about details than most people think. And there are not many important affairs in life for which a clear direction may not be found in God's Book. Take the matter of dress and we have 1 Peter 3:3-4 and 1 Timothy 2:9-10. Take the matter of conversation, and we have Ephesians 4:29 and 5:4. Take the matter of avenging injuries and standing up for your rights and we have Romans 12:19-21, Matthew 5:38-48 and 1 Peter 2:19-21. Take the matter of forgiving one another and we have Ephesians 4:32 and Mark 11:25-26. Take the matter of conformity to the world and we have Romans 12:2, 1 John 2:15-17 and James 4:4. Take the matter of anxieties of all kinds and we have Matthew 6:25-34 and Philippians 4:6-7.

I only give these as examples to show how very full and practical Bible guidance is. If, therefore, you find yourself in perplexity, first of all search and see whether the Bible speaks on the point in question, asking God to make plain to you by the power of His Spirit, through the Scripture, what is His mind. And whatever shall seem to you to be plainly taught there, that you must obey.

When we read and meditate upon this record of God's mind and will, with our understandings thus illuminated by the inspiring Spirit, our obedience will be as truly an obedience to a present, living word, as though it were afresh spoken to us today by our Lord from heaven. The Bible is not only an ancient message from God sent to us many ages ago, but it is a present message sent to us now each time we read it. "The words that I speak to you are spirit, and they are life" (John 6:63), and obedience to these words now is a living obedience to a present and personal command.

But it is essential in this connection to remember that the Bible is a book of principles, and not a book of disjointed aphorisms. Isolated texts may often be made to sanction things, to which the principles of Scripture are totally opposed.

I heard not long ago of a Christian woman in a Western meeting, who, having had the text, "For we walk by faith, not by sight" (2 Corinthians 5:7), brought very vividly before her mind, felt a strong impression that it was a command to be literally obeyed in the outward; and, blindfolding her eyes, insisted on walking up and down the aisle of the meeting-house as an illustration of the walk of faith. She very soon stumbled and fell against the stove, burning herself seriously, and then wondered at the mysterious dispensation. The principles of Scripture, and her own sanctified common sense, if applied to this case, would have saved her from the delusion.

The second test, therefore, to which our impressions must be brought, is that of our own higher judgment, or common sense.

It is as true now as in the days when Solomon wrote that "a man of understanding will attain wise counsel" (Proverbs 1:5); and his exhortation still continues binding upon us: "Wisdom is the principal thing; therefore get wisdom. And in all your getting, get understanding" (Proverbs 4:7).

As far as I can see, the Scriptures everywhere make it an essential thing for the children of God to use all the faculties which have been given them in their journey through this world. They are to use their outward faculties for their outward walk, and their inward faculties for their inward walk. And they might as well expect to be "kept" from dashing their feet against a stone in the outward, if they walk blindfolded, as to be "kept" from spiritual stumbling, if they put aside their judgment and common sense in their interior life.

I asked a Christian of "sound mind" lately how she distinguished between the voice of false spirits and the guidance of the Holy Spirit, and she replied promptly, "I rap them over the head, and see if they have any common sense."

Some, however, may say here, "But I thought we were not to depend on our human understanding in divine things." I answer to this, that we are not to depend on our unenlightened human understanding, but upon our human judgment and common sense, enlightened by the Spirit of God. That is, God will speak to us through the faculties He has Himself given us, and not independently of them. That is, just as we are to use our eyes when we walk, no matter how full of faith we may be, so also we are to use our mental faculties in our inward life.

The third and last test to which our impressions

must be brought is that of providential circumstances. If a "leading" is of God, a way will always open for it. Our Lord assures us of this when He says in John 10:4, "And when He brings out His own sheep, He goes before them; and the sheep follow Him, for they know His voice." He goes before to open a way, and we are to follow in the way thus opened. It is never a sign of a divine leading when the Christian insists on opening his own way, and riding roughshod over all opposing things. If the Lord "goes before" us, He will open all doors for us, and we shall not need ourselves to hammer them down.

The fourth point I would make is this: that, just as our impressions must be tested, as I have shown by the other three voices, so must these other voices be tested by our inward impressions; and if we feel a "stop in our minds" about anything, we must wait until that is removed before acting.

A Christian who had advanced with unusual rapidity in the divine life gave me as her secret this simple receipt: "I always mind the checks." We must not ignore the voice of our inward impressions, nor ride roughshod over them any more than we must the other three voices of which I have spoken.

These four voices, then, will always be found to agree in any truly divine leading ie the voice of our impressions, the voice of Scripture, the voice of our own sanctified judgment, and the voice of providential circumstances; and where these four do not all agree at first, we must wait until they do.

A divine sense of "oughtness," derived from the harmony of all God's various voices, is the only safe foundation for any action.

And now I have guarded the points of danger, do permit me to let myself out for a little to the blessedness and joy of this direct communication of God's will to us. It seems to me to be the grandest of privileges. In the first place, that God should love me enough to care about the details of my life is perfectly wonderful. And then that He should be willing to tell me all about it, and to let me know just how to live and walk so as to perfectly please Him, seems almost too good to be true.

We never care about the little details of people's lives unless we love them. It is a matter of indifference to us with the majority of people we meet as to what they do or how they spend their time; but as soon as we begin to love anyone, we begin at once to care. That God cares, therefore, is just a precious proof of His love; and it is most blessed to have Him speak to us about everything in our lives, about our duties, about our pleasures, about our friendships, about our occupations, about all that we do, or think, or say. You must know this in your own experience, dear reader, if you would come into the full joy and privilege of this life hid with Christ in God, for it is one of the most precious gifts!

God's promise is that He will work in us to will as well as to do of His good pleasure. This, of course, means that He will take possession of our will, and work it for us, and that His suggestions will come to us, not so much commands from the outside, as desires springing up within. They will originate in our will; we shall feel as though we wanted to do so and so, not as though we must. And this makes it a service of perfect liberty; for it is always easy to do what we desire to do, let the accompanying circumstances be as difficult as they may. Every mother knows that she could secure perfect and easy obedience in her child if she could only get into that child's will and work it for him, making him want himself to do the things she willed he should. And this is what our Father does for His children in the new dispensation; He writes His laws on our hearts and on our minds, and we love them, and are drawn to our obedience by our affections and judgment, not driven by our fears.

The way in which the Holy Spirit, therefore, usually works in His direct guidance is to impress upon the mind a wish or desire to do or leave undone certain things.

The soul when engaged, perhaps, in prayer, feels a sudden suggestion made to its inmost consciousness in reference to a certain point of duty. "I would like to do this or the other," it thinks, "I wish I could." Or perhaps the suggestion may come as question, "I wonder whether I had not better do so and so?" Or it may be only at first in the way of a conviction that such is the right and best thing to be done.

At once the matter should be committed to the Lord, with an instant consent of the will to obey Him; and if the suggestion is in accordance with the Scriptures, and a sanctified judgment, and with providential circumstances, an immediate obedience is the safest and easiest course. At the moment when the Spirit speaks, it is always easy to obey; if the soul hesitates and begins to reason, it becomes more and more difficult continually.

As a general rule, the first convictions are the right ones in a fully surrendered heart; for God is faithful in His dealings with us, and will cause His voice to be heard before any other voices. Such convictions, therefore, should never be met by reasoning. Prayer and trust are the only safe attitudes of the soul; and even these should be but momentary, as it were, lest the time for action should pass and the blessing be missed.

If, however, the suggestion does not seem quite clear enough to act upon, and doubt and perplexity ensue, especially if it is something about which one's friends hold a different opinion, then we shall need to wait for further light. The Scripture rule is, "Everything that does not come from faith is sin" (Romans 14:23 NIV); which means plainly that we must never act in doubt. A clear conviction of right is the only safe guide. But we must wait in faith, and in an attitude of entire surrender, saying, "Yes," continually to the will of our Lord, whatever it may be.

I believe the lack of a will thus surrendered lies at the root of many of our difficulties; and next to this lies the want of faith in any real divine guidance. God's children are amazingly skeptical here. They read the promises and they feel the need, but somehow they cannot seem to believe the guidance will be given to them; as if God should want us to obey His voice, but did not know how to make us hear and understand Him. It is, therefore, very possible for God to speak, but for the soul not to hear, because it does not believe He is speaking. No earthly parent or master could possibly guide his children or servants if they should refuse to believe he was speaking, and should not accept his voice as being really the expression of his will.

Every moment of our lives our Father is seeking to reveal Himself to us. "I, the one speaking to you – I am He" (John 4:26 NIV).

We must, therefore, have perfect confidence that the Lord's voice is speaking to us to teach and lead us, and that He will give us the wisdom needed for our right guidance; and when we have asked for light, we must accept our strongest conviction of "oughtness" as being the guidance we have sought.

A few guidelines will help us here:

(a) We must believe that God will guide us.
(b) We must surrender our own will to His guidance.
(c) We must hearken for the divine voice.
(d) We must wait for the divine harmony.
(e) When we are sure of the guidance, we must obey without question.

12

Conquering Temptation

*C*ERTAIN very great mistakes are made concerning this matter of temptation, in the practical working out of this life of faith.

First of all, people seem to expect that, after the soul has entered into its rest in God, temptations will cease; and to think that the promised deliverance is not only to be from yielding to temptation, but even also from being tempted. Consequently, when they find the Canaanite still in the land, and see the cities great and walled up to heaven, they are utterly discouraged, and think they must have gone wrong in some way, and that this cannot be the true land after all.

Then, next, they make the mistake of looking upon temptation as sin, and of blaming themselves for what in reality is the fault of the enemy only. This brings them into condemnation and discouragement; and discouragement, if continued in, always ends at last in actual sin. The enemy makes an easy prey of a discouraged soul; so that we fall often from the very fear of having fallen.

To meet the first of these difficulties it is only necessary to refer to the scriptural declarations, that the Christian life is to be throughout a warfare; and that, especially when seated in heavenly places in Christ Jesus (see Ephesians 2:6), we are to wrestle against spiritual enemies there, whose power and skill to tempt us must doubtless be far superior to any we have ever encountered before.

As a fact, temptations generally increase in strength tenfold after we have entered into the interior life, rather than decrease; and no amount or sort of them must ever for a moment lead us to suppose we have not really found the true abiding place. Strong temptations are generally a sign of great grace, rather than of little grace. When the children of Israel had first left Egypt, the Lord did not lead them through the country of the Philistines, although that was the nearest way; for God said, "Lest perhaps the people change their minds when they see war, and return to Egypt" (Exodus 13:17). But afterwards, when they learned better how to trust Him, He permitted their enemies to attack them.

Then also in their wilderness journey they met with but few enemies and fought but few battles, compared to those in the land, where they found seven great nations and thirty-one kings to be conquered, besides walled cities to be taken and giants to be overcome.

They could not have fought with the Canaanites and the Hittites and the Amorites and the Perizzites and the Hivites and the Jebusites (Exodus 3:8), until they had gone into the land where these enemies were. And the very power of your temptations, dear Christian, therefore, may perhaps be one of the strongest proofs that you really are in the land you have been seeking to enter, because they are temptations peculiar to that land. You must never allow your temptations to cause you to question the fact of your having entered the promised "heavenly places."

The second mistake is not quite so easy to deal with. It seems hardly worthwhile to say that temptation is not sin, and yet most of the distress about it arises from not understanding this fact. The very suggestion of wrong seems to bring pollution with it, and the evil agency not being recognized, the poor tempted soul begins to feel as if it must be very bad indeed, and very far off from God to have had such thoughts and suggestions.

It is as though a burglar should break into a man's house to steal, and, when the master of the house began to resist him and to drive him out, should turn round and accuse the owner of being himself the thief. It is the enemy's grand ruse for entrapping us. He comes and whispers suggestions of evil to us, doubts, blasphemies, jealousies, envy, and pride; and then turns round and says, "Oh, how wicked you must be to think of such things! It is very plain that you are not trusting the Lord; for if you were, it would have been impossible for these things to have entered your heart."

This reasoning sounds so very plausible that the soul often accepts it as true, and at once comes under condemnation, and is filled with discouragement; then it is easy for it to be led on into actual sin. One of the most fatal things in the life of faith is discouragement. One of the most helpful is cheerfulness.

A very wise man once said that in overcoming temptations, cheerfulness was the first thing, cheerfulness the second, and cheerfulness the third. We must expect to conquer. That is why the Lord said so often to Joshua, "Be strong and courageous. Do not be afraid; do not be discouraged" (Joshua 1:9 NIV); "Be strong and very courageous" (Joshua 1:7 NIV). And it is also the reason He says to us, "Do not let your hearts be troubled and do not be afraid" (John 14:27 NIV). The power of temptation is in the fainting of our own hearts. The enemy knows this well, and always begins his assaults by discouraging us, if it can in any way be accomplished.

Sometimes this discouragement arises from what we think is a righteous grief and disgust at ourselves that such things could be any temptation to us; but which is really a mortification arising from the fact that we have been indulging in a secret self-congratulation that our tastes were too pure, or our separation from the world was too complete for such things to tempt us. We have expected something from ourselves, and have been sorely disappointed not to find that something there, and are discouraged in consequence.

This mortification and discouragement is really a far worse condition than the temptation itself, though they present an appearance of true humility, for they are nothing but the results of wounded self-love. True humility can bear to see its own utter weakness and foolishness revealed, because it never expected anything from itself, and knows that its only hope and expectation must be in God. Therefore, instead of discouraging the soul from trusting, it drives it to a deeper and more utter trust. But the counterfeit humility which springs from self plunges the soul into the depths of a faithless discouragement, and drives it into the very sin which distressed it so.

I remember once hearing an allegory that illustrated this to me wonderfully. Satan called together a council of his servants to consult how they might make a good man sin. One evil spirit started up and said, "I will make him sin." "How will you do it?" asked Satan. "I will set before him the pleasures of sin," was the reply; "I will tell him of its delights and the rich rewards it brings." "Ah," said Satan, "that will not do; he has tried it, and knows better than that."

Then another spirit started up and said, "I will make him sin." "What will you do?" asked Satan. "I will tell him of the pains and sorrows of virtue. I will show him that virtue has no delights, and brings no rewards." "Ah, no!" exclaimed Satan, "that will not do at all; for he has tried it, and knows that wisdom's 'ways are ways of pleasantness, and all her paths are peace'" (Proverbs 3:17).

"Well," said another imp, starting up, "I will undertake to make him sin." "And what will you do?" asked Satan again. "I will discourage his soul," was the short reply. "Ah, that will do," cried Satan, "that will do! We shall conquer him now." And they did.

An old writer says, "All discouragement is from the devil"; and I wish every Christian would just take this as a pocket-piece, and never forget it. We must fly from discouragement as we would from sin.

But this is impossible if we fail to recognize the true agency in temptation. For if the temptations are our own fault, we cannot help being discouraged. But they are not. The Bible says, "Blessed is the man who endures temptation" (James 1:12); and we are exhorted to "count it all joy when you fall into various trials" (James 1:2).

Temptation, therefore, cannot be sin; and the truth is, it is no more a sin to hear these whispers and suggestions of evil in our souls, than it is for us to hear the swearing or wicked talk of bad men as we pass along the street. The sin only comes in either case by our stopping and joining in with them. If, when the wicked suggestions come, we turn from them at once, as we would from wicked talk, and pay no more attention to them, we do not sin.

But if we carry them on in our minds, and roll them under our tongues, and dwell on them with a half-consent of our will to them as true, then we sin. We may be enticed by evil a thousand times a day without sin, and we cannot help these enticings. But if the enemy can succeed in making us think that his enticing is our sin, he has accomplished half the battle, and can hardly fail to gain a complete victory. A dear lady once came to me under great darkness, simply from not understanding this. She had been living very happily in the life of faith for some time, and had been so free from temptation as almost to begin to think she would never be tempted any more. But suddenly a very peculiar form of temptation had assailed her, which had horrified her. She found that the moment she began to pray, dreadful thoughts of all kinds would rush into her mind. She had lived a very sheltered, innocent life, and these thoughts seemed so awful to her that she felt she must be one of the most wicked of sinners to be capable of having them. She began by thinking she could not possibly have entered into the rest of faith, and ended by concluding that she had never even been born again. Her soul was in an agony of distress.

I told her that these dreadful thoughts were altogether the suggestions of the enemy, who came to her the moment she kneeled in prayer, and poured them into her mind, and that she herself was not to blame for them at all; that she could not help them any more than she could help hearing if a wicked man should pour out his blasphemies in her presence.

I urged her to recognize and treat them as from the enemy; not to blame herself or be discouraged, but to turn at once to Jesus and commit them to Him. I showed her how great an advantage the enemy had gained by making her think these thoughts were originated by herself, and plunging her into condemnation and discouragement on account of them. And I assured her she would find a speedy victory if she would pay no attention to them; but, ignoring their presence, would simply turn her back on them and look to the Lord.

She grasped the truth, and the next time these thoughts came she said to the enemy, "I have found you out now. It is you who are suggesting these dreadful thoughts to me, and I hate them, and will have nothing to do with them. The Lord is my Savior; take them to Him, and settle them in His presence." Immediately the baffled enemy, finding himself discovered, fled in confusion, and her soul was perfectly delivered.

Another thing also. The enemy knows that if a Christian recognizes a suggestion of evil as coming from him, the Christian will recoil from it far more quickly than if it seems to be the suggestion of his own mind. If Satan prefaced each temptation with the words, "I am Satan, your relentless enemy; I have come to make you sin," I suppose we would hardly feel any desire at all to yield to his suggestions. He has to hide himself in order to make his baits attractive. And our victory will be far more easily gained if we are not ignorant of his devices, but recognize him at his very first approach.

We also make another great mistake about temptations in thinking that all time spent in combating them is lost. Hours pass, and we seem to have made no progress, because we have been so beset with temptations. But it often happens that we have been serving God far more truly during these hours than in our times of comparative freedom from temptation. Temptation is really more the devil's wrath against God than against us. He cannot touch our Savior, but he can wound our Savior by conquering us, and our ruin is important to him only as it accomplishes this. We are, therefore, really fighting our Lord's battles when we are fighting temptation, and hours are often worth days to us under these circumstances. We read, "Blessed is the man who endures temptation" (James 1:12); and I am sure this means enduring the continuance of it and its frequent recurrence. Nothing so cultivates the grace of patience as the endurance of temptation, and nothing so drives the soul to an utter dependence upon the Lord Jesus as its continuance.

Finally, nothing brings more praise and honor and glory to our dearest Lord Himself than the trial of our faith which comes through manifold temptations. We are told that it is more precious than gold, though it be tried with fire (see 1 Peter 1:7), and that we, who patiently endure the trial, shall receive for our reward "the crown of life which the Lord has promised to those who love Him" (James 1:12).

We cannot wonder, therefore, any longer at the exhortation with which the Holy Ghost opens the Book of James: "Consider it pure joy whenever you face trials of many kinds, because you know that the testing of your faith produces perseverance. Let perseverance finish its work so that you may be mature and complete, not lacking anything" (James 1:2-4 NIV).

Temptation is plainly to be the blessed instrument used by God to complete our perfection, and thus the enemy's own weapons are turned against himself, and we see how it is that all things, even temptations, can work together for good to those who love God.

As to the way of victory over temptations, it seems hardly necessary to say to those whom I am at this time especially addressing, that it is to be by faith. For this is, of course, the foundation upon which the whole interior life rests. Our one great motto is throughout, "We are nothing, Christ is all." And always and everywhere we have started out to stand, and walk, and overcome, and live by faith. We have discovered our own utter helplessness, and know that we cannot do anything for ourselves. Our only way, therefore, is to hand the temptation over to our Lord, and trust Him to conquer it for us. But when we put it into His hands we must leave it there. It must be as real a committing of ourselves to Him for victory as it was at first a committing of ourselves to Him for salvation. He must do all for us in the one case, as completely as in the other. It was faith only then, and it must be faith only now.

And the victories which the Lord works in conquering the temptations of those who thus trust Him are nothing short of miracles, as thousands can testify.

But into this part of the subject I cannot go at present, as my object has been rather to present temptation in its true light than to develop the way of victory over it. I want to deliver conscientious, faithful souls from the bondage into which they are sure to be brought if they fail to understand the true nature and use of temptation, and confound it with sin. I want that they should not be ignorant of the fact that temptations are, after all, an invaluable part of our soul's development; and that, whatever may be their original source, they are used by God to work out in us many blessed graces of character which would otherwise be lacking. Wherever temptation is, there is God also, superintending and controlling its power.

Temptations try us; and we are worth nothing if we are not tried. They develop our spiritual strength and courage and knowledge; and our development is the one thing God cries for. How shallow would all our spirituality be if it were not for temptations. "Blessed is the man who endures temptation; for when he has been approved, he will receive the crown of life which the Lord has promised to those who love Him" (James 1:12). This "crown of life" will be worth all that it has cost of trial and endurance to obtain it; and without these it could not be attained.

A frail lady procured once the cocoon of a very beautiful butterfly with unusually magnificent wings, hoping to have the pleasure of seeing it emerge from its cocoon in her sick-chamber. She watched it eagerly as spring drew on, and finally was delighted to see the butterfly beginning to emerge. But it seemed to have great difficulty. It pushed, and strained, and struggled, and seemed to make so little headway, that she concluded it must need some help, and with a pair of delicate scissors she finally clipped the tight cord that seemed to bind in the opening of the cocoon. Immediately the cocoon opened wide, and the butterfly escaped without any further struggle.

She congratulated herself on the success of her experiment, but found in a moment that something was the matter with the butterfly. It was all out of the co-coon it is true, but its great wings were lifeless and colorless, and dragged after it as a useless burden. For a few days it lived a miserable sickly life, and then died, without having once lifted its powerless wings. The lady was sorely disappointed and could not understand it.

When she related the circumstance to a naturalist, he told her that it had all been her own fault. That it required just that pushing and struggling to send the life fluid into the veins of the wings, and that her mistaken kindness in shortening the struggle had left the wings lifeless and colorless.

Just so do our spiritual wings need the struggle and effort of our conflict with temptation and trial; and to grant us an escape from it would be to weaken the power of our soul to "soar on wings like eagles" (Isaiah 40:31 NIV), and would deprive us of the "crown of life" (James 1:12) which is promised to those who endure.

Part 3

Results

13

Overcoming Failure

*T*HE very title of this chapter may perhaps startle some. "Failures," they will say, "we thought there were no failures in this life of faith!"

To this I would answer that there ought not to be, and need not be; but, as a fact, there sometimes are. And we have got to deal with facts, and not with theories. No teacher of this interior life ever says that it becomes impossible to sin; they only insist that sin ceases to be a necessity, and that a possibility of uniform victory is opened before us. And there are very few who do not confess that, as to their own actual experience, they have at times been overcome by momentary temptation. Of course, in speaking of sin here, I mean conscious, known sin. I do not touch on the subject of sins of ignorance, or what is called the inevitable sin of our nature, which are all covered by the atonement, and do not disturb our fellowship with God. I have no desire nor ability to treat of the doctrines concerning sin; these I will leave to the theologians to discuss and settle, while I speak only of the believer's experience in the matter. And I wish it to be fully understood that in all I shall say, I have reference simply to that which comes within the range of our consciousness.

Misunderstanding, then, on this point of known or conscious sin, opens the way for great dangers in the Higher Christian Life. When a believer, who has, as he trusts, entered upon the highway of holiness, finds himself surprised into sin, he is tempted either to be utterly discouraged, and to give everything up as lost; or else, in order to preserve the doctrine untouched, he feels it necessary to cover his sin up, calling it infirmity, and refusing to be honest and above-board about it.

Either of these courses is equally fatal to any real growth and progress in the life of holiness. The only way is to face the sad fact at once, call the thing by its right name, and discover, if possible, the reason and the remedy. This life of union with God requires the utmost honesty with Him and with ourselves. The communion which the sin itself would only momentarily disturb is sure to be lost by any dishonest dealing with it.

A sudden failure is no reason for being discouraged and giving up all as lost. Neither is the integrity of our doctrine touched by it. We are not preaching a state, but a walk. The highway of holiness is not a place, but a way. Sanctification is not a thing to be picked up at a certain stage of our experience, and forever after possessed, but it is a life to be lived day by day, and hour by hour. We may for a moment turn aside from a path, but the path is not obliterated by our wandering, and can be instantly regained. And in this life and walk of faith there may be momentary failures, which, although very sad and greatly to be deplored, need not, if rightly met, disturb the attitude of the soul as to entire consecration and perfect trust, nor interrupt, for more than the passing moment, its happy communion with its Lord.

The great point is an instant return to God. Our sin is no reason for ceasing to trust, but only an unanswerable argument why we must trust more fully than ever. From whatever cause we have been betrayed into failure, it is very certain that there is no remedy to be found for it in discouragement. As well might a child who is learning to walk, lie down in despair when he has fallen and refuse to take another step; so too might a believer who is seeking to learn how to live and walk by faith, give up in despair because of having fallen into sin.

The only way in both cases is to get right up and try again. When the children of Israel had met with that disastrous defeat, soon after their entrance into the land, before the little city of Ai, they were all so utterly discouraged that we read: "At this the hearts of the people melted in fear and became like water. Then Joshua tore his clothes and fell facedown to the ground before the ark of the LORD, remaining there till evening. The elders of Israel did the same, and sprinkled dust on their heads. And Joshua said, 'Alas, Sovereign LORD, why did You ever bring this people across the Jordan to deliver us into the hands of the Amorites to destroy us? If only we had been content to stay on the other side of the Jordan! Pardon Your servant, Lord. What can I say, now that Israel has been routed by its enemies? The Canaanites and the other people of the country will hear about this and they will surround us and wipe out our name from the earth. What then will You do for Your own great name?'" (Joshua 7:5-9 NIV).

What a wail of despair this was! And how exactly it is repeated by many a child of God in the present day, whose heart, because of a defeat, melts and becomes as water, and who cries out, "If only we had been content to stay on the other side of the Jordan" (Joshua 7:7 NIV) and predicts for itself further failures and even utter discomfiture before its enemies. No doubt Joshua thought then, as we are apt to think now, that discouragement and despair were the only proper and safe condition after such a failure. But God thought otherwise. "The LORD said to Joshua, 'Stand up! What are you doing down on your face?'" (Joshua 7:10 NIV).

The proper thing to do was not to abandon themselves thus to utter discouragement, humble as it might look, but at once to face the evil and get rid of it, and afresh and immediately to "sanctify themselves." "Get up, sanctify the people" (Joshua 7:13) is always God's command. "Lie down and be discouraged" is always the enemy's temptation. Our feeling is that it is presumptuous, and even almost impertinent, to go at once to the Lord, after having sinned against Him. It seems as if we ought to suffer the consequences of our sin first for a little while, and endure the accusations of our conscience. And we can hardly believe that the Lord can be willing at once to receive us back into loving fellowship with Himself.

A little girl once expressed the feeling to me, with a child's outspoken candor. She had asked whether the Lord Jesus always forgave us for our sins as soon as we asked Him, and I had said, "Yes, of course He does." "Just as soon" she repeated, doubtingly. "Yes," I replied, "the very minute we ask, He forgives us." "Well," she said deliberately, "I cannot believe that. I should think He would make us feel sorry for two or three days first. And then I should think He would make us ask Him a great many times, and in a very pretty way too, not just in common talk. And I believe that is the way He does it, and you need not try to make me think He forgives me right at once, no matter what the Bible says."

She only said what most Christians think, and, what is worse, what most Christians act on, making their discouragement and their very remorse separate them infinitely further off from God than their sin would have done. Yet it is so totally contrary to the way we like our children to act towards us that I wonder how we ever could have conceived such an idea of God. How a mother grieves when a naughty child goes off alone in despairing remorse, and doubts her willingness to forgive; and how, on the other hand, her whole heart goes out in welcoming love to the darling who runs to her at once and begs her forgiveness! Surely our God knew this yearning love when He said to us, "Return, you backsliding children, and I will heal your backslidings" (Jeremiah 3:22). The fact is, that the same moment which brings the consciousness of having sinned ought to bring also the consciousness of being forgiven. This is especially essential to an unwavering walk in the highway of holiness, for no separation from God can be tolerated here for an instant.

We can only walk in this path by looking continually unto Jesus (see Hebrews 12:2), moment by moment; and if our eyes are taken off of Him to look upon our own sin and our own weakness, we shall leave the path at once. The believer, therefore, who has, as he trusts, entered upon this highway, if he finds himself overcome by sin, must flee with it instantly to the Lord. He must act on 1 John 1:9: "If we confess our sins, He is faithful and just to forgive us our sins and to cleanse us from all unrighteousness."

He must not hide his sin and seek to salve it over with excuses, or to push it out of his memory by the lapse of time. But he must do as the children of Israel did and lay his sins out before the Lord. He must confess his sin. And then he must stone it with stones, and burn it with fire, and utterly put it away from him, and raise over it a great heap of stones, that it may be forever hidden from his sight. And he must believe, then and there, that God is, according to His Word, faithful and just to forgive him his sin, and that He does do it; and further, that He also cleanses him from all unrighteousness. He must claim an immediate forgiveness and an immediate cleansing by faith, and must go on trusting harder and more absolutely than ever. As soon as Israel's sin had been brought to light and put away, at once God's word came again in a message of glorious encouragement, "Do not be afraid, nor be dismayed. See, I have given into your hand the king of Ai, his people, his city, and his land" (Joshua 8:1). Our courage must rise higher than ever, and we must abandon ourselves more completely to the Lord, that His mighty power may the more perfectly work in us all the good pleasure of His will.

Moreover, we must forget our sin as soon as it is thus confessed and forgiven. We must not dwell on it, and examine it, and indulge in a luxury of distress and remorse. We must not put it on a pedestal, and then walk around it and view it on every side, and so magnify it into a mountain that hides our God from our eyes. We must follow the example of Paul, and "forgetting those things which are behind and reaching forward to those things which are ahead," we must, "press toward the goal for the prize of the upward call of God in Christ Jesus" (Philippians 3:13-14).

I would like to bring up two contrastive illustrations of these things. One was an earnest Christian man, an active worker in the church, who had been living for several months in the enjoyment of full salvation. He was suddenly overcome by a temptation to treat a brother unkindly. Not having supposed it possible that he could ever sin again, he was at once plunged into the deepest discouragement, and concluded he had been altogether mistaken, and had never entered into the life of full trust at all. Day by day his discouragement increased, until it became despair, and he concluded he had never even been born again, and gave himself up for lost. He spent three years of utter misery, going farther and farther away from God, and being gradually drawn off into one sin after another, until his life was a curse to himself and to all around him. His health failed under the terrible burden, and fears were entertained for his reason.

At the end of three years he met a Christian lady, who understood the truth about sin that I have been trying to explain. In a few moments' conversation she found out his trouble, and at once said, "You sinned in that act, there is no doubt about it, and I do not want you to try and excuse it. But have you never confessed it to the Lord and asked Him to forgive you?"

"Confessed it!" he exclaimed, "why, it seems to me I have done nothing but confess it, and entreat God to forgive me night and day for all these three dreadful years."

"And you have never believed He did forgive you?" asked the lady. "No," said the poor man, "how could I, for I never felt as if He did?"

"But suppose He had said He forgave you, would not that have done as well as for you to feel it?"

"Oh, yes," replied the man, "if God said it, of course I would believe it."

"Very well, He does say so," was the lady's answer, and she turned to the verse we have taken above (1 John 1:9) and read it aloud. "Now," she continued, "you have been all these three years confessing and confessing your sin, and all the while God's record has been declaring that He was faithful and just to forgive it and to cleanse you, and yet you have never once believed it. You have been 'making God a liar' all this while by refusing to believe His record."

The poor man saw the whole thing, and was dumb with amazement and consternation; and when the lady proposed they should kneel down, and that he should confess his past unbelief and sin, and should claim, then and there, a present forgiveness and a present cleansing, he obeyed like one in a maze. But the result was glorious. In a few moments the light broke in, and he burst out into praise at the wonderful deliverance. In three minutes his soul was enabled to traverse back by faith the whole long weary journey that he had been three years in making, and he found himself once more resting in Jesus, and rejoicing in the fullness of His salvation.

The other illustration was the case of a Christian lady who had been living in the land of promise about two weeks, and who had had a very bright and victorious experience. Suddenly, at the end of that time she was overcome by a violent burst of anger. For a moment a flood of discouragement swept over her soul. The enemy said, "There, now that shows it was all a mistake. Of course you have been deceived about the whole thing, and have never entered into the life of full trust at all. And now you may as well give up altogether, for you never can consecrate yourself any more entirely, nor trust any more fully, than you did this time; so it is very plain this life of holiness is not for you!" These thoughts flashed through her mind in a moment, but she was well taught in the ways of God, and she said at once, "Yes, I have sinned, and it is very sad. But the Bible says that if we confess our sins, God is faithful and just to forgive us our sins and to cleanse us from all unrighteousness, and I believe He will do it."

She did not delay a moment, but while still boiling over with anger, she ran – she could not walk – into a room where she could be alone, and kneeling down beside the bed, she said, "Lord, I confess my sin. I have sinned, I am even at this very moment sinning. I hate it, but I cannot get rid of it. I confess it with shame and confusion of face to You. And now I believe that, according to Your word, You forgive and You cleanse."

She said it out loud, for the inward turmoil was too great for it to be said inside. As the words "You forgive and You cleanse" passed her lips, the deliverance came. The Lord said, "Peace, be still," and there was a great calm. A flood of light and joy burst on her soul, the enemy fled, and she was more than conqueror through Him who loved her. The whole thing, the sin and the recovery from it, had occupied not five minutes, and her feet trod on more firmly than ever in the blessed highway of holiness. She sang afresh and with deeper meaning her song of deliverance, "I will sing to the LORD, for He has triumphed gloriously!" (Exodus 15:1).

The truth is, the only remedy, after all in every emergency, is to trust in the Lord. And if this is all we ought to do, and all we can do, is it not better to do it at once?

I have often been brought up short by the question, "Well, what can I do but trust?" And I have realized at once the folly of seeking deliverance in any other way, by saying to myself, "I shall have to come to simple trusting in the end, and why not come to it at once, now in the beginning?" It is a life and walk of faith we have entered upon, and if we fail in it our only recovery must lie in an increase of faith, not in a lessening of it. Let every failure, then, drive you instantly to the Lord, with a more complete abandonment and a more perfect trust; and you will find that, sad as they are, they will not take you out of the land of rest, nor permanently interrupt your sweet communion with Him.

And now, having shown the way of deliverance from failure, I want to say a little as to the causes of failure in this life of full salvation. The causes do not lie in the strength of the temptation nor in our own weakness, nor, above all, in any lack in the power or willingness of our Savior to save us. The promise to Israel was positive, "No one will be able to stand against you all the days of your life" (Joshua 1:5 NIV). And the promise to us is equally positive: "God is faithful; He will not let you be tempted beyond what you can bear. But when you are tempted, He will also provide a way out so that you can endure it" (1 Corinthians 10:13 NIV).

The men of Ai were "but few," and yet the people who had conquered the mighty Jericho "fled before the men of Ai" (Joshua 7:4). It was not the strength of their enemy, neither had God failed them. The cause of their defeat lay somewhere else, and the Lord Himself declares it, "Israel has sinned, and they have also transgressed My covenant which I commanded them. For they have even taken some of the accursed things, and have both stolen and deceived; and they have also put it among their own stuff. Therefore the children of Israel could not stand before their enemies, but turned their backs before their enemies" (Joshua 7:11-12).

It was a hidden evil that conquered them. Deep down under the earth, in an obscure tent in that vast army was hidden something against which God had a controversy, and this little hidden thing made the whole army helpless before their enemies. "You cannot stand before your enemies until you take away the accursed thing from among you" (Joshua 7:13).

The teaching here is simply that anything allowed in the heart which is contrary to the will of God, let it seem ever so insignificant, or be ever so deeply hidden, will cause us to fall before our enemies. Any root of bitterness cherished towards another, any self-seeking and harsh judgments indulged in, any slackness in obeying the voice of the Lord, any doubtful habits or surroundings, any one of these things will effectually cripple and paralyze our spiritual life.

We may have hidden the evil in the most remote corner of our hearts, and may have covered it over from our sight, refusing even to recognize its existence, of which, however, we cannot help being all the time secretly aware. We may steadily ignore it, and persist in declarations of consecration and full trust, we may be more earnest than ever in our religious duties, and have the eyes of our understanding opened more and more to the truth and the beauty of the life and walk of faith. We may seem to ourselves and to others to have reached an almost impregnable position of victory, and yet we may find ourselves suffering bitter defeats.

We may wonder, and question, and despair, and pray; nothing will do any good until the accursed thing is dug up from its hiding-place, brought out to the light, and laid before God. And the moment a believer who is walking in this interior life meets with a defeat, he must at once seek for the cause, not in the strength of that particular enemy, but in something behind, some hidden want of consecration lying at the very center of his being. Just as a headache is not the disease itself, but only a symptom of a disease situated in some other part of the body, so the sin in such a Christian is only the symptom of an evil hidden probably in a very different part of his being.

Sometimes the evil may be hidden even in that, which at a cursory glance, would look like good. Beneath apparent zeal for the truth may be hidden a judging spirit, or a subtle leaning to our own understanding. Beneath apparent Christian faithfulness may be hidden an absence of Christian love. Beneath an apparently rightful care for our affairs may be hidden a great want of trust in God. I believe our blessed Guide, the in-dwelling Holy Spirit, is always secretly discovering these things to us by continual little twinges and pangs of conscience, so that we are left without excuse. But it is very easy to disregard His gentle voice, and insist upon it to ourselves that all is right; and thus the fatal evil will continue hidden in our midst causing defeat in most unexpected quarters.

A capital illustration of this occurred to me once in my housekeeping. I had moved into a new house and, in looking over it to see if it was all ready for occupancy, I noticed in the cellar a very clean-looking cider-cask headed up at both ends. I debated with myself whether I should have it taken out of the cellar and opened to see what was in it, but concluded, as it seemed empty and looked nice, to leave it undisturbed, especially as it would have been quite a piece of work to get it up the stairs. I did not feel quite easy, but reasoned away my scruples and left it.

Every spring and fall, when house-cleaning time came on, I would remember that cask, with a little twinge of my housewifely conscience, feeling that I could not quite rest in the thought of a perfectly cleaned house, while it remained unopened, for how did I know but under its fair exterior it contained some hidden evil. Still I managed to quiet my scruples on the subject, thinking always of the trouble it would involve to investigate it; and for two or three years the innocent-looking cask stood quietly in my cellar.

Then, most unaccountably, moths began to fill my house. I used every possible precaution against them, and made every effort to eradicate them, but in vain. They increased rapidly and threatened to ruin every-thing I had. I suspected my carpets as being the cause, and subjected them to a thorough cleaning. I suspected my furniture, and had it newly upholstered. I suspected all sorts of impossible things. At last the thought of the cask flashed on me. At once I had it brought up out of the cellar and the head knocked in, and I think it is safe to say that thousands of moths poured out. The previous occupant of the house must have headed it up with something in it which bred moths, and this was the cause of all my trouble.

Now I believe that, in the same way, some innocent-looking habit or indulgence, some apparently unimportant and safe thing, about which we yet have now and then little twinges of conscience, something which is not brought out fairly into the light and investigated under the searching eye of God, lies at the root of most of the failure in this higher life. All is not given up. Some secret corner is kept locked against the entrance of the Lord. And therefore we cannot stand before our enemies, but find ourselves smitten down in their presence.

In order to prevent failure, or to discover its cause if we have failed, it is necessary that we should keep continually before us this prayer, "Search me, God, and know my heart; test me and know my anxious thoughts. See if there is any offensive way in me, and lead me in the way everlasting" (Psalm 139:23-24 NIV).

There may be something very deceptive in our sufferings over our failures. We may seem to ourselves to be wholly occupied with the glory of God, and yet in our inmost souls it may be self alone that occasions all our trouble. Our self-love is touched in a tender spot by the discovery that we are not so saintly as we thought we were; and this chagrin is often a greater sin than the original fault itself. The only safe way to treat our failures is neither to justify nor condemn ourselves on account of them, but to lay them quietly and in simplicity before the Lord, looking at them in peace and in the spirit of love.

All the old mystic writers tell us that our progress is aided far more by a simple, peaceful turning to God, than by all our chagrin and remorse over our lapses from Him. Only be faithful, they say, in turning quietly to Him alone, the moment you perceive what you have done, and His presence will deliver you from the snares which have entrapped you. To look at the self plunges you deeper into the slough, for this very slough is after all nothing but the self; while the gentlest look towards God will calm and deliver your heart.

Finally, let us never forget for one moment, no matter how often we may fail, that the Lord Jesus is able, according to the declaration concerning Him, to deliver us out of the hands of our enemies, that we may "serve Him without fear, in holiness and righteousness before Him all the days of our life" (Luke 1:74-75).

Let us then pray, every one of us, day and night, "Lord, keep us from sinning, and make us living witnesses of Your mighty power to save to the uttermost"; and let us never be satisfied until we are so pliable in His hands, and have learned so to trust Him, that He will be able to "make you complete in every good work to do His will, working in you what is well pleasing in His sight, through Jesus Christ, to whom be glory forever and ever. Amen" (Hebrews 13:21).

14

Defeating Doubt

A GREAT many Christians are slaves to doubting. No drunkard was ever more utterly bound by the chains of his fatal habit than they are by theirs. Every step of their whole Christian life is taken against the fearful odds of an army of doubts that are forever lying in wait to assail them. Their lives are made wretched, their usefulness is effectually hindered, and their communion with God is continually broken by their doubts. And although the entrance of the soul upon the life of faith, of which this book treats, does in many cases take it altogether out of the region where these doubts live and flourish; yet even here it sometimes happens that the old tyrant will rise up and reassert his sway, and will cause the feet to stumble and the heart to fail, even when he cannot succeed in utterly turning the believer back into the dreary wilderness again.

We all remember, doubtless, the childish fascination, and yet horror, in *The Pilgrim's Progress* of Christian's imprisonment in Doubting Castle by the wicked giant Despair, and our exultant sympathy in his escape through those massive gates and from that cruel tyrant. Little did we suspect then that we should ever find ourselves taken prisoner by the same giant, and imprisoned in the same castle. And yet I fear to every member of the church of Christ there has been at least one such experience. Turn to the account again, if it is not fresh in your minds, and see if you do not see pictured there experiences of your own that have been very grievous to bear at the time, and very sorrowful to look back upon afterwards.

It seems strange that people, whose very name of believers implies that their one chiefest characteristic is that they believe, should have to confess to such experiences. And yet it is such a universal habit that I feel if the majority of the church were to be named over again, the only fitting and descriptive name that could be given them would be that of doubters. In fact, most Christians have settled down under their doubts, as to a sort of inevitable malady, from which they suffer acutely, but to which they must try to be resigned as a part of the necessary discipline of this earthly life. And they lament over their doubts as a man might lament over his rheumatism, making themselves out as an "interesting case" of a special and peculiar trial, which requires the tenderest sympathy and the utmost consideration.

And this is too often true of believers who are earnestly longing to enter upon the life and walk of faith, and who have made perhaps many steps towards it. They have got rid, it may be, of the old doubts that once tormented them, as to whether their sins are really forgiven, and whether they shall, after all, get safe to heaven; but they have not got rid of doubting.

They have simply shifted the habit to a higher platform. They are saying, perhaps, "Yes, I believe my sins are forgiven, and I am a child of God through faith in Jesus Christ. I dare not doubt this any more. But then ..." And this "but then" includes an interminable array of doubts concerning every declaration and every promise our Father has made to His children.

One after another they fight with them and refuse to believe them, until they can have some more reliable proof of their being true, than the simple word of their God. And then they wonder why they are permitted to walk in such darkness, and look upon themselves almost in the light of martyrs, and groan under the peculiar spiritual conflicts they are compelled to endure.

Spiritual conflicts! Far better would they be named were we to call them spiritual rebellions! Our fight is to be a fight of faith, and the moment we doubt, our fight ceases and our rebellion begins.

I desire to put forth, if possible, one vigorous protest against this whole thing. Just as well might I join in with the lament of a drunkard and unite with him in prayer for grace to endure the discipline of his fatal indulgence, as to give way for one instant to the weak complaints of these enslaved souls, and try to console them under their slavery. To one and to the other I would dare to do nothing else but proclaim the perfect deliverance the Lord Jesus Christ has in store for them, and beseech, entreat, command them, with all the force of my whole nature, to avail themselves of it and be free. Not for one moment would I listen to their despairing excuses. You ought to be free, you can be free, you must be free!

Will you undertake to tell me that it is an inevitable necessity for God to be doubted by His children? Is it an inevitable necessity for your children to doubt you? Would you tolerate their doubts a single hour? Would you pity your son and condole with him, and feel that he was an interesting case if he should come to you and say, "Father, I cannot believe your word, I cannot trust your love"?

I remember once seeing the indignation of a mother I knew, stirred to its very depths by a little doubting on the part of one of her children. She had brought two little girls to my house to leave them while she did some errands. One of them, with the happy confidence of childhood, abandoned herself to all the pleasures she could find in my nursery, and sang and played until her mother's return.

The other one, with the wretched caution and mistrust of maturity, sat down alone in a corner to wonder whether her mother would remember to come back for her, and to fear she would be forgotten, and to imagine her mother would be glad of the chance to get rid of her anyhow, because she was such a naughty girl, and ended with working herself up into a perfect frenzy of despair. The look on that mother's face, when upon her return the weeping little girl told what was the matter with her, I shall not easily forget. Grief, wounded love, indignation, and pity, all strove together for mastery. But indignation gained the day, and I doubt if that little girl was ever so vigorously dealt with before. A hundred times in my life since has that scene come up before me with deepest teaching, and has compelled me, peremptorily, to refuse admittance to the doubts about my heavenly Father's love, and care, and remembrance of me, that have clamored at the door of my heart for entrance.

I am convinced that to many people doubting is a real luxury, and to deny themselves from indulging in it would be to exercise the hardest piece of self-denial they have ever known. It is a luxury that, like the indulgence in all other luxuries, brings very sorrowful results; and, perhaps, looking at the sadness and misery it has brought into your own Christian experience, you may be tempted to say, "Alas! This is no luxury to me, but only a fearful trial."

But pause for a moment. Try giving it up and you will soon find out whether it is a luxury or not. Do not your doubts come trooping to your door as a company of sympathizing friends, who appreciate your hard case, and have come to condole with you? And is it no luxury to sit down with them and entertain them, and listen to their arguments, and join in with their condolences? Would it be no self-denial to turn resolutely from them, and refuse to hear a word they have to say? If you do not know, try it and see.

Have you never tasted the luxury of indulging in hard thoughts against those who have, as you think, injured you? Have you never known what a positive fascination it is to brood over their unkindnesses, and to pry into their malice, and to imagine all sorts of wrong and uncomfortable things about them? It has made you wretched, of course, but it has been a fascinating sort of wretchedness that you could not easily give up.

And just like this is the luxury of doubting. Things have gone wrong with you in your experience. Dispensations have been mysterious, temptations have been peculiar, your case has seemed different from that of anyone's around you. What more natural than to conclude that for some reason God has forsaken you, and does not love you, and is indifferent to your welfare? And how irresistible is the conviction that you are too wicked for Him to care for, or too difficult for Him to manage.

You do not mean to blame Him, or accuse Him of injustice, for you feel that His indifference and rejection of you are fully deserved because of your unworthiness. And this very subterfuge leaves you at liberty to indulge in your doubts under the guise of a just and true appreciation of your own shortcomings. But all the while you are as really indulging in hard and wrong thoughts of your Lord as ever you did of a human enemy; for He says He came not to save the righteous, but sinners; and your very sinfulness and unworthiness are your chiefest claim upon His love and His care.

As well might the poor little lamb that has wandered from the flock and got lost in the wilderness say, "The shepherd does not love me, nor care for me, nor remember me, because I am lost. He only loves and cares for the lambs that never wander."

As well might the ill man say, "The doctor will not come to see me, nor give me any medicines, because I am ill. He only cares for and visits well people." Jesus says, "Those who are well have no need of a physician, but those who are sick" (Luke 5:31). And again He says, "Suppose one of you has a hundred sheep and loses one of them. Doesn't he leave the ninety-nine in the open country and go after the lost sheep until he finds it?" (Luke 15:4 NIV).

Any thoughts of Him, therefore, which are different from what He says of Himself, are hard thoughts; and to indulge in them is far worse than to indulge in hard thoughts of any earthly friend or foe. From the beginning to the end of your Christian life it is always sinful to indulge in doubts. Doubts are all from the devil, and are always untrue. And the only way to meet them is by a direct and emphatic denial.

And this brings me to the practical part of the whole subject, as to how to get deliverance from this fatal habit. My answer would be that the deliverance from this can be by no other means than the deliverance from any other sin. It is to be found in the Lord and in Him only. You must hand your doubting over to Him, as you have learned to hand your other temptations. You must do just what you do with your temper, or your pride. You must give it up to the Lord. I believe myself the only effectual remedy is to take a pledge against it as you would urge a drunkard to do against drink, trusting in the Lord alone to keep you steadfast.

Like any other sin, the stronghold is in the will and the will to doubt must be surrendered exactly as you surrender the will to yield to any other temptation. God always takes possession of a surrendered will. And if we come to the point of saying that we will not doubt, and surrender this central fortress of our nature to Him, His blessed Spirit will begin at once to work in us all the good pleasure of His will, and we shall find ourselves kept from doubting by His mighty and overcoming power.

The trouble is that in this matter of doubting the soul does not always make a full surrender, but is apt to reserve to itself a little secret liberty to doubt, looking upon it as being sometimes a necessity. "I do not want to doubt any more," we will say, or, "I hope I shall not"; but it is hard to come to the point of saying, "I will not doubt again." But no surrender is effectual until it reaches the point of saying, "I will not."

The liberty to doubt must be given up forever. And the soul must consent to a continuous life of inevitable trust. It is often necessary, I think, to make a definite transaction of this surrender of doubting, and to come to a point about it. I believe it is quite as necessary in the case of a doubter as in the case of a drunkard. It will not do to give it up by degrees. The total abstinence principle is the only effectual one here.

Then, the surrender once made, the soul must rest

absolutely upon the Lord for deliverance in each time of temptation. It must lift up the shield of faith the moment the assault comes. It must hand the very first suggestion of doubt over to the Lord, and must tell the enemy to settle the matter with Him. It must refuse to listen to the doubt a single moment. Let it come ever so plausibly, or under whatever guise of humility, the soul must simply say, "I dare not doubt; I must trust. The Lord is good, and He does love me. Jesus saves me; He saves me now."

Those three little words, repeated over and over, "Jesus saves me, Jesus saves me," will put to flight the greatest army of doubts that ever assaulted any soul. I have tried it times without number, and have never known it to fail. Do not stop to argue the matter out with your doubts, nor try to prove that they are wrong. Pay no attention to them whatever; treat them with the utmost contempt. Shut your door in their faces, and emphatically deny every word they say to you. Bring up some "It is written," and hurl it after them. Look right at Jesus, and tell Him you trust Him, and you mean to trust Him. Let the doubts clamor as they may; they cannot hurt you if you will not let them in.

This very day a perfect army of doubts stood awaiting my waking, and clamored at my door for admittance. Nothing seemed real, nothing seemed true; and least of all did it seem possible that I – miserable, wretched – could be the object of the Lord's love, or care, or notice. If I only had been at liberty to let these doubts in, and invite them to take seats and make themselves at home, what a luxury I should have felt it to be! But years ago I made a pledge against doubting; and I would as soon think of violating my pledge against intoxicating liquor as to violate this one. I dared not admit the first doubt. I therefore lifted up my shield of faith the moment I was conscious of these suggestions, and handing the whole army over to my Lord to conquer, I began to say, over and over, "The Lord does love me. He is my present and my perfect Savior; Jesus saves me, Jesus saves me now!" The victory was complete. The enemy had come in like a flood, but the Lord lifted up a standard against him, and he was routed and put to flight; and my soul is singing the song of Moses and the children of Israel, saying, "I will sing to the LORD, for He has triumphed gloriously! The horse and its rider He has thrown into the sea! The LORD is my strength and song, and He has become my salvation" (Exodus 15:1-2).

It will help you to resist the assaults of this temptation to doubt, to see clearly that doubting is sin. It is certainly a direct disobedience to our Lord, who commands us, "Let not your heart be troubled, neither let it be afraid" (John 14:27). And all through the Bible everywhere the commands to trust are imperative, and admit of no exceptions. Time and room would fail me to refer to one hundredth part of these, but no one can read the Psalms without being convinced that the man who trusts without a question, is the only man who pleases God and is accepted of Him.

The "provocation" of Israel was that they did not trust; "anger also came up against Israel, because they believed not in God, and trusted not in His salvation" (Psalm 78:21-22). And in contrast, we read in Isaiah concerning those who trust, "You will keep in perfect peace those whose minds are steadfast, because they trust in You" (Isaiah 26:3 NIV). Nothing grieves or wounds our hearts like doubting on the part of a friend, and nothing, I am convinced, grieves the heart of God more than doubting from us.

One of my children, who is now with the Lord, said to me one evening as I was tucking her up in bed, "Well, Mother, I have had my first doubt." "Oh, Ray," I said, "what was it?"

"Why," she replied, "Satan came to me and told me not to believe the Bible, for it was not a word of it true."

"And what did you say to him?" I asked. "Oh," she replied triumphantly, "I just said to him, 'Satan, I will believe it. So there!'"

I was delighted with the child's spiritual intelligence in knowing so well how to meet doubts, and encouraged her with all my heart, explaining to her how all doubts and discouragements are from the enemy, and how he is always a liar and must not be listened to for a moment.

The next night, I had forgotten all about it, however, and was surprised and startled when she said, as I was tucking her in bed, "Well, Mother, Satan has been at it again."

"Oh, Ray darling!" I exclaimed in dismay, "What did he say this time?" "Well," she replied, "he just told me that I was such a naughty little girl that Jesus could not love me, and I was foolish to think He did."

"And what did you say this time?" I asked. "Oh!" she replied, "I just looked at him cross and said, 'Satan, shut your mouth!'" And then she added, with a smile, "He can't make me unhappy one bit." A grander battle no soul ever fought than this little child had done, and no greater victory was ever won!

Dear doubting soul, go and do likewise; and a similar victory shall be yours. As you lay down this book take up your pen and write out your determination never to doubt again. Make it a real transaction between your soul and the Lord. Give up your liberty to doubt forever. Put your will in this matter over on the Lord's side, and trust Him to keep you from falling.

Tell Him all about your utter weakness and your long-encouraged habits of doubt, and how helpless you are before your enemy, and commit the whole battle to Him. Tell Him you will not doubt again; and then henceforward keep your face steadfastly looking unto Jesus, away from yourself and away from your doubts, holding fast the profession of your faith without wavering, because He is faithful who has promised.

And as surely as you do thus hold the beginning of your confidence steadfast unto the end, just so surely shall you find yourself in this matter made more than conqueror, through Him who loves you.

15

Living the Christian Life

*J*F all that has been said concerning the life hid with Christ in God be true, its results in the practical daily walk and conversation ought to be very marked, and the people who have entered into the enjoyment of it ought to be, in very truth, "His own special people, zealous for good works" (Titus 2:14).

My son at college once wrote to a friend that Christians are God's witnesses necessarily, because the world will not read the Bible, but they will read our lives; and that upon the report these give will very much depend their belief in the divine nature of the religion we profess. As we all know, this is an age of facts, and inquiries are being increasingly turned from theories to realities. If our religion is to make any headway now, it must be proved to be more than a theory, and we must present, to the investigation of the critical minds of our age, the grand facts of lives which have been actually and manifestly transformed by the mighty power of God working in us all the good pleasure of His will. Give us "forms of life," say the scientists, and we will be convinced. And when the church is able to present to them in all its members, the form of a holy life, their last stronghold will be conquered.

I desire, therefore, to speak very solemnly of what I conceive to be the necessary fruits of a life of faith, such as I have been describing, and to press home to the hearts of every one of my readers their responsibility to walk worthy of the high calling wherewith they have been called (see 2 Thessalonians 1:11).

And I would speak to some of you, at least, as personal friends, for I feel sure we have not gone this far together through this book without there having grown in your hearts, as there has in mine, a tender personal interest and longing for one another, that we may in everything show forth the praises of Him who has called us out of darkness into His marvelous light. As a friend, then, to friends, I am sure I may speak very plainly, and will be pardoned if I go into some particulars of life and character which are vital to all true Christian development.

The standard of practical holy living has been so low among Christians that any good degree of real devotedness of life and walk is looked upon with surprise, and even often with disapprobation, by a large portion of the church. And, for the most part, the professed followers of the Lord Jesus Christ are so little like

Him in character or in action that to an outside observer there would not seem to be much harmony between them.

But we, who have heard the call of our God to a life of entire consecration and perfect trust, must do differently from all this. We must come out from the world and be separate, and must not be conformed to it in our characters, nor in our purposes. We must no longer share in its spirit or its ways. Our conversation must be in heaven, and we must seek those things that are above, where Christ sits at the right hand of God (see Romans 8:34). We must walk through the world as Christ walked. We must have the mind that was in Him. As pilgrims and strangers we must abstain from fleshly lusts that war against the soul. As good soldiers of Jesus Christ, we must disentangle ourselves from the affairs of this life as far as possible, that we may please Him who has chosen us to be soldiers.

We must abstain from all appearance of evil. We must be kind to one another, tenderhearted, forgiving one another, even as God, for Christ's sake, has forgiven us. We must not resent injuries or unkindness, but must return good for evil, and turn the other cheek to the hand that smites us. We must take always the lowest place among our fellow-men; and seek not our own honor, but the honor of others. We must be gentle, and meek, and yielding; not standing up for our own rights, but for the rights of others. All that we do must be done for the glory of God. And, to sum it all up, since He who has called us is holy, so we must be holy in a manner of conversation; because it is written, "Be holy, for I am holy" (Leviticus 11:45).

Now, dear friends, this is all exceedingly practical and means, surely, a life very different from the lives of most professors around us. It means that we do really and absolutely turn our backs on self, and on self's motives and self's aims. It means that we are a special people, not only in the eyes of God, but in the eyes of the world around us; and that, wherever we go, it will be known from our Christlike lives and conversation that we are followers of the Lord Jesus Christ; and are not of the world, even as He was not of the world.

We shall no longer feel that our money is our own, but the Lord's, to be used in His service. We shall not feel at liberty to use our energies exclusively in the pursuit of worldly means, but, seeking first the kingdom of God and His righteousness, shall have all needful things added unto us. We shall find ourselves forbidden to seek the highest places, or to strain after worldly advantages. We shall not be permitted to be conformed to the world in our ways of thinking or of living. We shall feel no desire to indulge in the world's frivolous pursuits. We shall find our affections set upon heavenly things, rather than upon earthly things. Our days will be spent not in serving ourselves, but in serving our Lord; and all our rightful duties will be more perfectly performed than ever, because whatever we do will be done "not with eyeservice, as men-pleasers, but as bondservants of Christ, doing the will of God from the heart" (Ephesians 6:6).

Into all these things we shall undoubtedly be led by the blessed Spirit of God, if we give ourselves up to His guidance. But unless we have the right standard of Christian life set before us, we shall be hindered by our ignorance from recognizing His voice; and it is for this reason I desire to be very plain and definite in my statements.

I have noticed that wherever there has been a faithful following of the Lord in a consecrated soul, several things have inevitably followed, sooner or later.

Meekness and quietness of spirit become in time the characteristics of the daily life; a submissive acceptance of the will of God, as it comes in the hourly events of each day; pliability in the hands of God to do or to suffer all the good pleasure of His will; sweetness under provocation; calmness in the midst of turmoil and bustle; yieldingness to the wishes of others, and an insensibility to slights and affronts, absence of worry or anxiety; and deliverance from care and fear. All these, and many other similar graces are invariably found to be the natural outward development of that inward life which is hid with Christ in God.

Then, as to the habits of life, we always see such Christians sooner or later giving themselves up to some work for God and their fellow-men, willing to spend and be spent in the Master's service. They become indifferent to outward show in the furniture of their houses and the style of their living, and make all personal adornment secondary to the things of God. The voice is dedicated to God, to talk and sing for Him. The purse is placed at His disposal. The pen is dedicated to write for Him, the lips to speak for Him, the hands and the feet to do His bidding. Year after year such Christians are seen to grow more unworldly, more heavenly-minded, more transformed, more like Christ, until even their very faces express so much of the beautiful inward divine life, that all who look at them cannot but take knowledge of them that they live with God, and are abiding in Him.

I feel sure that to each one of you have come at least some divine intimations or foreshadowing of the life I here describe. Have you not begun to feel dimly conscious of the voice of God speaking to you in the depths of your soul about these things? Has it not been a pain and a distress to you of late to discover how much there is wrong in your life? Has not your soul been plunged into inward trouble and doubt about certain dispositions and ways, in which you have been formerly accustomed to indulge? Have you not begun to feel uneasy with some of your habits of life, and to wish that you could do differently in these respects? Have not paths of devotedness and of service begun to open out before you, with the longing thought, "Oh, that I could walk in them"?

All these longings and doubts, and this inward distress, are the voice of the Good Shepherd in your heart seeking to call you out of all that is contrary to His will. Oh! let me entreat of you not to turn away from His gentle pleadings. You little know the secret paths into which He means to lead you by these very steps, nor the wonderful stores of blessedness that lie at their end, or you would spring forward with an eager joy to yield to every one of His requirements. The heights of Christian perfection can only be reached by faithfully following the Guide who is to lead you there, and He reveals your way to you one step at a time in the teachings and providences of your daily lives, asking only on your part that you yield yourselves up to His guidance. If, then, in anything you are convinced of sin, be sure that it is the voice of your Lord, and surrender it at once to His bidding, rejoicing with a great joy that He has begun thus to lead and guide you. Be perfectly pliable in His wise hands, go where He entices you, turn away from all which He makes you shrink from, obey Him perfectly; and He will lead you out swiftly and easily into a wonderful life of conformity to Himself, that will be a testimony to all around you, beyond what you yourself will ever know.

I knew a soul thus given up to follow the Lord wherever He might lead her, who in three short months travelled from the depths of darkness and despair into the realization and conscious experience of the most blessed union with the Lord Jesus Christ. Out of the midst of her darkness, she consecrated herself to the Lord, surrendering her will up altogether to Him, that He might work in her to will and to do of His own good pleasure. Immediately He began to speak to her by His Spirit in her heart, suggesting to her some little acts of service for Him, and calling her out of all un-Christlike dispositions and ways. She recognized His voice, and yielded to Him each thing He asked for, following Him wherever He might lead her, with no fear but the one fear of disobeying Him. He led her rapidly on, day by day conforming her more and more to His will, and making her life such a testimony to those around her that even some who had begun by opposing and disbelieving were forced to acknowledge that it was of God, and were won to a similar surrender. And, finally, after three short months of this faithful following, it came to pass, so swiftly had she gone that her Lord was able to reveal to her wondering soul some of the deepest secrets of His love, and to fulfill to her the marvelous promise of Acts 1:5, baptizing her with the Holy Ghost.

Do you think she has ever regretted her wholehearted following of Him? Or that anything but thankfulness and joy can ever fill her soul when she reviews the steps by which her feet had been led to this place of wondrous blessedness, even though some of them may have seemed at the time hard to take? Ah! dear soul, if you would know a like blessing, abandon yourself, like her, to the guidance of the divine Master, and shrink from no surrender for which He may call.

Surely you can trust Him! And if some things may be called that look to you of but little moment, and not worthy of the Lord's attention, remember that He sees not as man sees, and that things small to you may be in His eyes the key and the clue to the deepest springs of your being. In order to mold you into entire conformity to His will, He must have you pliable in His hands, and this pliability is more quickly reached by yielding in the little things than even by the greater. Your one great desire is to follow Him fully; can you not say then a continual "Yes, Lord!" to all His sweet commands, whether small or great, and trust Him to lead you by the shortest road to your fullest blessedness?

My dear friend, this, and nothing less than this, is what your consecration meant, whether you knew it or not. It meant inevitable obedience. It meant that the will of God was henceforth to be your will under all circumstances and at all times. It meant that from that moment you surrendered your liberty of choice, and gave yourself up utterly into the control of the Lord. It meant an hourly following of Him wherever He might lead you, without any dream of turning back.

And now I appeal to you to make good your word. Let everything else go, that you may live out, in a practical daily walk and conversation, the divine life you have dwelling within you. You are united to the Lord by a wondrous tie; walk, then, as He walked, and show to the unbelieving world the blessed reality of His mighty power to save, by letting Him save you to the very uttermost. You need not fear to consent to this, for He is your Savior; and His power is to do it all. He is not asking you, in your poor weakness, to do it yourself; He only asks you to yield yourself to Him, that He may work in you to will and to do by His own mighty power. Your part is to yield yourself, His part is to work; and never, never will He give you any command which is not accompanied by ample power to obey it. Take no thought for tomorrow in this matter; but abandon yourself with a generous trust to the loving Lord, who has promised never to call His own sheep out into any path, without Himself going before them to make the way easy and safe. Take each onward step as He makes it plain to you. Bring all your life in each of its details to Him to regulate and guide. Follow gladly and quickly the sweet suggestions of His Spirit in your soul. And day by day you will find Him bringing you more and more into conformity with His will in all things; molding you and fashioning you, as you are able to bear it, into a vessel for His honor, sanctified and useful for the Master, and prepared for every good work (see 2 Timothy 2:21). So you will be given the sweet joy of being an epistle of Christ known and read of all men; and your light will shine so brightly that men seeing, not you, but your good works, will glorify, not you, but the Father who is in heaven.

We are predestined to be "conformed to the image" of God's Son (see Romans 8:29). This means, of course, not a likeness of bodily presence, but a likeness of character and nature. It means a similarity of thought, of feeling, of desire, of loves, of hates. It means that we are to think and act, according to our measure, as Christ would have thought and acted under our circumstances.

A little girl was once questioned about what it meant to be a Christian. She replied, "It means to be just what Christ would be, if He was a little girl and lived in my house."

The secret of Christ's life was the pouring out of Himself for others; and if we are like Him, this will be the secret of our lives also. He saved others, but Himself

He could not save. He "did not please Himself" (Romans 15:3), and therefore we are "not to please ourselves" (Romans 15:1), but rather our neighbor, when it is for his good.

A thoughtful Hindu religionist, who visited England and America lately to examine Christianity, said, as the result of his observations, "What Christians need is a little more of Christ's Christianity, and a little less of man's."

Man's Christianity teaches sacrifice to save ourselves; Christ's Christianity teaches sacrifice to save others. Man's Christianity produces the fruitless selfishness of too much of our religion. Christ's Christianity produces the blessed unselfishness of lives that are poured out for others, as was His.

In short, then, the one practical outcome of all that our Book has been teaching us is simply that we are to be Christlike Christians. And all our experiences amount to nothing if they do not produce this result. For "Not everyone who says to Me, 'Lord, Lord,' will enter the kingdom of heaven, but only the one who does the will of My Father who is in heaven'" (Matthew 7:21 NIV).

16

Joyful Obedience

I REMEMBER reading once somewhere this sentence, "Perfect obedience would be perfect happiness, if only we had perfect confidence in the power we were obeying."

I remember being struck with the saying, as the revelation of a possible, although hitherto undreamed-of way of happiness; and often afterwards, through all the lawlessness and willfulness of my life, did that saying recur to me as the vision of a rest, and yet of a possible development, that would soothe and at the same time satisfy all my yearnings.

Need I say that this rest has been revealed to me now, not as a vision, but as a reality; and that I have seen in the Lord Jesus, the Master to whom we may all yield up our implicit obedience, and, taking His yoke upon us, may find our perfect rest?

You little know, dear hesitating soul, of the joy you are missing. The Master has revealed Himself to you, and is calling for your complete surrender, and you shrink and hesitate. A measure of surrender you are willing to make, and think indeed it is fit and proper you should. But an utter abandonment, without any reserves, seems to you too much to be asked for. You are afraid of it. It involves too much, you think, and is too great a task. To be measurably obedient you desire; to be perfectly obedient appalls you.

And then, too, you see other souls who seem able to walk with easy consciences, in a far wider path than that which appears to be marked out for you, and you ask yourself why this need be. It seems strange, and perhaps hard to you, that you must do what they need not, and must leave undone what they have liberty to do. Ah! dear Christian, this very difference between you is your privilege, though you do not yet know it.

Your Lord says, "Whoever has My commands and keeps them is the one who loves Me. The one who loves Me will be loved by My Father, and I too will love them and show Myself to them" (John 14:21 NIV). You have His commandments; those you envy have them not. You know the mind of your Lord about many things, in which, as yet, they are walking in darkness. Is not this a privilege? Is it a cause for regret that your soul is brought into such near and intimate relations with your Master that He is able to tell you things which those who are farther off may not know? Do you not realize what a tender degree of intimacy is implied in this?

There are many relations in life which require from the different parties only very moderate degrees of devotion. We may have really pleasant friendships with one another, and yet spend a large part of our lives in separate interests, and widely differing pursuits. When together, we may greatly enjoy one another's society, and find many congenial points; but separation is not any especial distress to us, and other and more intimate friendships do not interfere.

There is not enough love between us, to give us either the right or the desire to enter into and share one another's most private affairs. A certain degree of reserve and distance is the suitable thing, we feel. But there are other relations in life where all this is changed. The friendship becomes love. The two hearts give themselves to one another, to be no longer two but one. A union of souls takes place, which makes all that belongs to one the property of the other.

Separate interests and separate paths in life are no longer possible. Things which were lawful before become unlawful now, because of the nearness of the tie that binds. The reserve and distance suitable to mere friendship becomes fatal in love. Love gives all, and must have all in return. The wishes of one become binding obligations to the other, and the deepest desire of each heart is that it may know every secret wish or longing of the other, in order that it may fly on the wings of the wind to gratify it.

Do such as these chafe under this yoke which love imposes? Do they envy the cool, calm, reasonable friendships they see around them, and regret the nearness into which their souls are brought to their beloved one, because of the obligations it creates? Do they not rather glory in these very obligations, and inwardly pity, with a tender yet exulting joy, the poor far-off ones who dare not come so near? Is not every fresh revelation of the mind of one another a fresh delight and privilege, and is any path found hard which their love compels them to travel?

Ah! dear souls, if you have ever known this even for a few hours in any earthly relation; if you have ever loved a fellow-human being enough to find sacrifice and service on their behalf a joy; if a whole-souled abandonment of your will to the will of another has ever gleamed across you as a blessed and longed-for privilege, or as a sweet and precious reality, then, by all the tender longing love of your heavenly Master, would I entreat you to let it be so towards God!

He loves you with more than the love of friendship. As a bridegroom rejoices over his bride, so does He rejoice over you, and nothing but a full surrender will satisfy Him. He has given you all, and He asks for all in return. The slightest reserve will grieve Him to the heart. He spared not Himself, and how can you spare yourself? For your sake He poured out in a lavish abandonment all that He had, and for His sake you must pour out all that you have without stint or measure.

Oh, be generous in your self-surrender! Meet His measureless devotion for you, with a measureless devotion to Him. Be glad and eager to throw yourself headlong into His dear arms, and to hand over the reins of government to Him. Whatever there is of you, let Him have it all. Give up forever everything that is separate from Him. Consent to resign from this time forward all liberty of choice; and glory in the blessed nearness of union which makes this enthusiasm of devotedness not only possible but necessary. Have you never longed to lavish your love and attentions upon someone far off from you in position or circumstances, with whom you were not intimate enough for any closer approach? Have you not felt a capacity for self-surrender and de-votedness that has seemed to burn within you like a fire, and yet had no object upon which it dared to lavish itself? Have not your hands been full of alabaster boxes of ointment, very precious, which you have never been near enough to any heart to pour out?

Will you shrink or hesitate if, then, you are hearing the sweet voice of your Lord calling you into a place of nearness to Himself, which will require a separation from all else, and which will make this enthusiasm of devotedness not only possible, but necessary? Will you think it hard that He reveals to you more of His mind than He does to others, and that He will not allow you to be happy in anything which separates you from Him-self? Do you want to go where He cannot go with you, or to have pursuits which He cannot share?

No! A thousand times, no! You will spring out to meet His dear will with an eager joy. Even His slightest wish will become a binding law to you, which it would fairly break your heart to disobey. You will glory in the very narrowness of the path He marks out for you, and will pity with an infinite pity the poor far-off ones who have missed this precious joy. The obligations of love will be to you its sweetest privileges; and the right you have acquired to lavish the uttermost abandonment of all that you have upon your Lord will seem to lift you into a region of unspeakable glory. The perfect happiness of perfect obedience will dawn upon your soul, and you will begin to know something of what Jesus meant when He said, "I delight to do Your will, O my God" (Psalm 40:8).

And do you think the joy in this will be all on your side? Has the Lord no joy in those who have thus surrendered themselves to Him, and who love to obey Him? Ah, my friends, we are not fit to speak of this but surely the Scriptures reveal to us glimpses of the delight, the satisfaction, the joy our Lord has in us, that ravish the soul with their marvelous suggestions of blessedness.

That we should need Him is easy to comprehend; that He should need us seems incomprehensible. That our desire should be towards Him is a matter of course; but that His desire should be towards us passes the bounds of human belief. And yet, over and over He says it, and what can we do but believe Him? He has made our hearts capable of this supreme, overmastering affection, and has offered Himself as the object of it. It is infinitely precious to Him, and He says, "The one who loves Me will be loved by My Father, and I too will love them and show Myself to them" (John 14:21 NIV). Continually at every heart He is knocking, and asking to be taken in as the supreme object of love. "Will you have Me," He says to the believer, "to be your Beloved? Will you follow Me into suffering and loneliness, and endure hardness for My sake, and ask for no reward but My smile of approval, and My word of praise? Will you throw yourself with an utter abandonment into My will? Will you give up to Me the absolute control of yourself and all that you are? Will you be content with pleasing Me and Me only? May I have My way with you in all things? Will you come into so close a union with Me as to make a separation from the world necessary? Will you accept Me for your only Lord, and leave all others, to cleave only unto Me?"

In a thousand ways He makes this offer of oneness with Himself to every believer. But all do not say "Yes" to Him. Other loves and other interests seem to them too precious to be cast aside. They do not miss heaven because of this. But they miss an unspeakable joy.

You, however, are not one of these. From the very first your soul has cried out eagerly and gladly to all His offers, "Yes, Lord; yes!" You are more than ready to pour out upon Him all your richest treasures of love and devotedness. You have brought to Him an enthusiasm of self-surrender that perhaps may disturb and distress the more prudent and moderate Christians around you.

Your love makes necessary a separation from the world, which a lower love cannot even conceive of. Sacrifices and services are possible and sweet to you, which could not come into the grasp of a more half-hearted devotedness. The life upon which you have entered gives you the right to a lavish outpouring of your all upon your beloved One. Services, of which more distant souls know nothing, become now your sweetest privilege. Your Lord claims from you, because of your union with Him, far more than He claims of them. What to them is lawful, love has made unlawful for you. To you He can make known His secrets, and to you He looks for an instant response to every requirement of His love.

Oh, it is wonderful! This glorious, unspeakable privilege upon which you have entered! How little it will matter to you if men shall hate you, or shall separate you from their company, and shall reproach you and cast out your name as evil for His dear sake! You may well "rejoice in that day and leap for joy" (Luke 6:23); for behold, your reward is great in heaven, and if you are a partaker of His suffering, you shall be also of His glory.

In you He sees the travail of His soul, and is satisfied. Your love and devotedness are His precious reward for all He has done for you. It is unspeakably sweet to Him.

Do not be afraid, then, to let yourself go in a heart-whole devotedness to your Lord that can brook no reserves. Others may not approve, but He will, and that is enough. Do not stint or measure your obedience or your service. Let your heart and your hand be as free to serve Him, as His heart and His hand were to serve you. Let Him have all there is of you, body, soul, and spirit, time, talents, voice, everything. Lay your whole life open before Him that He may control it. Say to Him each day, "Lord, how shall I regulate this day so as to please You? Where shall I go? What shall I do? Whom shall I visit? What shall I say?" Give your intellect up into His control and say, "Lord, tell me how to think so as to please You?" Give Him your reading, your pursuits, your friendships, and say, "Lord, give me the insight to judge concerning all these things with Your wisdom." Do not let there be a day nor an hour in which you are not intelligently doing His will, and following Him wholly. And this personal service to Him will give a halo to your life, and gild the most monotonous existence with a heavenly glow.

Have you ever grieved that the romance of youth is so soon lost in the hard realities of the world? Bring God thus into your life and into all its details, and a far grander enthusiasm will thrill your soul than the brightest days of youth could ever know, and nothing will seem hard or stern again. The meanest life will be glorified by this.

Often, as I have watched a poor woman at her washtub, and have thought of all the disheartening accessories of such a life, and have been tempted to wonder why such lives need to be, there has come over me, with a thrill of joy, the recollection of this possible glorification of it, and I have said to myself that even this life, lived in Christ, and with Christ, following Him wherever He may lead would be filled with an enthusiasm that would make every hour of it glorious. And I have gone on my way comforted to know that God's most wondrous blessings thus lie in the way of the poorest and the meanest lives. "For," says our Lord Himself, "whoever," whether they be rich or poor, old or young, bond or free, "does the will of My Father in heaven is My brother and sister and mother" (Matthew 12:50).

Pause a moment over these simple yet amazing words. His brother, and sister, and mother! What would we not have given to have been one of these! Oh, let me entreat of you, beloved Christian, to come, taste and see for yourself how good the Lord is, and what wonderful things He has in store for those who "keep His commandments and who do those things that are pleasing in His sight" (1 John 3:22).

"Now it shall come to pass, if you diligently obey the voice of the LORD your God, to observe carefully all His commandments which I command you today, that the LORD your God will set you high above all nations of the earth. And all these blessings shall come upon you and overtake you, because you obey the voice of the LORD your God:

"Blessed shall you be in the city, and blessed shall you be in the country. Blessed shall be the fruit of your body, the produce of your ground and the increase of your herds, the increase of your cattle and the offspring of your flocks. Blessed shall be your basket and your kneading bowl. Blessed shall you be when you come in, and blessed shall you be when you go out.

"The LORD will cause your enemies who rise against you to be defeated before your face; they shall come out against you one way and flee before you seven ways.

"The LORD will command the blessing on you in your storehouses and in all to which you set your hand, and

He will bless you in the land which the LORD your God is giving you.

"The LORD will establish you as a holy people to Himself, just as He has sworn to you, if you keep the commandments of the LORD your God and walk in His ways. Then all peoples of the earth shall see that you are called by the name of the LORD, and they shall be afraid of you.

"And the LORD will grant you plenty of goods, in the fruit of your body, in the increase of your livestock, and in the produce of your ground, in the land of which the LORD swore to your fathers to give you.

"And the LORD will make you the head and not the tail; you shall be above only, and not be beneath, if you heed the commandments of the LORD your God, which I command you today, and are careful to observe them" (Deuteronomy 28:1-11, 13).

For the Israelites this was outward and temporal, for us it is inward and spiritual; and, as such, infinitely more glorious. May our surrendered wills leap out to embrace it in all its fullness!

17

Unity with God

*A*LL the dealings of God with the soul of the believer are in order to bring it into oneness with Himself, that the prayer of our Lord may be fulfilled: "That they all may be one, as You, Father, are in Me, and I in You; that they also may be one in Us ... I in them, and You in Me; that they may be made perfect in one, and that the world may know that You have sent Me, and have loved them as You have loved Me" (John 17:21, 23).

This soul-union was the glorious purpose in the heart of God for His people before the foundation of the world. It was the mystery hid from ages and generations. It was accomplished in the incarnation of Christ. It has been made known by the Scriptures. And it is realized as an actual experience by many of God's dear children. But not by all. It is true of all, and God has not hidden it or made it hard, but the eyes of many are too dim and their hearts too unbelieving, and they fail to grasp it. And it is for the very purpose of bringing them into the personal and actual realization of this that the Lord is stirring up believers everywhere at the present time to abandon themselves to Him, that He may work in them all the good pleasure of His will.

All the previous steps in the Christian life lead up to this. The Lord has made us for it; and until we have intelligently apprehended it, and have voluntarily consented to embrace it, the travail of His soul for us is not satisfied, nor have our hearts found their destined and final rest (see Isaiah 53:11).

The usual course of Christian experience is pictured in the history of the disciples. First, they were awakened to see their condition and their need, and they came to Christ and gave in their allegiance to Him. Then they followed Him, worked for Him, believed in Him; and yet how unlike Him they were – seeking to be set up one above the other; running away from the cross; misunderstanding His mission and His words; forsaking their Lord in times of danger; but still sent out to preach, recognized by Him as His disciples, possessing power to work for Him. They knew Christ only "according to the flesh," (2 Corinthians 5:16) as outside of them, their Lord and Master, but not yet their Life.

Then came Pentecost, and these disciples came to know Him as inwardly revealed; as one with them in actual union, their very indwelling Life. Henceforth He was to them Christ within, working in them to will and to do of His good pleasure; delivering them by the law of the Spirit of His life from the bondage to the law of sin and death, under which they had been held. No longer was it between themselves and Him, a war of wills and a clashing of interests. One will alone animated them, and that was His will. One interest alone was dear to them, and that was His. They were made one with Him.

And surely all can recognize this picture, though perhaps as yet the final stage of it has not been fully reached. You may have left much to follow Christ, dear reader; you may have believed on him, and worked for Him, and loved Him, and yet may not be like Him.

Allegiance you know, and confidence you know, but not yet union. There are two wills, two interests, two lives. You have not yet lost your own life that you may live only in His. Once it was I and not Christ; then it was I and Christ; perhaps now it is even Christ and I. But has it come yet to be Christ only, and not I at all?

Perhaps you do not understand what this oneness means. Some people think it consists in a great emotion or a wonderful feeling of oneness, and they turn inward to examine their emotions, thinking to decide by the state of these, what is the state of their interior union with God. But nowhere is the mistake of trusting feelings greater than here.

Oneness with Christ must, in the very nature of things, consist in a Christlike life and character. It is not what we feel, but what we are that settles the question. No matter how exalted or intense our emotions on the subject may be, if there is not a likeness of character with Christ, a unity of aim and purpose, a similarity of thought and of action, there can be no real oneness.

We speak of two people being one, and we mean that their purposes, and actions, and thoughts, and desires are alike. A friend may pour out upon us enthusiastic expressions of love, and unity and oneness, but if that friend's aims, and actions, and ways of looking at things are exactly opposite to ours, we cannot feel there is any real oneness between us, notwithstanding all our affection for one another. To be truly one with another, we must have the same likes and dislikes, the same joys and sorrows, the same hopes and fears. As it was said, we must look through one another's eyes, and think with one another's brains.

And oneness with Christ can be judged by no other rule. It is out of the question to be one with Him in any way other than in the way of nature, and character, and life. Unless we are Christlike in our thoughts and our ways, we are not one with Him, no matter how we feel.

I have seen Christians, with hardly one Christlike attribute in their whole characters, who yet were so emotional and had such ecstatic feelings of love for Christ, as to think themselves justified in claiming the closest oneness with Him. I scarcely know a sadder sight. Surely our Lord meant to reach such cases when He said in Matthew 7:21, "Not everyone who says to Me, 'Lord, Lord,' shall enter the kingdom of heaven, but he who does the will of My Father in heaven."

He was not making here any arbitrary statement of God's will, but a simple announcement of the nature of things. Of course it must be so. It is like saying, "No man can enter the ranks of astronomers who is not an astronomer." Emotions will not make a man an astronomer, but life and action. He must be one, not merely feel that he is one.

There is no escape from this inexorable nature of things, and especially here. Unless we are one with Christ as to character and life and action, we cannot be one with Him in any other way, for there is no other way. We must be "partakers of His nature" or we cannot be partakers of His life, for His life and His nature are one.

But emotional souls do not always recognize this. They feel so near Christ and so united to Him that they think it must be real; and overlooking the absolute necessity of Christlikeness of character and walk, they are building their hopes and their confidence on their delightful emotions and exalted feelings, and think they must be one with Him, or they could not have such rich and holy experiences.

Now it is a psychological fact that these or similar emotions can be produced by other causes than a purely divine influence, and that they are largely dependent upon temperament and physical conditions. It is most dangerous, therefore, to make them a test of our spiritual union with Christ.

It may result in just such a grievous self-deception as our Lord warns against in Luke 6:46-49. "Why do you call Me 'Lord, Lord,' and not do the things which I say?" (Luke 6:46). Our soul delights perhaps in calling Him "Lord, Lord," but are we doing the things which He said?

For this, He tells us, is the important point, after all.

If, therefore, led by our feelings, we are saying in meetings, or among our friends, or even in our own heart before the Lord, that we are abiding in Him, let us take home to ourselves in solemn consideration these words of the Holy Ghost, "Whoever claims to live in Him must live as Jesus did" (1 John 2:6 NIV). Unless we are thus walking, we cannot possibly be abiding in Him, no matter how much we may feel as if we were.

If you are really one with Christ you will be sweet to those who are cross to you; you will bear everything and make no complaints; when you are reviled you will not revile again; you will consent to be trampled on, as Christ was, and feel nothing but love in return; you will seek the honor of others rather than your own; you will take the lowest place, and be the servant of all, as Christ was; you will literally and truly love your enemies and do good to them that despitefully use you; you will, in short, live a Christlike life, and manifest outwardly as well as feel inwardly a Christlike spirit, and will walk among men as He walked among them. This, dear friends, is what it is to be one with Christ. And if all this is not your life according to your measure, then you are not one with Him, no matter how ecstatic or exalted your feelings may be.

To be one with Christ is too wonderful and solemn and mighty an experience to be reached by any overflow or exaltation of mere feeling. He was holy, and those who are one with Him will be holy also. There is no escape from this simple and obvious fact.

When our Lord tried to make us understand His oneness with God, He expressed it in such words as these, "I always do those things that please Him" (John 8:29). "The Son can do nothing by Himself; He can do only what He sees His Father doing, because whatever the Father does the Son also does" (John 5:19 NIV). "I can of Myself do nothing. As I hear, I judge; and My judgment is righteous, because I do not seek My own will but the will of the Father who sent Me" (John 5:30). "If I do not do the works of My Father, do not believe Me; but if I do, though you do not believe Me, believe the works, that you may know and believe that the Father is in Me, and I in Him" (John 10:37-38).

The test of oneness, then, was the doing of the same works, and it is the test of oneness now. And if our Lord could say of Himself that if He did not the works of his Father, He did not ask to be believed, no matter what professions or claims He might make, surely His disciples must do no less.

It is forever true in the nature of things that "a good tree cannot bear bad fruit, and a bad tree cannot bear good fruit" (Matthew 7:18 NIV). It is not that they will not, but they cannot. And a soul that is one with Christ will just as surely bring forth a Christlike life, as a grapevine will bring forth grapes and not thistles.

Not that I would be understood to object to emotions. On the contrary, I believe they are very precious gifts, when they are from God, and are to be greatly rejoiced in. But what I do object to is the making them a test or proof of spiritual states, either in ourselves or others, and depending on them as the foundation of our faith. Let them come or let them go, just as God pleases, and make no account of them either way. But always see to it that the really vital marks of oneness with Christ, the marks of likeness in character, and life, and walk, are ours, and all will be well. For "He who says, 'I know Him,' and does not keep His commandments, is a liar, and the truth is not in him. But whoever keeps His word, truly the love of God is perfected in him. By this we know that we are in Him" (1 John 2:4-5).

It may be, my dear reader, that the grief of your life has been the fact that you have so few good feelings. You try your hardest to get up the feelings which you hear others talking about, but they will not come. You pray for them fervently, and are often tempted to upbraid God because He does not grant them to you. And you are filled with an almost unbearable anguish because you think your want of emotion is a sign that there is not any interior union of your soul with Christ. You judge altogether by your feelings, and think there is no other way to judge.

Now my advice to you is to let your feelings go, and pay no regard to them whatever. They really have nothing to do with the matter. They are not the indicators of your spiritual state, but are merely the indicators of your temperament, or of your present physical condition. People in very low states of grace are often the subjects of very powerful emotional experiences. We all know this from the scenes we have heard of or witnessed at camp-meetings and revivals. I myself had a colored servant once who would become unconscious under the power of her wonderful experiences whenever there was a revival meeting at their church, who yet had hardly a token of any spiritual life about her at other times, and who was, in fact, not even moral. Now surely, if the Bible teaches nothing else, it does teach this, that a Christlike life and walk must accompany any experience which is really born of His spirit. It could not be otherwise in the very nature of things. But I fear some Christians have separated the two things so entirely in their conceptions as to have exalted their experiences at the expense of their walk, and have come to care far more about their emotions than about their character.

A certain colored congregation in one of the Southern States was a plague to the whole neighborhood by their open disregard of even the ordinary rules of morality: stealing, and lying, and cheating, without apparently a single prick of conscience on the subject. And yet their nightly meetings were times of the greatest emotion and "power." Someone finally spoke to the preacher about it, and begged him to preach a sermon on morality, which would lead his people to see their sins. "Ah, missus," he replied, "I knows dey's bad, but den it always brings a coldness like over de meetings when I preaches about dem things."

You are helpless as to your emotions, but character you can have if you will. You can be so filled with Christ as to be Christlike, and if you are Christlike, then you are one with Him in the only vital and essential way, even though your feelings may tell you that it is an impossibility.

Having thus settled what oneness with Christ really is, the next point for us to consider is how to reach it for ourselves. We must first of all find out what are the facts in the case, and what is our own relation to these facts.

If you read such passages as 1 Corinthians 3:16, "Don't you know that you yourselves are God's temple and that God's Spirit dwells in your midst?" and then look at the opening of the chapter to see to whom these wonderful words are spoken, even to "babes in Christ," who were "yet carnal," and walked according to man, you will see that this soul-union of which I speak, this unspeakably glorious mystery of an indwelling God, is the possession of even the weakest and most failing believer in Christ. So that it is not a new thing you are to ask for, but only to realize that which you already have. Of every believer in the Lord Jesus it is absolutely true, that his body is a temple of the Holy Spirit, who is in him and whom he received from God (see 1 Corinthians 6:19).

It seems to me just in this way; as though Christ were living in a house, shut up in a far-off closet, unknown and unnoticed by the dwellers in the house, longing to make Himself known to them and be one with them in all their daily lives, and share in all their interests, but unwilling to force Himself upon their notice; as nothing but a voluntary companionship could meet or satisfy the needs of His love. The days pass by over that favored household, and they remain in ignorance of their marvelous privilege. They come and go about all their daily affairs with no thought of their wonderful Guest. Their plans are laid without reference to Him. His wisdom to guide, and His strength to protect, are all lost to them. Lonely days and weeks are spent in sadness, which might have been full of the sweetness of His presence.

But suddenly the announcement is made, "The Lord is in the house!"

How will its owner receive the intelligence? Will he call out an eager thanksgiving, and throw wide open every door for the entrance of his glorious Guest; or will he shrink and hesitate, afraid of His presence and seek to reserve some private corner for a refuge from His all-seeing eye?

Dear friend, I make the glad announcement to thee that the Lord is in your heart. Since the day of your conversion He has been dwelling there, but you have lived on in ignorance of it. Every moment during all that time might have been passed in the sunshine of His sweet presence, and every step has been taken under His advice. But because you knew it not, and have never looked for Him there, your life has been lonely and full of failure. But now that I make the announcement to you, how will you receive it?

Are you glad to have Him? Will you throw wide open every door to welcome Him in? Will you joyfully and thankfully give up the government of your life into His hands? Will you consult Him about everything, and let Him decide each step for you, and mark out every path?

Will you invite Him to your innermost chambers, and make Him the sharer in your most hidden life? Will you say, "YES!" to all His longing for union with you, and with a glad and eager abandonment, hand yourself and all that concerns you over into His hands? If you will, then will your soul begin to know something of the joy of union with Christ.

And yet, after all, this is but a faint picture of the blessed reality. For far more glorious than it would be to have Christ a dweller in the house or in the heart, is it to be brought into such a real and actual union with Him as to be one with Him, one will, one purpose, one interest, one life. Human words cannot express such glory as this. And yet I want to express it.

I want to make your souls so unutterably hungry to realize it, that day or night you cannot rest without it. Do you understand the words "one with Christ"? Do you catch the slightest glimpse of their marvelous meaning? Does not your whole soul begin to exult over such a wondrous destiny? For it is a reality. It means to have no life but His life, to have no will but His will, to have no interests but His interests, to share His riches, to enter into His joys, to partake of His sorrows, to manifest His life, to have the same mind as He had, to think, and feel, and act, and walk as He did. Oh, who could have dreamed that such a destiny could have been ours!

Will you have it, dear soul? Your Lord will not force it on you, for He wants you as His companion and His friend, and a forced union would be incompatible with this. It must be voluntary on your part.

The bride must say a willing "Yes" to her bridegroom, or the joy of their union is utterly wanting. Can you say a willing "Yes" to the Lord?

It is such a simple transaction, and yet so real! The steps are but three. First, be convinced that the Scriptures teach this glorious indwelling of God; then surrender your whole being to Him to be possessed by Him; and finally believe that He has taken possession, and is dwelling in you. Begin to reckon yourself dead, and to reckon Christ as your only life. Maintain this attitude of soul unwaveringly. Say, "I have been crucified with Christ; it is no longer I who live, but Christ lives in me" (Galatians 2:20), over and over, day and night, until it becomes the habitual breathing of your soul.

Put off your self-life by faith and in fact continually, and put on practically the life of Christ. Let this act become, by its constant repetition, the attitude of your whole being. And as surely as you do this day by day, you will find yourself continually bearing about in your body the dying of the Lord Jesus, that the life also of Jesus may be made manifest in your mortal flesh. You will learn to know what salvation means; and will have opened out to you astonished gaze secrets of the Lord, of which you have hitherto hardly dreamed.

18

Every Cloud Has
a Silver Lining

*I*N many of our store windows at Christmas time there stands a most significant picture. It is a dreary, desolate winter scene. There is a dark, stormy, wintry sky, bare trees, and brown grass and dead weeds, with patches of snow over them.

On a leafless tree at one side of the picture is an empty and snow-covered nest, and on a branch near sits a little bird.

All is cold, and dark, and desolate enough to daunt any bird, and drive it to some fairer clime, but this bird is sitting there in an attitude of perfect contentment, and has its little head bravely lifted up towards the sky, while a winter song is evidently about to burst forth from its tiny throat. This picture, which always stands on my shelf, has preached me many a sermon. And the test is always the same, and finds its expression in the two words, "although" and "yet."

"Though the fig tree may not blossom, nor fruit be on the vines; though the labor of the olive may fail, and the fields yield no food; though the flock may be cut off from the fold, and there be no herd in the stalls — yet I will rejoice in the LORD, I will joy in the God of my salvation" (Habakkuk 3:17-18).

There comes a time in many lives, when, like this bird in the winter, the soul finds itself bereft of every comfort both outward and inward; when all seems dark, and all seems wrong, even; when everything in which we have trusted seems to fail us; when the promises are apparently unfulfilled, and our prayers gain no response; when there seems nothing left to rest on in earth or heaven.

And it is at such times as these that the brave little bird with its message is needed. "Although" all is wrong everywhere, "yet" there is still one thing left to rejoice in, and that is God; the "God of our salvation," who changes not, but is the same good, loving, tender God yesterday, today, and forever. We can joy in Him always, whether we have anything else to rejoice in or not.

By rejoicing in Him, however, I do not mean rejoicing in ourselves, although I fear most people think this is really what is meant. It is their feelings or their revelations or their experiences that constitute the groundwork of their joy, and if none of these are satisfactory, they see no possibility of joy at all.

But the lesson the Lord is trying to teach us all the time is the lesson of self-effacement. He commands us to look away from self and all self's experiences, to crucify self and count it dead, to cease to be interested in self, and to know nothing and be interested in nothing but God.

The reason for this is that God has destined us for a higher life than the self-life. That just as He has destined the caterpillar to become the butterfly and therefore has appointed the caterpillar life to die in order that the butterfly life may take its place, so He has appointed our self-life to die in order that the divine life may become ours instead. The caterpillar effaces itself in its grub form that it may evolve or develop into its butterfly form. It dies that it may live. And just so must we.

Therefore, the one most essential thing in this stage of our existence must be the death to self and the resurrection to a life only in God. And it is for this reason that the lesson of joy in the Lord, and not in self, must be learned. Every advancing soul must come sooner or later to the place where it can trust God, the bare God, if I may be allowed the expression, simply and only because of what He is in Himself, and not because of His promises or His gifts. It must learn to have its joy in Him alone, and to rejoice in Him when all else in heaven and earth shall seem to fail.

The only way in which this place can be reached, I believe, is by the soul being compelled to face in its own experience the loss of all things both inward and out-ward. I do not mean necessarily that all one's friends must die, or all one's money be lost: but I do mean that the soul shall find itself, from either inward or outward causes, desolate and bereft, and empty of all consolation. It must come to the end of everything that is not God; and must have nothing else left to rest on within or without. It must experience just what the prophet meant when he wrote that "although."

It must wade through the slough, and fall off of the precipice, and be swamped by the ocean, and at last find in the midst of them, and at the bottom of them, and behind them, the present, living, loving, omnipotent God! And then, and not until then, will it understand the prophet's exulting shout of triumph, and be able to join it: "YET I will rejoice in the LORD; I will joy in the God of my salvation" (Habakkuk 3:18).

And then, also, and not until then, will it know the full meaning of the verse that follows: "The LORD God is my strength; He will make my feet like deer's feet, and He will make me walk on my high hills" (Habakkuk 3:19).

The soul often walks on what seem like high places, which are, however, largely self-evolved and emotional, and have but little of God in them; and in moments of loss and failure and darkness, these high places become precipices of failure. But the high places to which the Lord brings the soul that rejoices only in Him can be touched by no darkness or loss, for their very foundations are laid in the midst of an utter loss and death of all that is not God.

If we want an unwavering experience, therefore, we can find it only in the Lord, apart from all else; apart from His gifts, apart from His blessings, apart from all that can change or be affected by the changing conditions of our earthly life.

The prayer which is answered today may seem to be unanswered tomorrow; the promises once so gloriously fulfilled may cease to be a reality to us; the spiritual blessing which was at one time such a joy may be utterly lost; and nothing of all we once trusted to and rested on may be left us, but the hungry and longing memory of it all. But when all else is gone, God is still left. Nothing changes Him. He is the same yesterday, today, and forever, and in Him is no variableness, neither shadow of turning. And the soul that finds its joy in Him alone can suffer no wavering.

It is grand to trust in the promises, but it is grander still to trust in the Promiser. The promises may be misunderstood or misapplied, and at the moment when we are leaning all our weight upon them, they may seem utterly to fail us. But no one ever trusted in the Promiser and was confounded.

The God who is behind His promises and is infinitely greater than His promises can never fail us in any emergency, and the soul that is stayed on Him cannot know anything but perfect peace.

The little child does not always understand its mother's promises, but it knows its mother, and its childlike trust is founded not on her word, but upon herself. And just so it is with those of us who have learned the lesson of this "although" and "yet." There may not be a prayer answered or a promise fulfilled to our own consciousness, but what of that? Behind the prayers and behind the promises, there is God, and He is enough. And to such a soul the simple words "God is" answer every question and solve every doubt.

To the little trusting child the simple fact of the mother's existence is the answer to all its need. The mother may not make one single promise, or detail any plan, but she is, and that is enough for the child. The child rejoices in the mother; not in her promises, but in herself. And to the child, as to us, there is behind all that changes and can change, the one unchangeable joy of the mother's existence. While the mother lives, the child must be cared for, and the child knows this, instinctively if not intelligently, and rejoices in knowing it.

And while God lives, His children must be cared for as well, and His children ought to know this, and rejoice in it as instinctively and far more intelligently than the child of human parents. For what else can God do, being what He is? Neglect, indifference, forgetfulness, ignorance are all impossible to Him. He knows everything, He cares about everything, He can manage everything, and He loves us. What more could we ask for? Therefore, come what may, we will lift our faces to our God, like our brave little bird teacher, and, in the midst of our darkest "although" will sing our glad and triumphant "yet."

All of God's saints in all ages have done this. Job said, out of the depths of sorrow and trial which few can equal, "Though He slay me, yet will I trust Him" (Job 13:15).

David could say in the moment of his keenest anguish, "Yea, though I walk through the valley of the shadow of death," yet "I will fear no evil; for You are with me" (Psalm 23:4). And again he could say, "God is our refuge and strength, an ever-present help in trouble. Therefore we will not fear, though the earth give way and the mountains fall into the heart of the sea, though its waters roar and foam and the mountains quake with their surging … God is within her, she will not fall; God will help her at break of day" (Psalm 46:1-3, 5 NIV).

Paul could say in the midst of his sorrows, "We are hard-pressed on every side, yet not crushed; we are perplexed, but not in despair; persecuted, but not forsaken; struck down, but not destroyed … Therefore we do not lose heart. Even though our outward man is perishing, yet the inward man is being renewed day by day. For our light affliction, which is but for a moment, is working for us a far more exceeding and eternal weight of glory, while we do not look at the things which are seen, but at the things which are not seen. For the things which are seen are temporary, but the things which are not seen are eternal" (2 Corinthians 4:8-9, 16-18).

All this and more can the soul say that learned this lesson of rejoicing in God alone. Spiritual joy is not a thing, not a lump of joy, so to speak, stored away in one's heart to be looked at and rejoiced over. Joy is only the gladness that comes from the possession of something good, or the knowledge of something pleasant. And the Christian's joy is simply his gladness in knowing Christ, and in his possession of such a God and Savior. We do not on an earthly plane rejoice in our joy, but in the thing that causes our joy. And on the heavenly plane it is the same. We are to rejoice in the Lord, and joy in the God of our salvation (see Habakkuk 3:18); and this joy no man nor devil can take from us, and no earthly sorrows can touch.

A writer on the interior life says, in effect, that our spiritual pathway is divided into three regions, very different from one another and yet each one a necessary stage in the onward progress. First, there is the region of beginnings, which is a time full of sensible joys and delights, of fervent aspirations, of emotional experiences, and of many secret manifestations of God. Then comes a vast extent of wilderness, full of temptation, and trial, and conflict, of the loss of sensible manifestations, of dryness, and of inward and outward darkness and distress. And then, finally, if this desert period is faithfully traversed, there comes on the further side of it a region of mountain heights of uninterrupted union and communion with God, of superhuman detachment from everything earthly, of infinite contentment with the divine will, and of marvelous transformation into the image of Christ.

Whether this order is true or not, I cannot here discuss, but of one thing I am very sure, that to many souls who have tasted the joy of the "region of beginnings" here set forth, there has come afterwards a period of desert experience at which they have been sorely amazed and perplexed. And I cannot but think such might, perhaps, in this explanation, find the answer to their trouble. They are being taught the lesson of detachment from all that is not God, in order that their souls may at last be brought into that interior union and oneness with Him who is set forth in the picture given of the third and last region of mountain heights of blessedness.

The soul's pathway is always through death to life. The caterpillar cannot in the nature of things become the butterfly in any other way than by dying to the one life in order to live in the other. And neither can we. Therefore, it may well be that this region of death and desolation must need be passed through if we would reach the calm mountain heights beyond. And if we know this, we can walk triumphantly through the darkest experience, sure that all is well, since God is God.

In the lives of many who read this paper there is, I feel sure, at least one of these desert "althoughs," and in some lives there are many.

Dear friends, is the "yet" there also? Have you learned the prophet's lesson? Is God enough for you?

19

Interior Kingdoms vs. Exterior Kingdoms

*O*NCE, on being asked by the Pharisees when the kingdom of God would come, Jesus replied, 'The coming of the kingdom of God is not something that can be observed, nor will people say, *Here it is*, or *There it is*, because the kingdom of God is in your midst'" (Luke 17:20-21 NIV).

The expressions "kingdom of God" and "kingdom of heaven" are used in Scripture concerning the divine life in the soul. They mean simply the place or condition where God rules and where His will is done. It is an interior kingdom, not an exterior one. Its thrones are not outward thrones of human pomp and glory, but inward thrones of dominion and supremacy over the things of time and sense. Its kings are not clothed in royal robes of purple and fine linen, but with the interior garments of purity and truth. And its reign is not in outward show, but in inward power. Neither is it in one place rather than another, nor in one form of things above another. It is not here nor there, not in this mountain nor yet at Jerusalem that we are to find Christ, and enter into His kingdom. It is not a matter of place at all, but one of condition. And in every place and under every name, and through every form, all who seek God and work righteousness shall find His kingdom within them.

But this is very little understood. In our childish fashion of literalism we have too much imbibed the idea that a kingdom must necessarily be in a particular place and with outward observation; and have therefore expected that the kingdom of heaven would mean for us an outward victory of heaven over earth in some particular place, or under some special form; and that to sit on a throne with Christ would be to have an outward uplifting in power and glory before the face of all around us.

But as the inner sense of Scripture unfolds to us, we see that this would be but a poor and superficial fulfilling of the real meaning of these wonderful symbols. And the vision of their true significance grows and strengthens before the "eyes that see," until at last we know that our Lord's words were truer than ever we had dreamed before, that the "kingdom of God is not something that can be observed, nor will people say, 'Here it is,' or 'There it is,' because the kingdom of God is in your midst" (Luke 17:20-21 NIV).

In Daniel we have the announcement of the kingdom, and in Isaiah, the announcement of the King:

"The God of heaven will set up a kingdom that will never be destroyed, nor will it be left to another people. It will crush all those kingdoms and bring them to an end, but it will itself endure forever" (Daniel 2:44 NIV).

"For unto us a Child is born, unto us a Son is given; and the government will be upon His shoulder. And His name will be called Wonderful, Counselor, Mighty God, Everlasting Father, Prince of Peace. Of the increase of His government and peace there will be no end, upon the throne of David and over His kingdom, to order it and establish it with judgment and justice from that time forward, even forever. The zeal of the LORD of hosts will perform this" (Isaiah 9:6-7).

This kingdom is to break in pieces and consume all other kingdoms by right of the law by which the inward always rules the outward. If there is peace within, no outward turmoil can affect the soul; but outward peace can never quiet an inward tempest. A happy heart can walk in triumphant indifference through a sea of external trouble; while internal anguish cannot find happiness in the most favorable surroundings. What a man is within himself makes or unmakes his joy, and not what he possesses outside of himself.

No act of kings or emperors or any other man can degrade a soul that retains its own dignity; no tyrant can enslave a man who is inwardly free. Therefore to have this divine kingdom set up within means that all other powers to conquer or enslave are broken, and the soul reigns triumphant over them all. Men and devils may try to hold such a one in bondage, but they are powerless before the might of this interior kingdom. No longer will fashion, or conventionality, or the fear of man, or the love of ease, or any other of the many tyrants to which Christians cringe and bow, rule a soul that has been raised to a throne in this inward kingdom.

No sin or temptation can overcome, no sorrow can crush, no discouragement can hinder. Let a man or woman have been bound in ever so tyrannical chains of sinful habits, this kingdom will set them free. Circumstances make men kings in the outward life, but in this hidden life men become kings over circumstances. And the soul that has aforetime been the slave of a thousand outward things, finds itself here utterly independent of them, every one.

For the King in this kingdom is One whom no circumstances can affect or baffle. It is He indeed who makes circumstances. And since the government is upon His shoulders, we cannot doubt that He will order the kingdom with a judgment and justice that will leave nothing for any subject in His kingdom to desire.

In the expression "the government shall be upon His shoulder," we have the whole secret of this wonderful kingdom – upon His shoulder, not upon ours. The care is His, the burdens are His, the responsibility belongs to Him, the protection rests upon Him, the planning, and providing, and controlling, and guiding, all are in His hands. No one can question as to His perfect fulfillment of every requirement of His kingship. Therefore those who are in His kingdom, are utterly delivered from any need to be anxious, or burdened, or perplexed, or troubled. And by this deliverance they become kings. The government is not upon their shoulders, and they have no business to interfere with it. Their King has assumed the whole responsibility, and if He can but see His subjects happy and prosperous, He is content Himself to bear all the weight and care of kingship. How often we speak of the responsibilities of earthly kings, and pity them for the burdens that kingship imposes. We recognize, even on an earthly plane, that to be a king means, or ought to mean, the bearing of the burdens of even the lowliest of his subjects.

From this instinctive sense of every human heart as to the rightful duties and responsibilities of kingship, we may learn what it means to be in a kingdom over which God is King, and where He has Himself declared all things shall be ordered with judgment and justice from henceforth and forever. Surely no care or anxiety can ever enter here, if the heart but knows its kingdom and its King!

In John 18:36, our King tells us the tactics of His kingdom: "Jesus answered, 'My kingdom is not of this world. If My kingdom were of this world, My servants would fight, so that I should not be delivered to the Jews; but now My kingdom is not from here.'"

Earthly kings and earthly kingdoms gain and keep their supremacy by outward conflict; God's kingdom conquers by inward power. Earthly kings subdue enemies; God subdues enmity. His victories must be interior before they can be exterior. He does not subjugate, but He conquers. Even we, on our earthly plane, know something of this principle, and do not value any victory over another which only reaches the body and has not subdued the heart. No true mother cares for an outward obedience merely; nothing will satisfy her but the inward surrender. Unless the citadel of the heart is conquered, the conquest seems worthless.

And with God how much more will this be the case, since we are told that "the LORD does not see as man sees; for man looks at the outward appearance, but the LORD looks at the heart" (1 Samuel 16:7). We speak of "subduing hearts" and we mean not that they are overpowered or forced into an unwilling and compulsory surrender, but that they are conquered by being won, and are willingly yielded up to another's control. And it is after this fashion and no other that God subdues. So that to read that "His kingdom rules over all" (Psalm 103:19) means that all hearts are won to His service in a glad and willing surrender.

For again I repeat, His reign must be inward before it can be outward. And in truth it is no reign at all unless it is within. If we think of it a moment we shall see that this must be so in the very nature of things, and that it is impossible to conceive of God reigning in a kingdom where the subduing reaches no further than the outside actions of His subjects. His kingdom is not of this world, but is in a spiritual sphere where its power is over the souls and not the bodies of men; and therefore only when the soul is conquered can it be set up.

Understood in this light, how full of love and blessing do all those declarations and prophecies become, which tell us that God is to subdue His enemies under His feet, and is to rule them in righteousness and power! And how glorious with hope does the voice of that great multitude heard by John sound, saying, "Alleluia! For the Lord God Omnipotent reigns!" (Revelations 19:6).

In confirmation of all this we have two passages descriptive of this kingdom, in Romans 14:17 and 1 Corinthians 4:20: "For the kingdom of God is not eating and drinking, but righteousness and peace and joy in the Holy Spirit." "For the kingdom of God is not in word but in power."

Not outward things, but inward. Not what a man eats and drinks, not where he lives, nor what is his nationality, nor the customs of his race, not even what he thinks nor what he says; but what are the inward characteristics of his nature, and the inward power of his spiritual life. For these alone constitute this kingdom of God. Not what I do, but what I am, is to decide whether I belong to it or not. And only as inward righteousness, and inward peace, and inward joy, and inward power are bestowed and experienced, can this kingdom be set up. Therefore no outward subjugation can accomplish results like these, but only the interior work of the all-subduing spirit of God.

We who have entered this kingdom, or, rather, in whom this kingdom is set up, sit upon the throne with our King and share His dominion. The world was His footstool, and it becomes our footstool also (see Acts 7:49).

Over the things of time and sense He reigned triumph-ant by the power of a life lived in a plane above them and superior to them, and so may we (see Revelations 20:4-6). We are all of us familiar with the expression that such and such a person "rises superior to his surround-ings," and we mean that there is in that soul a hidden power that controls its surroundings, instead of being controlled by them. Our King essentially rose superior to His surroundings; and it is given to us who are reigning with Him to do the same.

But, just as He was not a King in outward appearance, but only in inward power, so shall we be. He reigned, not in this, that He had all the treasures and riches of the world at His command, but that He had none of them, and could do without them. And so shall our reigning be. We shall not have all men bowing down to us, and all things bending to our will; but with all men opposing and all things adverse, we shall walk in a royal triumph of soul through the midst of them. We shall suffer the loss of all things, and by that loss be set forever free from their power to bind. We shall hide ourselves in the impregnable fortress of the will of our King, and shall reign there in a perpetual kingdom.

All this is contrary to man's thought of kingship. The only idea the human heart can compass is that outward circumstances must bend and bow to the soul that is seated on a throne with Christ. Friends must approve, enemies must be silenced, obstacles must be overcome, affairs must prosper, or there can be no reigning. If man had had the ordering of Daniel's business, or of that matter of the three Hebrew children in the burning fiery furnace, he would have said the only way of victory would be for the minds of the kings to have been so changed that Daniel should not have been cast into the den of lions (see Daniel 6), and the Hebrew children should have been kept out of the furnace (see Daniel 3).

But God's way was infinitely grander. He suffered Daniel to be cast among the lions, in order that he might reign triumphant over them when in their very midst, and He allowed Shadrach, Meshach and Abednego to be cast into the burning, fiery furnace, in order that they might walk through it without so much as the smell of fire upon them. He tells us not that we shall walk in paths where there are no serpents and scorpions, but that we shall walk through the midst of serpents and scorpions, and shall tread them under our feet (see Luke 10:19).

And how much more glorious a kingdom is this than any outward rule or control could be! To be inwardly a king, while outwardly a slave, is one of the grandest heights of triumph of which our hearts can conceive. To be destitute, afflicted, tormented, to be stoned and torn asunder, and slain with the sword; to wander in sheepskins and goatskins, and in deserts and mountains, and in dens and caves of the earth, and yet to be through it all kings in interior kingdoms of righteousness, peace and joy in the Holy Ghost is surely a kingdom that none but God could give, and none but God-like souls receive.

A few such kings we have at some time or other seen or heard of in this world of ours, and all hearts have acknowledged their unconscious sway. One I read of among the brethren of the monastery of St. Cyr. Because of their piety, these brethren incurred the hatred of the monasteries around them, and the anger of their superiors, and were cast out as evil from their community.

One of them was sent as prisoner to a monastery where his chief enemies dwelt, and was there subjected to the most cruel and degrading treatment. Although he was of gentle birth, and had been an abbot in the community he had left, he was compelled to do the most menial work, was forced to carry a noisome burden on his back, and was driven out to beg with a placard on his bosom declaring him to be the vilest of the vile.

But through it all the spirit of the saint reigned triumphant, and nothing disturbed his calm, or soured for a moment his Christlike sweetness. For his persecutors he never had anything but words of kindness and smiles of love. And at last by the mighty power of the divine kingdom in which he lived, he subdued all hearts around him to himself, and became the trusted friend and adviser, and the beloved ruler over the very enemies who had once so delighted to persecute and revile him. "Blessed are the meek, for they shall inherit the earth" (Matthew 5:5). By his meekness he conquered and became king.

At one time a dangerous criminal was sent to the monastery for imprisonment. He was so violent that no bonds sufficed to bind him, and no strength could control him. At last he was taken to the cell of this brother from St. Cyr, and they were shut up together; even the stolid monks themselves recognizing in that divine meekness a power to conquer that surpassed all the powers with which they were acquainted. The saint received the violent man as a beloved brother, and smiled upon him with heavenly kindness. But the criminal returned it with abuse and violence. He broke the monk's furniture and destroyed his bed, he kicked him, and beat him, and tore his hair, and spat upon him. He exhausted himself in his violence against him.

Through it all the monk made no resistance, and said no word but words of love; and when at length the criminal, worn out with his fury, paused to take breath, the beaten man looked upon his persecutor with a smile of ineffable love and tender compassion, as though he would gather him to his bosom and comfort him for his misery. It was more than the criminal could bear. Hatred, and revenge, and anger he could repay in kind, but against love and meekness like this he had no weapons, and his heart was conquered. He fell at the feet of the saint and washed them with his tears, as he entreated forgiveness for his cruelty, and vowed a lifelong loyalty to his service.

And from that moment all trouble with that criminal was over. He followed the saint about like a loving and faithful dog, eager to do or to be anything the other might desire. And when the time of his imprisonment was over, and the gates of his prison were opened for his release, he could not be induced to go, because he could not bear to leave the man who had saved him by love.

Of such a nature is kingship in this kingdom of

heaven. Each soul can make the application for itself, without need of comment from me.

In Matthew 5-7, we have the King of this kingdom describing the characteristics of His kingdom and giving the laws for His subjects. "Blessed are the poor in spirit," He says, "for theirs is the kingdom of heaven" (Matthew 5:3). Not the rich, or great, or wise, or learned, but the poor in spirit, the meek, the merciful, the pure in heart, those who mourn, and those who hunger and thirst, those who are persecuted, and reviled, and spoken evil against, all such belong to this kingdom. Gentleness, yieldingness, meekness, and charity are the characteristics of these kings, and they reign in the power of them.

One Christian asked another, "How can I make people respect me?"

"I would command their respect," was the reply. And this meant not that he should stand up and say in tones of authority, "Now I command you all to respect me," but that he should so act, and live, and be, that no one could help respecting him. Men sometimes win an outward show of respect and submission by an overbearing tyranny, but he who would rule the heart of his subjects must try other methods.

Our Lord developed this thought to some who wished to share His throne. He called them to Him, and said, "You know that those who are considered rulers over the Gentiles lord it over them, and their great ones exercise authority over them. Yet it shall not be so among you; but whoever desires to become great among you shall be your servant. And whoever of you desires to be first shall be slave of all. For even the Son of Man did not come to be served, but to serve, and to give His life a ransom for many" (Mark 10:42-45).

From the human standpoint, man alone reigns who is able to exercise lordship over those around him. From the divine standpoint the soul that serves is the soul that reigns. Not he who demands most receives this inward crowning, but he who gives up most.

What grander kingship can be conceived of than that which Christ sets forth in the Sermon on the Mount, "But I tell you not to resist an evil person. But whoever slaps you on your right cheek, turn the other to him also. If anyone wants to sue you and take away your tunic, let him have your cloak also. And whoever compels you to go one mile, go with him two" (Matthew 5:39-41)?

Surely only a soul that is in harmony with God can mount such a throne of dominion as this! But this is our destiny. We are made for this purpose. We are born of a kingly race, and are heirs to this ineffable kingdom; "heirs of God and joint heirs with Christ" (Romans 8:17).

I would that we could realize this; and could see in every act of service or surrender to which we might find ourselves called, an upward step in the pathway that leads us to our kingdom and our throne!

I mean this in a very practical sense. I mean that the homely services of our daily lives, and the little sacrifices which each day demands, will be, if faithfully fulfilled, actual rounds in the ladder by which we are mounting to our thrones. I mean that if we are faithful over the "few things" of our earthly kingdom, we shall be made ruler over the "many things" of the heavenly kingdom.

He that follows Christ in this ministry of service and of suffering will reign with Him in the glory of supreme self-sacrifice, and will be the "chiefest" in His divine kingdom of love. Knowing this, who would hesitate to "turn the other cheek," since by the turning a kingdom is to be won and a throne is to be gained?

Joseph was a type of all this. In slavery and in prison he reigned as king, as truly as when seated on Pharaoh's throne or riding in Pharaoh's chariot (see Genesis 39:6, 22-23). He became the greatest by being the least, the chiefest by being servant of all.

Dear reader, are you reigning after this fashion, and in this sort of kingdom? Are you the greatest in your little world of home, or church, or social circle by being the least, and chiefest by being the servant of all? If not, your kingdom is not Christ's kingdom, and your throne is not one shared by Him.

To enter into the secrets of this interior kingdom and to partake of its heavenly power is no notional victory, no fancied supremacy. It is a real and actual reigning, which will cause thee as a matter of fact to "rise superior" to the world and the things of it, and to walk through it independent of its smiles or frowns, dwelling in a region of heavenly peace and heavenly triumph which earth can neither give nor take away. "For the kingdom of God is not in word but in power" (1 Corinthians 4:20). It is not a talk but a fact; and those who are in it recognize their kingship and prove it by reigning.

But perhaps you will say, "How can I enter into this kingdom, if I am not already in?" Let our Lord Himself answer you: "At that time the disciples came to Jesus and asked, 'Who, then, is the greatest in the kingdom of heaven?' He called a little child to Him, and placed the child among them. And He said: 'Truly I tell you, unless you change and become like little children, you will never enter the kingdom of heaven'" (Matthew 18:1-3 NIV). It is a kingdom of childlike hearts, and only such can enter it.

To be a "little child" means simply to be one. I cannot describe it better than this. We all have known little children in our lives, and have delighted ourselves in their simplicity and their trustfulness, their lighthearted carelessness, and their unquestioning obedience to those in authority over them. And to be the greatest in this divine kingdom means to have the most of this guileless, tender, trustful, self-forgetting, obedient heart of a child.

"Not everyone who says to Me, 'Lord, Lord,' shall enter the kingdom of heaven, but he who does the will of My Father in heaven" (Matthew 7:21). It is not saying, but doing, that will avail us here. We must be a child, or we cannot sit on the child's throne. And to be a child means to do the Father's will, since the very essence of true childhood is the spirit of obedience united to the spirit of trust.

Become a little child, then, by laying aside all your greatness, all your self-assertion, all your self-dependence, all your wisdom, and all your strength, and consenting to die to your own self-life, be born again into the kingdom of God. The only way out of one life and into another is by a death to one and a new birth into the other. It is the old story, therefore, reiterated so often and in so many different ways, of through death to life.

Die, then, that you my live. Lose your own life that you may find Christ's life. The caterpillar can only enter into the butterfly's kingdom by dying to its caterpillar life, and emerging into the resurrection life of the butterfly; and just so can we also only enter into the kingdom of God by the way of a death out of the kingdom of self, and an emergence into the resurrection life of Christ.

Let everything go, then, that belongs to the natural – all your own notions, and plans, and ways, and thoughts – and accept in their stead God's plans, and ways, and thoughts. Do this faithfully and do it persistently, and you shall come at last to sit on His throne, and to reign with Him in an interior kingdom which shall break in pieces and consume all other kingdoms, and shall stand for ever and ever.

There is no other way. This kingdom cannot be entered by pomp, and show, and greatness, and strength; but by littleness, and helplessness, and childlikeness, and babyhood, and death. He that humbles himself, and he only, shall be exalted here; and to mount the throne with Christ requires that we shall first have followed Him in the suffering, and loss, and crucifixion. If we suffer with him, we shall also reign with Him. Not as an arbitrary reward for our suffering, but as the result that will follow in the very nature of things. Christ's loss must necessarily bring Christ's gain, Christ's death must bring Christ's resurrection, and to follow Him in the regeneration will surely and inevitably bring the soul that follows to His crown and His throne.

The Kingdom is not a place, but character, those who have not the character cannot by any possibility be in it. We pray daily, "Your kingdom come." Do we know what we are praying for? Do we comprehend the change it will make in us if it comes in us? Are we willing to be so changed?

What is the kingdom of God but the rule of God? And what is the rule of God but the will of God? Therefore when we pray, "Your will be done on earth as it is in heaven," we have touched the secret of it all.

A horde of savages might conquer a civilized kingdom by sheer brute force; but if they would conquer the civilization of that kingdom, they could only do so by submitting to its control. And just so is it with the kingdom of heaven. It yields its scepter to none but those who render obedience to its laws.

"To him who overcomes I will grant to sit with Me on My throne, as I also overcame and sat down with My Father on His throne" (Revelations 3:21).

"He always reigns who sides with God," says an old writer. And again, "He who perfectly accepts the will of God, dwells in a perpetual kingdom." Are you reigning after this fashion and in this sort of a kingdom?

Are you the "chiefest" by being the "servant of all"?

Are you a king over your circumstances, or do your

circumstances reign over you?

Do you triumph over your temptations, or do they triumph over you?

Can you sit on an inward throne in the midst of outward defeat and loss?

Can you conquer by yielding, and become the greatest by being the least?

If you can answer yes to all these questions, then you have come into your kingdom; and whatever your outward lot may be, or the estimation in which men may hold you, you are in very truth among the number of those concerning whom our Lord declares "shall be called great in the kingdom of heaven" (Matthew 5:19).

20

God's Chariots

*T*HE chariots of God are twenty thousand, even thousands of thousands; the Lord is among them as in Sinai, in the Holy Place" (Psalm 68:17).

Chariots are for conveyance and progress. Earthly chariots carry the bodies of those who ride in them over all intervening distances or obstacles to the place of their destination, and God's chariots carry their souls.

No words can express the glorious places to which that soul shall arrive who travels in the chariots of God. And our verse tells us they are many. All around us on every side they wait for us; but we do not always see them. Earth's chariots are always visible, but God's chariots are invisible.

2 Kings 6:14-17

The king of Syria came up against the man of God with horses and chariots that were visible to every one, but God had chariots that could be seen by none, save the eye of faith. The servant of the prophet could only see the outward and visible, and he cried, as so many have done since, "Alas, my master! What shall we do?" But the prophet himself sat calmly within his house without fear, because his eyes were opened to see the invisible. And all that he asked for his servant was, "LORD, I pray, open his eyes that he may see."

This is the prayer we need to pray for ourselves and for one another, "Lord, open our eyes that we may see." For the world all around us is full of God's horses and chariots, waiting to carry us to places of glorious victory. But they do not look like chariots. They look instead like enemies, sufferings, trials, defeats, misunderstandings, disappointments, unkindness. They look like Juggernaut cars of misery and wretchedness, but they really are chariots of triumph in which we may ride to those very heights of victory for which our souls have been longing and praying.

Deuteronomy 32:12-13

If we would "ride on the high places of the earth" we must get into the chariots that can take us there; and only the "chariots of God" are equal to such lofty riding as this.

Isaiah 58:14

We may make out of each event in our lives either a Juggernaut car to crush us, or a chariot in which to ride to heights of victory. It all depends upon how we take them; whether we lie down under our trials and let them roll over and crush us, or whether we climb up into them as into a chariot, and make them carry us triumphantly onward and upward.

2 Kings 2:11-12

Whenever we mount into God's chariots the same thing happens to us spiritually that happened to Elisha. We shall have a translation. Not into the heavens above us, as Elisha did, but into the heaven within us, which, after all, is almost a grander translation than his. We shall be carried up and away from the low earthly groveling plane of life, where everything hurts and everything is unhappy, up into the heavenly places in Christ Jesus, where we shall ride in triumph over all below.

Ephesians 2:6

These "heavenly places" are interior, not exterior, and the road that leads to them is interior also. But the chariot that carries the soul over this road is generally some outward loss, or trial or disappointment; some chastening that does not indeed seem for the present to be joyous, but grievous; but that nevertheless afterward yields the peaceable fruits of righteousness to them that are exercised thereby.

Hebrews 12:5-11

Look upon these chastening, no matter how grievous it may be for the present, as God's chariots sent to carry your souls into the "high places" of spiritual achievement and uplifting, and you will find that they are after all paved with love.

Song of Songs 3:9-10

Your own individual chariot may look very unlovely. It may be a cross-grained relative or friend; it may be the result of human malice, or cruelty, or neglect; but every chariot sent by God must necessarily be paved with love, since God is love, and God's love is the sweetest, softest, tenderest thing to rest one's self upon that was ever found by any soul anywhere. It is His love indeed that sends the chariot.

Habakkuk 3:8, 12-13

Here the prophet tells us that it was God's displeasure against the obstacles which beset the path of His people that made Him come to their rescue, riding in His "chariots of salvation." Everything becomes a "chariot of salvation" when God rides upon it. The "clouds" that darken our skies and seem to shut out the shining of the sun of righteousness are, after all, if we only knew it, His chariots, into which we may mount with Him, and "ride prosperously" over all the darkness.

Psalm 45:3-4; Psalm 18:10; Deuteronomy 33:26

A late writer said that we cannot, by even the most vigorous and toilsome efforts, sweep away the clouds, but we can climb so high above them as to reach the clear atmosphere overhead; and he who rides with God rides upon the heavens far above all earth-borne clouds.

Psalm 68:32-34

This may sound fanciful, but it is really exceedingly practical when we begin to act it out in our daily lives. I knew a lady who had a very slow servant. She was an excellent girl in every other respect, and very valuable in the household, but her slowness was a constant source of irritation to her mistress, who was naturally quick, and who always chafed at slowness. The lady would consequently get out of temper with the girl twenty times a day, and twenty times a day would repent of her anger, and resolve to conquer it, but in vain.

Her life was made miserable by the conflict. One day it occurred to her that she had for a long while been praying for patience, and that perhaps this slow servant was the very chariot the Lord had sent to carry her soul over into patience. She immediately accepted it as such, and from that time used the slowness of her servant as a chariot for her soul. And the result was a victory of patience that no slowness of anybody was ever after able to disturb.

Another instance: I knew a sister at one of our conventions who was put to sleep in a room with two others on account of the crowd.

She wanted to sleep, but they wanted to talk, and the first night she was greatly disturbed, and lay there fretting and fuming long after the others had hushed and she might have slept. But the next day she heard something about God's chariots, and that night she accepted these talking sisters as her chariots to carry her over into sweetness and patience, and she lay there feeling peaceful and at rest.

When, however, it grew very late, and she knew they all ought to be sleeping, she ventured to say slyly, "Sisters, I am lying here riding in a chariot," and the effect was instantaneous in producing perfect quiet. Her chariot had carried her over to victory, not only inwardly, but at last outwardly as well.

If we would ride in God's chariots, instead of in our own, we should find this to be the case continually.

Isaiah 31:1-3; Psalm 20:7-8

Our constant temptation is to trust in the "chariots of Egypt." We can see them; they are tangible and real, and they look so substantial; while God's chariots are invisible and intangible, and it is hard to believe they are there. Our eyes are not opened to see them.

2 Kings 19:23

We try to reach the high places with the multitude of our chariots. We depend first on one thing, and then on another, to advance our spiritual condition and to gain our spiritual victories. We go to Egypt for help. And God is obliged often to destroy all our own chariots before he can bring us to the point of mounting into His.

Micah 5:10; Haggai 2:22

We lean too much upon a dear friend to help us onward in the spiritual life, and the Lord is obliged to separate us from that friend.

We feel that all our spiritual prosperity depends on our continuance under the ministry of a favorite preacher, and we are mysteriously removed. We look upon our prayer-meeting or our Bible-class as the chief source of our spiritual strength, and we are shut up from attending it.

And the "chariot of God," which alone can carry us to the places where we hoped to be taken by the instrumentalities upon which we have been depending, is to be found in the very deprivations we have so mourned over. God must burn up with the fire of His love every chariot of our own that stands in the way of our mounting into His.

Isaiah 66:15-16

Let us be thankful, then, for every trial that will help to destroy our chariots, and will compel us to take refuge in the chariot of God, which stands ready and waiting beside us.

Psalm 62:5-8

We have to be brought to the place where all other refuges fail us, before we can say, "He only." We say, "He, and something else." "He, and my experience," or "He, and my church relationships," or "He, and my Christian work"; and all that comes after the "and" must be taken away from us, or must be proved useless before we can come to the "He only." As long as visible chariots are at hand, the soul will not mount into the invisible ones.

Psalm 68:4

If we want to ride with God "on the clouds," we have to be brought to an end of all riding upon the earth.

Psalm 68:24

To see God's "procession," we must get into the "sanctuary" of His presence; and to share in His "procession" and go with Him, we must abandon all earthly "processions."

Proverbs 20:24; Psalm 17:5; Psalm 40:1-2

When we mount into God's chariot our steps are "established," for no obstacles can hinder its triumphal course. All losses therefore are gains that bring us to this.

Philippians 3:7-9

Paul understood this, and he gloried in the losses which brought him such unspeakable gain.

2 Corinthians 12:7-10

Even the "thorn in the flesh," the messenger of Satan sent to buffet him, became only a chariot to his willing soul, that carried him to heights of triumph which he could have reached in no other way. To "take pleasure" in one's trials, what is this but turning them into the grandest of chariots?

Joseph had a revelation of his future triumphs and reigning, but the chariots that carried him there looked to the eye of sense like the bitterest failures and defeats. It was a strange road to a kingdom, through slavery and a prison, and yet by no other road could Joseph have reached his triumph. His dream, Genesis 37:5-10; his chariots, Genesis 37:19-20, 27-28 and Genesis 39:19-20; how he rode in his chariots, Genesis 39:1-6, 21-23; his triumph, Genesis 41:38-43.

And now a word as to how one is to mount into these chariots. My answer would be simply this: Find out where God is in each one of them, and hide yourself in Him. Or, in other words, do what the little child does when trouble comes, who finds its mother and hides in her arms. The real chariot after all that takes us through triumphantly is the carrying of God.

Isaiah 46:4

The baby carried in the chariot of its mother's arms rides triumphantly through the hardest places, and does not even know they are hard.

Isaiah 63:9

And how much more we, who are carried in the chariot of the arms of God!

Get into your chariot, then. Take each thing that is wrong in your lives as God's chariot for you. No matter who the builder of the wrong may be, whether men or devils, by the time it reaches your side it is God's chariot for you, and is meant to carry you to a heavenly place of triumph. Shut out all the second causes, and find the Lord in it. Say, "Lord, open my eyes that I may see, not the visible enemy, but Your unseen chariots of deliverance."

Accept His will in the trial, whatever it may be, and hide yourself in His arms of love. Say, "Your will be done; Your will be done!" over and over. Shut out every other thought but the one thought of submission to His will and of trust in His love. Make your trial thus your chariot, and you will find your soul "riding on the clouds" with God in a way you never dreamed could be.

I have not a shadow of doubt that if all our eyes were opened today we would see our homes, and our places of business, and the streets we traverse filled with the chariots of God. There is no need for any one of us to walk for lack of chariots. That cross inmate of your household, who has hitherto made life a burden to you, and who has been the Juggernaut car to crush your soul into the dust, may henceforth be a glorious chariot to carry you to the heights of heavenly patience and longsuffering. That misunderstanding, that mortification, that unkindness, that disappointment, that loss, that defeat – all these are chariots waiting to carry you to the very heights of victory you have so longed to reach.

Mount into them, then, with thankful hearts, and lose sight of all second causes in the shining of His love who will "carry you in His arms" safely and triumphantly over it all.

21

In God's Hands

*N*OT long ago I was driving with a Quaker preacher through our beautiful Philadelphia Park when our conversation turned on the apparent fruitlessness of a great deal of the preaching in the church at the present time.

We had spoken, of course, of the foundation cause in the absence of the power of the Holy Ghost, but we still felt that this could not account for it all, as both of us knew many preachers really baptized with the Spirit, who yet seemed to have no fruit to their ministry.

And then I suggested that one reason might be in the fact that so many ministers, when preaching or talking on religious subjects, put on a different tone and manner from the one they ordinarily use, and by this very manner remove religion so far from the range of ordinary life as to fail of gaining any real hold on the hearts of the men and women whose whole lives are lived on the plane of ordinary and homely pleasures and duties. "Now, for instance," I said, "if in your preaching from the friends' gallery you could use the same tone and manner as your present one, how much more effectual and convincing your preaching would be." "Oh, but I could not do that," was the reply, "because the preacher's gallery is so much more solemn a place than this."

"But why is it more solemn?" I asked. "Is it not the presence of God only that makes the gallery or the pulpit solemn, and have we not the presence of God equally here? Is it not just as solemn to live in our everyday life as it is to preach, and ought we not to do the one to His glory just as much as the other?" And then I added, as the subject seemed to open out before me, "I verily believe a large part of the difficulty lies in the unscriptural and unnatural divorce that has been brought about between our so-called religious life and our so-called temporal life; as if our religion were something apart from ourselves, a sort of outside garment that was to be put on and off according to our circumstances and purposes. On Sundays, for instance, and in church, our purpose is to seek God, and worship and serve Him, and therefore on Sundays we bring out our religious life and put it on in a suitably solemn manner, and live it with a strained gravity and decorum which deprives it of half its power. But on Mondays our purpose is to seek our own interests and serve them, and so we bring out our temporal life and put it on with a sense of relief, as from an unnatural bondage, and live it with ease and naturalness, and consequently with far more power."

The thoughts thus started remained with me and gathered strength. Not long afterward I was present at a meeting where the leader opened with reading John 15, and the words, "Without Me you can do nothing" (John 15:5) struck me with amazement. Hundreds of times before I had read those words, and had thought that I understood them thoroughly. But now it seemed almost as though they must have been newly inserted in the Bible, so ablaze were they with wondrous meaning.

"There it is," I said to myself, "Jesus Himself said so, that apart from Him we have no real life of any kind, whether we call it temporal or spiritual, and that, therefore, all living or doing that is without Him is of such a nature that God, who sees into the realities of things, calls it 'nothing.'" And then the question forced itself upon me as to whether any soul really believed this statement to be true; or, if believing it theoretically, whether any one made it practical in their daily walk and life.

And I saw, as in a flash almost, that the real secret of divine union lay quite as much in this practical aspect of it as in any interior revealing or experiences. For if I do nothing, literally nothing, apart from Christ, I am of course united to Him in a continual oneness that cannot be questioned or gainsaid; while if I live a large part of my daily life and perform a large part of my daily work apart from Him, I have no real union, no matter how exalted and delightful my emotions concerning it may be. It is to consider this aspect of the subject, therefore, that the present paper is written. For I am very sure that the wide divorce made between things spiritual and things temporal, of which I have spoken, has done more than almost anything else to hinder a realized interior union with God, and to put all religion so outside of the pale of common life as to make it an almost unattainable thing to the ordinary mass of mankind. Moreover, it has introduced an unnatural constraint and stiltedness into the experience of Christians that seems to shut them out from much of the free, happy, childlike ease that belongs of right to the children of God.

I feel, therefore, that it is of vital importance for us to understand the truth of this matter. And the thought that makes it clearest to me is this: that the fact of our oneness with Christ contains the whole thing in a nutshell. If we are one with Him, then of course in the very nature of things we can do nothing without Him.

For that which is one cannot act as being two. And if I therefore do anything without Christ, then I am not one with Him in that thing, and like a branch severed from the vine I am withered and worthless. It is as if the branch should recognize its connection with and dependence upon the vine for most of its growth, and fruit-bearing, and climbing, but should feel a capacity in itself to grow and climb over a certain fence or around the trunk of a certain tree, and should therefore sever its connection with the vine for this part of its living. Of course that which thus sought an independent life would wither and die in the very nature of things. And just so is it with us who are branches of Christ, the true vine. No independent action, whether small or great, is possible to us without withering and death, any more than to the branch of the natural vine.

This will show us at once how fatal to the realized oneness with Christ, for which our souls hunger, is the divorce I have spoken of. We have all realized, more or less, that without Him we cannot live our religious life, but when it comes to living our so-called temporal life, to keeping house or transacting business, or making calls, or darning stockings, or sweeping a room, or trimming a bonnet, or entertaining company, who is there that even theoretically thinks such things as these are to be done for Christ, and can only be rightly done as we abide in Him and do them in His strength?

But if it is Christ working in the Christian who is to lead the prayer-meeting, then, since Christ and the Christian are one, it must be also Christ working in and through the Christian who is to keep the house and make the bargain; and one duty is therefore in the very essence of things as religious as the other.

It is the man that makes the action, not the action the man. And as much solemnity and sweetness will thus be brought into our everyday domestic and social affairs as into the so-called religious occasions of life, if we will only acknowledge God in all our ways (see Proverbs 3:6), and do whatever we do, even if it be only eating and drinking, to His glory (see 1 Corinthians 10:31). If our religion is really our life, and not merely something extraneous tacked on to our life, it must necessarily go into everything in which we live; and no act, however human or natural it may be, can be taken out of its control and guidance.

If God is with us always, then He is just as much with us in our business times and our social times as in our religious times, and one moment is as solemn with His presence as another. If it is a fact that in Him we "live and move and have our being" (Acts 17:28), then it is also a fact, whether we know it or not, that without Him we cannot do anything. And facts are stubborn things, thank God, and do not alter for all our feelings.

In Psalm 127:1-2, we have a very striking illustration of this truth. The psalmist says, "Unless the LORD builds the house, they labor in vain who build it; unless the LORD guards the city, the watchman stays awake in vain. It is vain for you to rise up early, to sit up late, to eat the bread of sorrows; for so He gives His beloved sleep." The two things here spoken of as being done in vain, unless the Lord is in the doing of them, are purely secular things; simple business matters on the human plane of life. And whatever spiritual lesson they were intended to teach gains its impressiveness only from this, that these statements concerning God's presence in temporal things were statements of patent and incontrovertible facts.

In truth the Bible is full of this fact, and the only wonder is how any believer in the Bible could have overlooked it. From the building of cities down to the numbering of the hairs of our head and the noting of a sparrow's fall, throughout the whole range of homely daily living, God is declared to be present and to be the mainspring of it all. Whatever we do, even if it be such a purely physical thing as eating and drinking, we are to do for Him and to His glory (see 1 Corinthians 10:31), and we are exhorted to so live and so walk in the light in everything, as to have it made manifest of our works, temporal as well as spiritual that "they have been done in God" (John 3:21).

There is unspeakable comfort in this for every loving Christian heart, in that it turns all of life into a sacrament, and makes the kitchen, or the workshop, or the nursery, or the parlor, as sweet and solemn a place of service to the Lord, and as real a means of union with Him, as the prayer-meeting, or the mission board, or the charitable visitation.

A dear young Christian mother and housekeeper came to me once with a sorely grieved heart, because of her engrossing temporal life. "There seems," she said, "to be nothing spiritual about my life from one week's end to the other. My large family of little children are so engrossing that day after day passes without my having a single moment for anything but simply attendance on them and on my necessary household duties, and I go to bed night after night sick at heart because I have felt separated from my Lord all day long, and have not been able to do anything for Him." I told her of what I have written above, and assured her that all would be changed if she would only see and acknowledge God in all these homely duties, and would recognize her utter dependence upon Him for the doing of them. Her heart received the good news with gladness, and months afterward she told me that from that moment life had become a transformed and glorified thing, with the abiding presence of the Lord, and with the sweetness of continual service to Him.

Another Christian, a young lady in a fashionable family, came to me also in similar grief that in so much of her life she was separated from God and had no sense of His presence. I told her she ought never to do anything that could cause such a separation; but she assured me that it was impossible to avoid it, as the things she meant were none of them wrong things. "For instance," she said, "it is plainly my duty to pay calls with my mother, and yet nothing seems to separate me so much from God as paying calls."

"But how would it be," I asked, "if you paid the calls as service to the Lord and for His glory?" "What!" she exclaimed, "pay calls for God! I never heard of such a thing." "But why not?" I asked. "If it is right to pay calls at all it ought to be done for God, for we are commanded whatever we do to do it for His glory, and if it is not right you ought not to do it. As a Christian," I continued, "you must not do anything that you cannot do for Him." "I see! I see!" she exclaimed, "and it makes all life look so different! Nothing can separate me from Him that is not sin, but each act done to His glory, whatever it may be, will only draw me closer and make His presence more real."

These two instances will illustrate my meaning. And

I feel sure there are thousands of other burdened and weary lives that would be similarly transformed if these truths were but realized and acted on.

An old spiritual writer says something to this effect, that in order to become a saint it is not always necessary to change our works, but only to put an interior purpose towards God in them all; that we must begin to do for His glory and in His strength that which before we did for self and in self's capacity; which means, after all, just what our Lord meant when He said, "Without Me you can do nothing" (John 15:5).

There is another side of this truth also which is full of comfort, and which the psalmist develops in the verses I have quoted. "It is vain," he says, "for you to rise up early, to sit up late, to eat the bread of sorrows" (Psalm 127:2). Or, in other words, what is the use of all this worry and strain? For the work will after all amount to nothing unless God is in it, and if He is in it, what folly to fret or be burdened, since He of course, by the very fact of His presence, assumes the care and responsibility of it all.

Ah, it is vain indeed, and I would that all God's children knew it! We mothers at least ought to know it, for our own ways with our children would teach us something of it every day we live, if we had but the "eyes to see" (see 2 Kings 6:17). How many mothers have risen early, and sat up, late, and eaten the bread of sorrows, just that they might give sleep to their beloved children. And how grieved their hearts would have been if, after all their pains, the children had refused to rest. I can appeal to some mother hearts, I am sure, as thoroughly understanding my meaning. Memories will arise of the flushed and rosy boy coming in at night, tired with his play or his work, with knees out and coat torn, and of the patient, loving toil to patch and mend it all, sitting up late and rising early, that the dearly loved cause of all the mischief might rest undisturbed in childhood's happy sleep.

How "vain," and worse than vain, would it have been for that loved and cared-for darling to have himself also sat up late, and risen early, and eaten the bread of sorrows, when all the while his mother was doing it for him just that he might not have it to do. And if this is true of mothers, how much more true must it be of Him who made the mothers, and who came among us in bodily form to bear our burdens, and carry our sorrows, and do our work, just that we might enter His rest (see Hebrews 4:10).

Beloved, have you entered into this rest?

"For anyone who enters God's rest also rests from their works, just as God did from His" (Hebrews 4:10 NIV). That is, he has learned at last the lesson that without Christ or apart from Him he can do nothing, but that he can do all things through Christ strengthening him; and therefore he has laid aside all self-effort, and has abandoned himself to God that He may work in him both to will and to do of His good pleasure. This and this only is the rest that remains for the people of God.

Scientific men are seeking to resolve all forces in nature into one primal force. Unity of origin is the present cry of science. Light, heat, sound are all said to be the products of one force differently applied, and that force is motion. All things, say the scientists, can be resolved back to this. Whether they are right or wrong I cannot say; but the Bible reveals to us one grand primal force which is behind motion itself, and that is God-force. God is at the source of everything, God is the origin of everything, God is the explanation of everything. Without Him was not anything made that was made, and without Him is not anything done that is done (see John 1:3).

Surely, then, it is not the announcement of any mystery, but the simple statement of a simple fact, when our Lord says, "Without Me you can do nothing" (John 15:5). Even of Himself He said, "I can of Myself do nothing" (John 5:30), and He meant that He and His Father were so one that any independent action was impossible. Surely it is the revelation of a glorious necessity existing between our souls and Christ that He should say we could do nothing without Him; for it means that He has made us so one with Himself that independent action is as impossible with us towards Him, as it was with Him towards His Father.

Dear Christian, do you not catch a glimpse here of a region of wondrous glory? Let us believe, then, that without Him we can literally do nothing. We must believe it, for it is true. But let us recognize its truth, and act on it from this time forward. Let us make a hearty renunciation of all living apart from Christ, and let us begin from this moment to acknowledge Him in all our ways, and do everything, whatsoever we do, as service to Him and for His glory, depending upon Him alone for wisdom, and strength, and sweetness, and patience, and everything else that is necessary for the right accomplishing of all our living.

As I said before, it is not so much a change of acts that will be necessary as a change of motive and of dependence. The house will be kept, or the children cared for, or the business transacted, perhaps, just the same as before as to the outward, but inwardly God will be acknowledged, and depended on, and served; and there will be all the difference between a life lived at ease in the glory of His presence, and a life lived painfully and with effort apart from Him. There will result also from this bringing of God into our affairs a wonderful accession of divine wisdom in the conduct of them, and a far greater quickness and dispatch in their accomplishment, a surprising increase in the fertility of resource, an ease in apprehending the true nature and bearing of things, and an enlargement on every side that will amaze the hitherto cramped and cabined soul.

I mean this literally. I mean that the house will be kept more nicely and with greater ease, the children will be trained more swiftly, the stockings will be darned more swiftly, the guest will be entertained more comfortably, the servants will be managed more easily, the bargain will be made more satisfactorily, and all life will move with far more sweetness and harmony. For God will be in every moment of it, and where He is all must go well.

Moreover the soul itself, in this natural and simple

way, will acquire such a holy habit of abiding in Christ that at last His presence will become the most real thing in life to our consciousness, and a habitual, silent, and secret conversation with Him will be carried on that will yield a continual joy.

Sometimes the child of God asks eagerly and hungrily, "What is the shortest and quickest way by which I can reach the highest degree of union and communion with God, possible to human beings in this life?" No shorter or quicker way can be found than the one I have been declaring. By the homely path of everyday duties done thus in God and for God, the most sublime heights are reached. Not as a reward, however, but as an inevitable and natural result, for if we thus abide in Him and refuse to leave Him, where He is there shall we also be, and all that He is will be ours.

If, then, you would know, beloved reader, the interior divine union realized in your soul, begin from this very day to put it outwardly in practice as I have suggested. Offer each moment of your living and each act of your doing to God, and say to Him continually, "Lord, I am doing this in You and for Your glory. You are my strength, and my wisdom, and my all-sufficient supply for every need. I depend only upon You." Refuse utterly to live for a single moment or to perform a single act apart from Him. Persist in this until it becomes the established habit of your soul. And sooner or later you will surely know the longings of your soul satisfied in the abiding presence of Christ, your indwelling Life.

22

God's Omnipresence

"*I*F I go up to the heavens, You are there; if I make my bed in the depths, You are there. If I rise on the wings of the dawn, if I settle on the far side of the sea, even there Your hand will guide me, Your right hand will hold me fast" (Psalm 139:8-10 NIV).

Very few of us understand the full meaning of the words in Matthew 1:23, "They shall call His name Immanuel, which is translated, 'God with us.'" In this short sentence is revealed to us the grandest fact the world can ever know: that God, the Almighty God, the Creator of heaven and earth, is not a far-off God, dwelling in a heaven of unapproachable glory, but is living with us right here in this world, in the midst of our poor, ignorant, helpless lives, as close to us as we are to ourselves. This seems so incredible to the human heart that we are very slow to believe it; but that the

Bible teaches it as a fact, from cover to cover, cannot be denied by any honest mind. In Genesis 3:8 we read of the "presence of the LORD God among the trees of the garden." And from that time on He is revealed to us always as in the most familiar and daily interaction with His people everywhere.

In Exodus 25:8 we find Him asking them to make Him a sanctuary that He may dwell among them. He taught them to rely on Him as an ever-present Friend and Helper, to consult Him about all their affairs, and to abandon the whole management of their lives to Him. And finally He came in Christ in bodily form and dwelt in the world as a man among men, making Himself bone of our bone and flesh of our flesh (see Genesis 2:23), taking upon Him our nature, and revealing to us, in the most tangible and real way possible, the grand, and blessed, and incomprehensible fact that He intended to be with us always, even unto the end of the world.

Whoever will believe this fact with all their hearts will find in it the solution of every difficulty of their lives. I remember when I was a little girl and found myself in any trouble or perplexity, the coming in of my father or mother on the scene would always bring me immediate relief. The moment I heard the voice of one of them saying, "Daughter, I am here," that moment every burden dropped off and every anxiety was stilled. It was their simple presence that did it. They did not need to promise to relieve me, they did not need to tell me their plans of relief; the simple fact of their presence was all the assurance I required that everything now would be set straight and all would go well for me, and my only interest after their arrival was simply to see how they would do it all. Perhaps they were exceptional parents to have created such confidence in their children's hearts. I think myself they were. But as our God is certainly an exceptional God, the application has absolute force, and His presence is literally all we need. It would be enough for us, even if we had not a single promise, nor a single revelation of His plans.

How often in the Bible He has stilled all questions and all fears by the simple announcement, "I will be with you" (see Isaiah 43:2 and 41:10), and who can doubt that in these words He meant to assure us that all His wisdom, and love, and omnipotent power would therefore, of course, be engaged on our side?

Over and over again in my childhood have the magic words, "Oh, there is mother!" brought me immediate relief and comfort; and over and over again in my later years have almost the same words reverently spoken, "Oh, there is God!" brought me a far more blessed deliverance. With Him present, what could I have to fear?

Since He has said, "Never will I leave you; never will I forsake you" (Hebrews 13:5 NIV), surely I may boldly say, "The Lord is my helper; I will not be afraid. What can mere mortals do to me?" (Hebrews 13:6 NIV). I remember to this day the inspiring sense of utter security that used to come to me with my earthly father's presence. I never feared anything when he was near. And surely with my heavenly Father there can be no possible room for fear.

It is because of its practical help and comfort, therefore, that I desire to make this wonderful fact of "Immanuel, God with us" (Matthew 1:23), clear and definite, for I am very sure but few, even of God's own children, really believe it. They may say they do, they may repeat a thousand times in the conventional, pious tone considered suitable to such a sentiment, "Oh, yes, we know that God is always present with us, but ..." And in this "but" the whole story is told.

There are no "buts" in the vocabulary of the soul that accepts His presence as a literal fact. Such a soul is joyously triumphant over every suggestion of fear or of doubt. It has God, and that is enough for it. His presence is its certain security and supply, always, and for everything.

Let me, then, beg my readers to turn with me for a while to the 139th Psalm, where we shall find a most blessed revelation of this truth. The central thought of the Psalm is to be found in verses 7 to 13: "Where can I go from Your Spirit? Or where can I flee from Your presence? If I ascend into heaven, You are there; if I make my bed in hell, behold, You are there. If I take the wings of the morning, and dwell in the uttermost parts of the sea, even there Your hand shall lead me, and Your right hand shall hold me. If I say, 'Surely the darkness shall fall on me,' even the night shall be light about me; indeed, the darkness shall not hide from You, but the night shines as the day; the darkness and the light are both alike to You. For You formed my inward parts; You covered me in my mother's womb."

I cannot conceive of a more definite or sweeping declaration of His continual presence with us, wherever we may be or whatever we may do, than is contained in this passage. People talk about seeking to get into the presence of the Lord, but here we see that they cannot get out of it; that there is no place in the whole universe where He is not present; neither heaven, nor hell, nor the uttermost parts of the sea; and no darkness so great as to hide for one moment from Him. And the reason of this is that He has created our inmost beings (see Psalm 139:13 NIV), which means that He is not only with us, but within us, and consequently must accompany us wherever we ourselves go.

We must accept it as true, therefore, that the words of our Lord, "Lo, I am with you always, even to the end of the age" (Matthew 28:20) were the expression, not of a beautiful sentiment merely, but of an incontrovertible fact. He is with us, and we cannot get away from Him.

We may be in such thick darkness as to be utterly unable to see Him, and may think, probably often have thought, that, therefore, He does not see us. But our Psalm assures us that the darkness hides us not from Him, and that, in fact, darkness and light are both alike to Him (see Psalm 139:12).

We are as present to His view and as plainly seen when our own souls are in the depths of spiritual darkness, as when they are basking in the brightest light. The darkness may hide Him from us, but it does not hide us from Him. Neither does any apparent spiritual distance or wandering take us out of His presence; not even if we go into the depths of sin in our wandering. In the uttermost parts of the sea, or wherever we may be, He is ever present to hold and to lead us. There is not a moment, nor a place where we can be left without His care.

There are times in our lives when delirium makes us utterly unaware of the presence of our most careful and tender nurses. A child in delirium will cry out in anguish for its mother, and will harrow her heart by its piteous lamentations and appeals, when all the while she is holding its fevered hand, and bathing its aching head, and caring for it with all the untold tenderness of a mother's love. The darkness of disease has hidden the mother from the child, but has not hidden the child from the mother.

And just so it is with our God and us. The darkness of our doubts or our fears, of our sorrows or our despair, or even of our sins, cannot hide us from Him, although it may, and often does, hide Him from us. He has told us that the darkness and the light are both alike to Him; and if our faith will only lay hold of this as a fact, we will be enabled to pass through the darkest seasons in quiet trust, sure that all the while, though we cannot see nor feel Him, our God is caring for us, and will never leave nor forsake us.

Whether, however, this abiding presence of our God will be a joy to us or a sorrow will depend upon what we know about Him. If we think of Him as a stern tyrant, intent only on His own glory, we shall be afraid of His continual presence. If we think of Him as a tender, loving Father, intent only on our blessing and happiness, we shall be glad and thankful to have Him thus ever with us. For the presence and the care of love can never mean anything but good to the one beloved.

The Psalm we are considering shows us that the presence of our God is the presence of love, and that it brings us an infinitude of comfort and rest. He says in verses 1 to 5, "O LORD, You have searched me and known me. You know my sitting down and my rising up; You understand my thought afar off. You comprehend my path and my lying down, and are acquainted with all my ways. For there is not a word on my tongue, but behold, O LORD, You know it altogether. You have hedged me behind and before, and laid Your hand upon me."

Our God knows us and understands us, and is acquainted with all our ways. No one else in all the world understands us. Our actions are misinterpreted, it may be, and our motives misjudged. Our natural characteristics are not taken into account, nor our inherited tendencies considered. No one makes allowances for our ill health; no one realizes how much we have to contend with. But our Father knows it all. He understands us, and His judgment of us takes into account every element, conscious or unconscious, that goes to make up our character and to control our actions.

Only an all-comprehending love can be just, and our God is just. No wonder Faber can say: "There is no place where earth's sorrows are more felt than up in heaven; there is no place where earth's failings have such kindly judgment given." Some of you have been afraid of His justice, perhaps, because you thought it would be against you. But do you not see now that it is all on your side, just as a mother's justice is, because "He knows our frame; He remembers that we are dust" (Psalm 103:14)?

No human judge can ever do this; and to me this comprehension of God is one of my most blessed comforts. Often I do not understand myself; all within looks confused and hopelessly tangled. But then I remember that He has searched me, and that He knows me and understands the thoughts which so perplex me, and that, therefore, I may just leave the whole miserable tangle to Him to unravel. And my soul sinks down at once, as on downy pillows, into a place of the most blissful rest.

Then, further, because of this complete knowledge and understanding of our needs, what comfort it is to be told that He knows our sitting down and our rising up; that He compasses our path, and takes note of our lying down (see Psalm 139:2-3).

Just what a mother does for her foolish, careless, ignorant, but dearly loved little ones, this very thing does our God for us. When a mother is with her children she thinks of their comfort and well-being always before her own. They must have comfortable seats where no draught can reach them, no matter what amount of discomfort she may herself be compelled to endure. Their beds must be soft and their blankets warm, let hers be what they may. Their paths must be smooth and safe, even though she is obliged herself to walk in rough and dangerous ways. Her own comfort, as compared to that of her children, is of no account in a loving mother's eyes. And surely our God has not made the mothers in this world more capable of a self-sacrificing love than He is Himself. He must be better and greater on the line of love and self-sacrifice than any mother He ever made.

Then, since He has assured us that He knows our sitting down and our rising up, that He compasses our path and our lying down, we may be perfectly and blessedly sure that in even these little details of our lives we get the very best that His love, and wisdom, and power can compass. I mean this in a very literal sense. I mean that He cares for our literal seats and our literal beds, and sees that we, each one, have just that sort of a seat or that sort of a bed which is best for us and for our highest development.

And just on this last point is where He is so much better than any mother can be. His love is a wise love that sees the outcome of things, and cares more for our highest good than for that which is lower. So that, while a mother's weak love cannot see beyond the child's present comfort, and cannot bear to inflict or allow any discomfort, the strong, wise love of our God can bear to permit the present discomfort, for the sake of the future glory that is to result there from.

At home and abroad, therefore, let us commit the choosing of our seats, and of our beds, and of all the other little homely circumstances of our daily lives and surroundings, to the God who has thus assured us that

He knows all about every one of them. For we are told in our Psalm that He "hedges" our path (see Psalm 139:5). We have some of us known what it was to be "hedged" by unwelcome and unpleasant people or things. But we never have thought, perhaps, that we were beset by God, that He loves us so that He cannot leave us alone, and that no coldness nor rebuffs on our part can drive Him away.

Yet it is gloriously true! And, moreover, He hedges us "behind" as well as "before." Just as a mother does. She goes after her children and picks up all they have dropped, and clears away all the rubbish they have left behind them.

We mothers begin this in the nursery with the blocks and playthings, and we go on with it all our lives long; seeking continually to set straight that which our children have left crooked behind them; often at the cost of much toil and trouble, but always with a love that makes the toil and trouble nothing in comparison to caring for the children we love.

What good mother ever turned away the poor little tearful darling who came with a tangled knot for her unraveling, or refused to help the eager rosy boy to unwind his kite-strings? Suppose it has been their own fault that the knots and tangles have come, still her love can sympathize with and pity the very faults themselves, and all the more does she seek to atone for them.

All this and more does our God do for us from our earliest infancy, long even before we know enough to be conscious of it, until the very end of our earthly lives.

We have seen Him before us perhaps, but we have never thought of Him as behind us as well. Yet it is a blessed fact that He is behind us all the time, longing to make crooked things straight, to untangle our tangled skeins, and to atone continually for the wrong we have done and the mistakes we have made. If any of us, therefore, have that in our past which has caused us anxiety or remorse, let us lift up our heads in a happy confidence from henceforth, that the God who is behind us will set it all straight somehow, if we will but commit it to Him, and can even make our very mistakes and misdoings work together for good. Ah! It is a grand thing to be "hedged" by God.

Then again what depths of comfort there are in verses 14 to 16 of Psalm 139: "I will praise You, for I am fearfully and wonderfully made; marvelous are Your works, and that my soul knows very well. My frame was not hidden from You, when I was made in secret, and skillfully wrought in the lowest parts of the earth. Your eyes saw my substance, being yet unformed. And in Your Book they all were written, the days fashioned for me, when as yet there were none of them."

One of the things which often troubles us more than we care to confess is our dislike of the way we have been put together. Our mental or moral "make-up" does not suit us. We think if we had only been created with less of this or more of that, if we were less impulsive or more enthusiastic, if we had been made more like someone else whom we admire, that then our chances of success would have been far greater; that we could have served God far more acceptably; and could have been more satisfactory in every way to ourselves and to Him. And we are tempted sometimes to think that with our miserable make-up, it is hopeless to expect to please Him.

If we really realized that God Himself had made us, we should see the folly of all this at once, but we secretly feel as if somehow He had not had much hand in the matter, but as if we had been put together in a haphazard sort of way that had left our characters very much to chance. We believe in creation in the general, but not in the particular, when it comes to ourselves.

In this Psalm we see that God has presided over the creation of each one of us, superintending the smallest details; even, to speak figuratively, writing down what each "member" was to be, when as yet there was none of them. Therefore we, just as we are naturally, with just the characteristics that we were born with, are precisely what God would have us to be, and were planned out by His own hand to do the special work that He has prepared for our doing. I mean, of course, our natural characteristics, not the perversion of them by sin on our parts.

There is something very glorifying to the Creator in this way of looking at it. Genius always seeks expression, and seeks, too, to express itself in as great a variety of forms and ways as possible. No true artist repeats himself, but each picture he paints or statue he carves is a new expression of his creative power. When we go to an exhibition of pictures, we should feel it a lowering of art if two were exactly alike; and just so is it with us who are God's workmanship (see Ephesians 2:10). His creative power is expressed differently in each one of us. And in the individual "make-up" which sometimes so troubles us, there is a manifestation of this power different from every other, and without which the day of exhibition, when we are, each one, to be to the praise of His glory, would be incomplete. All He asks of us is that, as He has had the making of us, so He may also have the managing, since He alone understands us, and is, therefore, the only one who can do it.

The man who makes an intricate machine is the best one to manage it and repair it; any one else who meddles with it is apt to spoil it. And when we think of the intricacy of our inward machinery and the continual failure of our own management of it, we may well be thankful to hand it all over to the One who created it, and to leave it in His hands. We may be sure He will then make the best out of us that can be made, and that we, even we, with our "peculiar temperaments," and our apparently unfortunate characteristics, will be made vessels unto honor, sanctified and meet for the Master's use, and fitted to every good work.

I met once with a saying in an old Quaker writer which I have never forgotten: "Be content to be just what your God has made you." It has helped me to understand the point upon which I am dwelling; and I feel sure contentment that our own "make-up" is as essential a part of our submission to God as contentment with any other of the circumstances of our daily life. If we did not each one of us exist just as we are by nature, then one expression of God's creative power would be missing, and one part of His work would be left undone. And besides, to complain of ourselves is to complain of the One who has made us, and cannot but grieve Him. Let us be content, then, and only see to it that we let the Divine Potter make out of us the very best He can, and use us according to His own good pleasure.

Verses 17 and 18 bring out another view of God's continual presence with us, and that is that He is always thinking about us, and that His thoughts are kind and loving thoughts, for the psalmist calls them precious. "How precious also are Your thoughts to me, O God! How great is the sum of them! If I should count them, they would be more in number than the sand; when I awake, I am still with You" (Psalm 139:17-18).

So many people are tempted to think that God is not paying any attention to them. They think that their interests and their affairs are altogether beneath His notice, and that they are too unworthy to hope for His attention. But they wrong Him grievously by such thoughts.

A mother pays as much attention to her smallest infant as to her oldest children, and is as much interested in its little needs and pleasures as in theirs. I am not sure but she is more. Her thoughts dwell around the one who needs them most; and He who made the mother's heart will not Himself be less attentive to the needs and pleasures of the meanest and most helpless of His creatures. He even hears the young lions when they cry, and not a sparrow can fall to the ground without Him; therefore, we, who are of more value than many sparrows (see Matthew 10:31), need not be afraid of a moment's neglect.

In fact, the responsibilities of creating anything requires an unintermitting care of it on the part of the Creator; and it is the glory of omnipotence that it can attend at once to the smallest details and to the grandest operations as well.

I do not know why it is that we consider a man or woman weak who attends to large affairs to the neglect of little details, and then turn around and accuse our God of doing this very thing. But if any of my readers have hitherto been guilty of this folly, let it end now and here, and let each one from henceforth believe, without any questioning, that always and everywhere "the LORD thinks upon me" (Psalm 40:17).

The remainder of Psalm 139 develops the perfect accord of thought between the soul and God, where this life of simple faith has been entered upon. Having learned the transforming fact of God's continual presence and unceasing care, the soul is brought into so profound a union with Him as to love what He loves, and hate what He hates; and eagerly appeals to Him to search it, and try it, that there may be no spot left anywhere in all its being which is out of harmony with Him (see Psalm 139:23-24).

In the sunlight of His presence darkness must flee, and the heart will soon feel that it cannot endure to have any corner shut away from His shining; for in His presence is "fullness of joy," and at His right hand "are pleasures forevermore" (Psalm 16:11).

An old woman, living in a rather desolate part of England, made considerable money by selling ale and beer to chance travelers who passed her lonely cottage. But her conscience troubled her about it. She wanted to be a Christian and to go to heaven when she died, but she had an inward feeling that if she did become a Christian she would have to give up her profitable business, and this she thought would be more than she could do; so that between the two things she was brought into great conflict.

But one night, at a meeting she attended, a preacher from a distance told about the sweet and blessed fact of God's continual presence with us, and of the joy this was sure to bring when it was known. Her soul was enraptured at the thought of such a possibility for her, and forgetting all about the beer, she began at once with a very simple faith to claim it as a blessed reality. Over and over again she exclaimed in her heart, as the preacher went on with his sermon, "Why, Lord Jesus, I didn't know that You are always with me! Why, Lord, how good it is to know that I have got You all the time to live with me and take care of me! Why, Lord, I will not be lonely no more!" And when the meeting closed and she took her way home across the moors, all the time the happy refrain went on, "Ah, Lord Jesus, You are going home with me tonight. Never mind, Lord Jesus, old Betty will never let You go again now, I know I have got You!"

As her faith thus laid hold of the fact of His presence she began to rejoice in it more and more, until finally, when she had reached her cottage door, her soul was full of delight. As she opened the door, the first object her eyes rested upon was a great pot of ale on the table ready for selling. At once it flashed into her mind, "The Lord will not like to have that ale in the house where He lives," and her whole heart responded eagerly, "That ale shall go." She knew the pot was heavy, and she kneeled beside it saying, "Lord, You have come home with me, and You are going to live with me always in this cottage, and I know You don't like this ale. Please give me strength to tip it over into the road."

Strength was given, and the ale was soon running down the lane. Then the old woman came back into her cottage, and kneeling down again thanked the Lord for the strength given, and added, "Now, Lord, if there is anything else in this cottage that You do not like, show it to me, and it shall be tipped out too."

Is not this a perfect illustration of the close of our Psalm? "Do I not hate them, O LORD, who hate You? And do I not loathe those who rise up against You? I hate them with perfect hatred; I count them my enemies. Search me, O God, and know my heart; try me, and know my anxieties; and see if there is any wicked way in me, and lead me in the way everlasting" (Psalm 139:21-24).

Just as light drives out darkness, so does the realized presence of God drive out sin, and the soul that by faith abides in His presence knows a very real and wonderful deliverance. And now I trust that some will ask, "How can I find this presence to be real to myself?" I will close, therefore, with a few practical directions.

First, convince yourself from the Scriptures that it is a fact. Facts must always be the foundation of our experiences, or the experiences are worthless. It is not the feeling that causes the fact, but the fact that produces the feeling. And what every soul needs in this case first of all is to be convinced beyond question, from God's own words about it, that His continual presence with us is an unalterable fact.

Then, this point having been settled, the next thing to do is to make it real to ourselves by "practicing His presence," as an old writer expresses it, always and everywhere, and in everything. This means simply that you are to obey the Scripture command and "in all your ways acknowledge Him" (Proverbs 3:6), by saying over each hour and moment, "The Lord is here," and by doing everything you do, even if only eating and drinking, in His presence and for Him. Literally, "whether you eat or drink, or whatever you do, do all to the glory of God" (1 Corinthians 10:31).

By this continual "practice of His presence," the soul at last acquires a habit of faith; and it becomes, finally, as difficult to doubt His presence as it was at first to believe it. No great effort is required for this, but simply an unwavering faith. It is not studied reasoning or elaborate meditation that will help you here. The soul must recognize, by an act of simple faith, that God is present, and must then accustom itself to a continual conversation with Him about all its affairs, in freedom and simplicity.

He does not require great things of us. A little remembrance of His presence, a few words of love and confidence, a momentary lifting of the heart to Him from time to time as we go about our daily affairs, a constant appeal to Him in everything as to a present and loving friend and helper, an endeavor to live in a continual sense of His presence, and a letting of our hearts "dwell at ease" because of it – this is all He asks; the least little remembrance is welcome to Him, and helps to make His presence real to us.

Whoever will be faithful in this exercise will soon be led into a blessed realization of all I have been trying to tell in this book, and of far more that I cannot tell; and will understand in a way beyond telling, those wonderful words concerning our Lord, "They shall call His name Immanuel, which is translated, 'God with us'" (Matthew 1:23).